A Quick Index of Essential Questions

10. Special equipment
What special equipment is required, and what are its space requirements? Is security a factor?
25, 53, 62, 64–72, 108–9, 111–24, 125–50, 170–72, 182–84, 187, 191–94

11. Materials
What materials need to be uniquely considered or rejected?
151–90

12. Acoustic control
What special acoustical considerations affect the design?
103

13. Lighting design
What special lighting (day and artificial) considerations affect the design?
104–7, 150, 155–57, 163–65, 167, 175–76, 188–90

14. Interiors issues
What special considerations (scale, color, texture, finishes, furnishings, special features) affect the planning of interiors?
72–79, 81–82, 87–94, 151–90

15. Wayfinding
What special factors determine signing systems?
18–20, 59–60, 150, 153–54, 161–63, 179, 184–87, 165–71, 175, 177, 179, 184–87

16. Preservation/modernization
What special considerations (historical authenticity, infrastructure retrofit) arise when renovating a facility of this type?
72–82, 157–59, 180–86, 188–90

17. Operation and maintenance
How will design decisions influence the operation and maintenance of the completed facility?
109, 163–65

18. Key cost factors
What are the principal determinants of the total construction cost?
94–95, 165

19. Emerging technologies
What new technologies are especially relevant to the building type?
8, 24, 191–94

BUILDING TYPE BASICS FOR

banks and financial institutions

Other titles in the
BUILDING TYPE BASICS
series

HEALTHCARE FACILITIES, Second Edition
Michael Bobrow and Julia Thomas;
Thomas Payette; Ronald Skaggs; Richard Kobus

ELEMENTARY AND SECONDARY SCHOOLS, Second Edition
Bradford Perkins

MUSEUMS
Arthur Rosenblatt

HOSPITALITY FACILITIES
Brian McDonough; John Hill and Robert Glazier;
Winford "Buck" Lindsay; Thomas Sykes

RESEARCH LABORATORIES, Second Edition
Daniel Watch

OFFICE BUILDINGS
A. Eugene Kohn and Paul Katz

COLLEGE AND UNIVERSITY FACILITIES
David J. Neuman

JUSTICE FACILITIES
Todd S. Phillips
Michael A. Griebel

SENIOR LIVING
Bradford Perkins

RETAIL AND MIXED-USE FACILITIES
The Jerde Partnership

TRANSIT FACILITIES
Kenneth W. Griffin

PLACES OF WORSHIP
Nicholas W. Roberts

HOUSING, Second Edition
Robert Chandler, John Clancy, David Dixon,
Joan Goody, Geoffery Wooding

RECREATIONAL FACILITIES
Richard J. Diedrich

PERFORMING ARTS FACILITIES
Hugh Hardy

BUILDING TYPE BASICS FOR

banks and financial institutions

HOMER L. WILLIAMS
Williams Spurgeon Kuhl & Freshnock Architects

JOHN WILEY & SONS, INC.

This book is printed on acid-free paper. ∞

Copyright © 2010 by John Wiley & Sons, Inc. All rights reserved

Published by John Wiley & Sons, Inc., Hoboken, New Jersey
Published simultaneously in Canada

No part of this publication may be reproduced, stored in a retrieval system, or transmitted in any form or by any means, electronic, mechanical, photocopying, recording, scanning, or otherwise, except as permitted under Section 107 or 108 of the 1976 United States Copyright Act, without either the prior written permission of the Publisher, or authorization through payment of the appropriate per-copy fee to the Copyright Clearance Center, 222 Rosewood Drive, Danvers, MA 01923, (978) 750-8400, fax (978) 646-8600, or on the web at www.copyright.com. Requests to the Publisher for permission should be addressed to the Permissions Department, John Wiley & Sons, Inc., 111 River Street, Hoboken, NJ 07030, (201) 748-6011, fax (201) 748-6008, or online at www.wiley.com/go/permissions.

Limit of Liability/Disclaimer of Warranty: While the publisher and the author have used their best efforts in preparing this book, they make no representations or warranties with respect to the accuracy or completeness of the contents of this book and specifically disclaim any implied warranties of merchantability or fitness for a particular purpose. No warranty may be created or extended by sales representatives or written sales materials. The advice and strategies contained herein may not be suitable for your situation. You should consult with a professional where appropriate. Neither the publisher nor the author shall be liable for any loss of profit or any other commercial damages, including but not limited to special, incidental, consequential, or other damages.

For general information about our other products and services, please contact our Customer Care Department within the United States at (800) 762-2974, outside the United States at (317) 572-3993 or fax (317) 572-4002.

Wiley also publishes its books in a variety of electronic formats. Some content that appears in print may not be available in electronic books. For more information about Wiley products, visit our web site at www.wiley.com.

Library of Congress Cataloging-in-Publication Data:

Williams, Homer.
  Building type basics for banks and financial institutions / Homer Williams.
     p. cm.
  Includes bibliographical references and index.
  ISBN 978-0-470-27862-8 (cloth : alk. paper) 1. Bank buildings—United States—Designs and plans. I. Title.
  NA6241.W55 2010
  725'.24—dc22
                                         2009031376

Printed in the United States of America
10 9 8 7 6 5 4 3 2 1

CONTENTS

Preface *John Czarnecki* — ix

Acknowledgments — xi

Introduction — xiii

1. A Brief History of Banking — 1
Banking in the United States — 1
The Great Depression — 6
World War II and the Postwar Era — 7
From the 1960s to the Present — 8

2. The Structure of the Financial System — 9
Regulatory Agencies and Legislation — 9
Banking Institutions — 13

3. Brand Identification — 17
Branding — 17
Case Studies — 18
The Use and Future of Technology in Branding — 24

4. Programming — 27
Programming Guide Checklist — 27

5. Drive-Up Banks — 33
Early Drive-Up Banks — 33
Contemporary Drive-Up Facilities — 37

6. Site Selection and Planning — 39
Planning and Zoning — 39
Temporary Facilities — 42
Conventional Drive-Up — 44
Face-Up Lanes — 47
Tandem Island Customer Units — 50
Direct-Bury and Trench Installations for Remote Lanes — 51
Commercial Lanes — 52
ATM Facilities — 53
Canopy Design — 55
Site Signage — 59

CONTENTS

7. Building Design — 61
- The Floor Plan — 61
- Existing Branch Transformation — 72
- The Boutique Bank/Shop — 79
- Prototypical Design — 80
- Malls, Airports, and In-Store Locations — 81
- Call Centers — 81
- Online Banking and Tellers — 82
- Select-Market Banks — 83
- New Products and Services — 84
- Single- or Multifloor — 84
- The Community Meeting Room — 86
- Operational Space Needs — 87
- Building Codes — 91
- Utilities — 94
- Construction Cost Comparisons — 94
- Sustainability — 95

8. Mechanical, Electrical, and Plumbing Systems — 97
- HVAC Systems — 97
- Special Interior Conditions — 102
- Plumbing — 103
- Electrical — 104
- Specialized Bank Equipment — 108
- Building Commissioning and Verification — 109

9. Teller Rooms, Workrooms, and Associated Equipment — 111
- Teller Areas — 111
- Workrooms — 116
- Teller Equipment — 122
- Other Equipment — 122

10. Specialized Equipment — 125
- Drive-Up Units — 125
- Remote Drive-Up Systems — 126
- Personal Teller Machines — 127
- Window and Drawer Units — 131
- Night Depositories — 134
- Safe Deposit Vaults — 135
- Automated Teller Machines — 145
- Alarm and Building Security Systems — 148
- Other Equipment — 150
- Forms Dispenser — 150

CONTENTS

11. Case Studies — 151

Noralco Credit Union; Fort Collins, Colorado — 152
Farmers Bank of North Missouri; Saint Joseph — 154
Freestar Bank; Downs, Illinois — 155
Hyde Park Bank; Chicago, Illinois — 157
Madison National Bank, Signature Branch; Merrick, New York — 160
Pilot Bank; Tampa, Florida — 161
Old National Bancorp Headquaters; Evansville, Indiana — 163
River Bank; Osceola, Wisconsin — 165
Mountain State Bank; Cumming, Georgia — 167
Rock Springs National Bank; Rock Springs, Wyoming — 168
Frandsen Bank & Trust; Forest Lake, Minnesota — 170
Home State Bank; Willmar, Minnesota — 172
Colonial Bank, Anthem Branch; Henderson, Nevada — 175
Wachovia Bank at Eagles Landing Financial Center; Stockbridge, Georgia — 176
St. Cloud Federal Credit Union; Sartell, Minnesota — 178
North Fork Bank, Long Beach Branch; Long Beach, New York — 180
Aloha Pacific Credit Union; Honolulu, Hawaii — 182
Watermark Credit Union Headquarters Facility; Seattle, Washington — 184
Fivepoint Credit Union; Bridge City, Texas — 186
Banner Bank; Boise, Idaho — 188

12. The Future of Bank Architecture — 191

Appendices

Appendix A. Federal Bank Regulators — 195
Appendix B. State Banking Association Websites — 199
Appendix C. Bank Equipment Manufacturers — 201
Appendix D. Financial Websites — 208
Appendix E. Featured Project Architects and Designers — 210

Bibliography and References — 212

Index — 215

PREFACE

Wiley's Building Type Basics series, conceived more than a decade ago by the late Stephen A. Kliment, FAIA, series founder and editor, who had served as editor in chief of *Architectural Record* magazine from 1990 to 1996, includes one book on each of the major building types that architects design.

Early in the development of the series, Kliment called upon expert architects to each author a volume based on the typology that they had built a career or firm upon.

Who is this series intended for, and what purpose will it serve in your practice? Building Type Basics books are written primarily for architects—from recent graduates working on their first project in a building type, to experienced architects who want the latest information on a building type they already know, to seasoned associates and principals looking to add a new building type to their firm's portfolio. Beyond architects, the series is useful to developers, builders, clients, urban planners urban designers, and related professional consultants working with a given building type. As Kliment had written in the preface to the first editions of the Building Type Basics series: "As architectural practice becomes more generalized and firms pursue and accept commissions for a widening range of building types, the books in this series will comprise a convenient, hands-on resource providing basic information on the initial design phases of a project and answers to the questions design professionals routinely encounter in those crucial early phases."

Each volume of the Building Type Basics series covers what architects need to know about the unique features of a given typology—from site selection and site planning issues related to landscape and parking to predesign programming, project delivery processes, building codes and accessibility, engineering systems, lighting and acoustics, wayfinding, costs, feasibility, financing, and more. The latest editions in this series, including this volume, offer information about sustainable design solutions, the contemporary design trends related to that building type, as well as the most current updates in both information technology and building technology that impact a building type.

Case studies of the best contemporary projects of a given building type help to illustrate the concepts presented in each book. Selected projects are geographically diverse across North America and vary in scale so that one can glean lessons from a given case study that can be applied to the architect's or designer's own work, whether a small-scale project in a remote setting in a southern climate or a large-scale building in a dense, urban setting in a harsh northern climate or somewhere in-between. That is, wherever your project is located and whatever its scale, the case studies in this book offer valuable lessons.

PREFACE

Richly illustrated with diagrams, drawings, and photographs, the Building Type Basics series—through both visual information and narrative—will serve as both a guide and reference with its presentation of relevant concepts, design principles, and techniques to guide your projects.

John E. Czarnecki, Assoc. AIA
Senior Editor, Architecture and Design
John Wiley & Sons

ACKNOWLEDGMENTS

This book has been in the making since I first worked on an early drive-up branch bank project in the early 1960s and could find no reference guide or source available that described bank design (except for some limited product literature from bank equipment companies). It would fill many more pages to acknowledge every person since then who has assisted me in the course of compiling this body of work, but I wish to mention the following people who have assisted me in past and recent years in this effort:

From Diebold Inc. are Brad Stephenson, vice president of the Physical Securities Group; Dan McIntyre, senior product manager; and Mike Petcavage; also Elizabeth Bray and Robert Kelly of Diebold's Kansas City office; Stuart Chun of Diebold's Hawaii office. Mark Thatcher and Darwin Fest of Bankers Security Company of Kansas City; Ron Apgar of Oppliger Equipment Company of Kansas City; Brian Strautman of the Hamilton Safe Co.; and Ron Parsley of ADT.

From ComCo Inc. are Neal Broussard and Perry Manley, together with a special thanks to ComCo's president, Gary Paul, and its chair, Melissa Carder. For valuable information gained from firsthand tours of the manufacturing process in much of the specialized equipment featured in this work, I am indebted to Steve Cunningham of American Vault Inc.

My bank board colleagues at Northland National Bank include Gordon Peterson, John Hagen, Dr. Ross Sciara, Frank Palermo, chairman Kenneth Reidemann, and former chairman Floyd Anderson. Of great help were Northland staff members Ken Roberson, Bill Vaughan, Ralph Puglisi, Tina Johnson, Tracey Gulley, Cindy Green, Geri Saint Clair, and the entire operations staff.

Other bankers who gave me the opportunity to work on their bank projects, and learn more in the process, include E. J. Rolfs, the late Marc Dittman, Lee Walker, Ken Hollander, Rhonda Dugan, Steve Rowton, Ron Barbossa, Larry Ellington, Bruce Davis, Jerry James, Joseph James, Jim Farley, the late J. W. Farley, Larry Janacaro, Dr. Steve McRae, the late Dr. Joseph Kelly, Bruce Davis, Bill Esry, G. L. Thomas, Tim Rice, Ted Wilson, Jeff Elsea, Paul Degenhardt, Mark Smith, David DeShon, Jim Fowler, and Ann Dickinson. Outside bank directors Mack Porter, Jim Trimble, and Jim Chappell were also very important in my continuing efforts.

Assistance from WSKF staff includes Cathy Smith, Jennifer Elliott, Brian Dostal, Kellie Fitzgerald, Alison Broochert, Dustin Watkins, Tricia Ingram, Miranda White, Dalyn Novak, and Vince Magers; and my utmost appreciation must go to architect Greg Porter. To Tino South, a special thanks. To my former partners at WSKF, Mark Spurgeon, ALA; Rick Kuhl, MBA; and John Freshnock, AIA, thanks for tolerating my time away to teach, study, and write.

ACKNOWLEDGMENTS

Engineer Kurt Ewart, PE, of Hoss & Brown, assisted me with his insight into the particular needs of HVAC, electrical, and plumbing systems and applications for financial institutions. From PKMR Engineers, Jerot Pearson, PE, and Mike Raaf, PE, also contributed their insight. I owe a special thanks to Dr. John Vanderford, who assisted me with facts about geotechnical energy systems and their increasing importance.

The participation from numerous colleagues involved with financial institution design begins with Paul Siebert, CMC, and Naomi Webb of EHS Design; Ellen Dickson, AIA, of BE Design; Jack Boarman, AIA, and David Kroos, AIA, of BKV Group Architects; Paul Florian, FAIA, and Jane Allen of Florian Architects; Kathleen Gaffney and Salma Baahramy of Gensler Architects; Joe Robertson, AIA, VP, Barbara Cronn, Senior Associate, and Mike Plotnick of HOK Architects/Saint Louis; Scott Veazey, AIA, of VPS Architecture; Jennifer Albrecht of HTG Architects; Robert Foreman, AIA, of Foreman Seeley Fountain Architects; John Myefski, ALA, and Heather Hammerle of Myefski Cook Architects; Wyatt Porter Brown of McHarry Architects; John R. Sorrenti, FAIA, and W. C. Jack Miller of JRS Architects; Stacy Downs, Dave Broesdar, and Sean Lathrop of KKE Architects; Kevin Blair, Tom Auer, AIA, and Roxanne Barr of NewGround; Sofia Galadza of IA Interior Architects; Dr. Robert A. Fielden, NCARB, FAIA, of RAFI Architects; Katie Sosnowchik of HDR Architects, and their associates Suzie Hall, ASID, LEED AP, of Cornerstone Design, and Elizabeth Cooper, LEED AP, of The Architects Office. Another thanks goes to Honolulu-based Ushijima Architects, and Glen Mason, AIA, Architects.

Wallace Watanabe and Rita Ornelas gave me the opportunity to go behind the scenes at Aloha Pacific and observe its cutting-edge financial service operations. Gary Lewis Evans, President of Bank of the Internet, contributed his keen insight. Calvin Kleinman, Paul Clendening, and Derek Kleinman of Private Bank allowed me to see their impressive operation and facilities.

At the University of Hawaii were Harumi Leong, Keefe Ch'ng, Tiffany Nahinu, Jonathan Ching, Yishan Yu, Mireille Turin, and Barbara Ho, all of whom assisted me in this project. A special thanks to Dean Clark Llewellyn and Associate Dean David Rockwood at the School of Architecture.

My utmost appreciation must go to my doctoral committee from the University of Hawaii: Professor Leighton Liu, chair; Dr. Robert A. Fielden, NCARB, FAIA; Patrick T. Onishi, AIA; and banking expert Mr. Leland M. Walker. It was that doctoral dissertation that paved the way for this publication.

Finally, my great appreciation must extend to senior editor Amanda Miller; editor John Czarnecki, Assoc. AIA; and editorial assistant Sadie Abuhoff at John Wiley & Sons in Hoboken for their patience and valuable assistance.

INTRODUCTION

Although banks and other financial institutions have been a significant building type in the developed world for many years, there are few reference guides or books about planning, designing, or constructing them. Architects understand the programming and design process but often know little about the operational functionality and specialized equipment needed in a new bank. Similarly, most bankers know a great deal about banking operations and departmental functions, but very little about the design process or how to achieve a desired architectural goal.

Across the globe, financial services are offered by many different methods and in many different physical settings. A study of such differences would be of great interest, and could perhaps fill several volumes. This work, however, is of more limited and practical intent: it is meant to provide a hands-on, single-source reference for bankers, their architects, interior designers, builders, subcontractors, and suppliers embarking on a new project. Although the case studies offered here are limited to projects in the United States (with one Canadian exception), they have international applicability.

A brief history of banking in the United States is helpful in providing background on the evolution of bank design, from the earliest examples to the advent of the motor bank. The impact of banking regulators and their immense influence on banks today is outlined. Next is presented the automobile access that pneumatic tubes greatly enhanced, continuing to the evolution of current motor-bank design. The material presented herein will lead the reader to the new design directions now possible.

A study of current planning practices, recommendations, and commonly used and newly available equipment is presented. Here are listed the spatial needs, uses, and relationships common in today's bank planning, as well as typical equipment needs. Although many illustrations of suggested equipment and assemblies are offered, these should be taken as a general guide only, as such equipment is constantly being improved and changed.

A major concern in this post-9/11 era is security. Banks may become a preferred target of terrorists, some of whom are overwhelmingly opposed to the very idea of modern western banking (Sullivan 2007). There are also the familiar threat of the bank robber and the new and the increasingly troublesome electronic identity thief. The Bank Protection Act now assigns a great deal of responsibility for the security of financial institutions to their boards of directors. Thus architects, designers, and their banker clients must be familiar with the systems needed to insure security in these structures.

The trend toward a paperless and cashless society continues apace. New directions in electronic commerce are rapidly changing the older brick-and-mortar edifices that have long been the image of banking. Remote Deposit Capture, which eliminates the "float" time for a check to clear, is increasingly used by merchants and soon will be by consumers as well. While the automobile remains important in American bank planning, remote teller machines with

INTRODUCTION

closed-circuit televised teller assistance are increasingly popular at drive-up locations. New "smart" ATMs that will sometimes be directly connected by pneumatic tube service are about to enter the marketplace. Other newly developed equipment is available to bankers and their customers.

Although most facilities retain some measure of personal teller service, some new facilities are being constructed to be "tellerless," with the majority of customer access through new teller machines employing televised and pneumatic conveyance, providing both customer service and a vivid new marketing theme. The tellers are available but are out of sight and may not even be in the same building. Boutique espresso café–Internet bank shops are also providing call-center access as well as online and direct financial services.

Personal bankers are now being provided to some clients by the larger banking organizations, and some new banks are accepting only those customers who have a high net worth. Many banks have continued to offer trust advisors and services. Also offered today are new products such as annuities, securities and investments, insurance, real estate, risk management, and other services. These were not on offer earlier because of regulations that have only recently changed. It remains to be seen, in this era of global economic meltdown stemming in part from subprime mortgage difficulties, if banking laws will again change in the direction of much greater federal and state regulation.

Some new planning concepts feature multiple computer station operators who provide online teller services for their customers without ever seeing or meeting them in person. Banking via mobile devices such as cell phones and personal digital assistants is now being implemented, with the potential of replacing many of the brick-and-mortar bank functions that have so long been required. In a more dense urban area, a bank may have a central facility with a call center and/or an online staff only, and that facility becomes more akin to a high-tech office building than a traditional bank. These usually have multiple full-service branches of a prototypical design as well, but in some cases they only have a coffee shop that features phone and Internet service to a call or data center.

With the ever-increasing competition that now occurs in the financial world, brand identification is becoming increasingly important. Brand images are more than just the institutional logo, as they translate to all forms of advertising inside the building and out. In many cases the building itself may become a major part of the brand image.

This work presents twenty banks that have been recently constructed and illustrates the features that distinguish them. Included is a wide range of types that can be found in the United States today, from small neighborhood branch designs, to complete functional conversions (e.g., from a restaurant to bank), to large headquarters facilities. Not included are the skyscraper bank towers that are primarily office buildings, although two multistory banks recognized for their sustainability in design are examined. Also included are listings of equipment manufacturers, financial institution organizations, and the regulatory agencies with jurisdiction over them, as well as the architects and designers whose projects are featured.[1]

1. Much of the information offered in this work comes from the important financial equipment manufacturers in the United States, from the expert architects and designers whose projects are featured, and from this writer's more than forty years of experience in financial-institution (principally branch-bank) design.

BUILDING TYPE BASICS FOR

banks and financial institutions

CHAPTER 1
A BRIEF HISTORY OF BANKING

There is no certainty as to when banking began, but the act of exchanging various forms of payment dates from prior to the third millennium BC (Heathcote 2000, p. 9). The first banks were likely temples, where people could exchange items such as cattle, implements, or precious metals, before the use of coins. When coins of precious metals began to be used as payment, "money changers" were those who understood the relative value of various coins and could provide the means for a desired exchange.

Banking then declined in medieval Europe because of religious opposition to "usury," which is the collection of interest added to a loaned amount. The Renaissance brought a revival of banking, most prominently in Italy where Marco Polo had introduced a trade route to the east, and with that, its exotic products. In the fourteenth century, the famous banking houses in Venice and Florence brought about the modern practice of banking as it came to be known. In fact, the English *bank* derives from the Italian *banco*, meaning "bench"—the tables where early banking transactions occurred (Mayer 1987, p. 26).

As trade increased and more people traveled greater distances to exchange goods, the need for an accurate means of monetary measure increased as well. Coins soon became difficult and unwieldy to carry in large numbers, and the need for an alternative resulted in the creation of paper money, which was first used in China (Williams 1997, p. 149).

In England, the safekeeping of precious coins or objects was entrusted to goldsmiths, who had the only safe storage vaults or boxes. Their customers knew that was how the goldsmiths kept safe their valuables and began to ask if their own could be kept in the smiths' vaults as well. Written receipts allowed both customers and the goldsmiths to know what was stored at a given time. Soon, customers, and then the goldsmiths, began to exchange these written receipts, instead of the actual stored items. Thus began an early form of monetary note (Moore 1987, p. 9).

The practice became so commonplace that in 1694 the Bank of England was chartered by the government and allowed to issue its own notes, early forms of paper currency. This originally private bank was later to become England's Central Bank (Mayer 1987, p. 27).

BANKING IN THE UNITED STATES

Banking in the United States developed relatively late. The economy in colonial America was principally agricultural, and credit was extended to farmers by merchants in cities such as Boston or Philadelphia. These merchants then bought on credit from their British suppliers, and when the harvest came in, the whole chain was paid off. Because the British credit system was cut off during the Revolutionary War, the need for indigenous banks became clear. Several of the colonies had previously established "land banks." These issued notes to make loans against land, but they very soon experienced

A BRIEF HISTORY OF BANKING

▶ *First Bank of the United States, Philadelphia, Pennsylvania, 1797; attributed to Samuel Blodgett. Greek temple–inspired architecture was selected for many early bank projects.* Historic American Buildings Survey.

problems with over-issue and depreciation of their notes. The few that did not fail were closed by the British Colonial administration in 1741 (Kohn 2004, p. 134).

In 1781, the Bank of North America was chartered within the Commonwealth of Pennsylvania, to help finance the Revolutionary War, but for another ten years there was no nationally chartered bank. In 1791, Congress granted the First Bank of the United States a twenty-year charter at the behest of Alexander Hamilton, the first Secretary of the Treasury. The bank building's design was attributed to Samuel Blodgett, although this has been questioned (Belfoure 2005, p. 16). The early colonial banks—which had since become state institutions—were then competing with the First Bank of the United States. They objected to its continuation, and in 1811 Congress failed to renew its charter.

Economic complications resulting from the War of 1812 prompted Congress to create the Second Bank of the United States in 1816, also with a twenty-year charter. The building was designed by William Strickland. Continuing political differences resulted in President Andrew Jackson's veto of the extension of that charter in 1836. From then until the Civil War era, free banks could be established by anyone who could provide a minimum capital outlay and deposit specified amounts, in the form of bonds, with a state agent. With such minimal restraint, however, many of these failed, often because of defaults on the states' bonds they were holding. By 1860, eighteen of the then thirty-two states had enacted "free charter" laws, and these contributed significantly to the westward expansion of the country.

For the most part, banks of this era were

Banking in the United States

◀ *Second Bank of the United States, Philadelphia, Pennsylvania, 1820; William Strickland. Simple Doric columns were used here.* Historic American Buildings Survey.

designed in the classical Greek, Italianate, French Second Empire, Victorian Gothic, or English Queen Anne style. Then the work of Henry H. Richardson brought about a revival of the eleventh-century Romanesque style in the 1870s. Surprisingly, Richardson only designed one bank, the Agawam Bank in Springfield, Massachusetts, and it was not in the style for which he became famous. His many other commissions, however, were the inspiration for countless banks throughout the United States well into the early twentieth century (Belfoure 2005, p. 104).

In 1863, Congress enacted the National Banking Act to finance the Civil War, and by 1866 there were 1,600 nationally chartered banks, which accounted for 75 percent of all bank deposits in the United States. This act also brought about the first uniform national currency and established the Office of the Comptroller of the Currency (OCC),[1] the bureau that has authority over all national banks to this day. (See chapter 2 for a description of the duties and responsibilities of the OCC.)

The new banks were required to back their notes with federal government securities, and the numbers of new banks quickly grew. Severe financial panics occurred, despite these safeguards, in 1893 and again in 1907. These led to the establishment of the National Monetary Commission, which then recommended passage of the Federal Reserve Act (1913).[2]

The Federal Reserve was then established in order to provide a central bank as the

---

1. http://www.occ.gov (accessed September 15, 2007).
2. http://federalreserve.gov (accessed September 17, 2007).

lender of last resort, and to establish monitory policy for the entire country. (Chapter 2 provides a description of the Federal Reserve and its responsibilities.)

Louis Sullivan and the Prairie Style

Louis Sullivan was already a noted architect when he designed his first bank project in 1907, the famous National Farmers Bank in Owatonna, Minnesota.

Sullivan's design philosophy of "form follows function," which his even more renowned protégé Frank Lloyd Wright also espoused, influenced other, lesser-known but significant architects of the upper Midwest. These early twentieth-century architects believed American architecture should cease copying the classical styles. George G. Elmslie, who had worked for Sullivan on the National Farmers Bank project, together with William G. Purcell, formed Purcell and Elmslie, Architects. They produced several important bank projects, including the Merchants Bank of Winona, in Minnesota (Belfoure 2005, pp. 194–211). Completed in 1912, it was significant for its innovative, Sullivan-inspired exterior.

Frank Lloyd Wright, who produced so many significant buildings in his long career, designed relatively few banks. The architectural significance of the early Prairie-style banks is acknowledged by critics and historians alike, but unfortunately this design movement did not spread to the rest of the country, where the majority of banks continued to be designed in a classical revival style. It was not until the late 1920s that architects and their banker

▶ National Farmers Bank, Owatonna, Minnesota, 1908; Louis Sullivan. Louis Sullivan's most famous bank is still beautiful more than 100 years later. Historic American Buildings Survey.

Banking in the United States

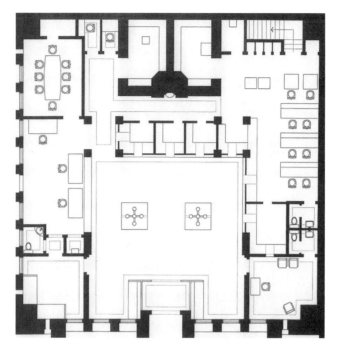

◀ *Merchants Bank of Winona, Minnesota, 1912; Purcell and Elmslie. This plan is remarkably similar to bank plans that became popular many years later. Some branch facilities today are reminiscent in their use of lobby, teller, and desk space. Illustration by the author, after an image from* Western Architect, *January 1915.*

◀ *Merchants Bank of Winona, Minnesota, 1912; Purcell and Elmslie. The terra-cotta ornament made popular by Louis Sullivan is clearly visible on the facade of this bank building, perhaps the best work of Purcell and Elmslie.*

A BRIEF HISTORY OF BANKING

clients would consider a more modern style for bank design.

THE GREAT DEPRESSION

The stock market crash of 1929 marked the beginning of the Great Depression, which soon became a worldwide circumstance. Bank construction came to a halt, and market events led to the insolvency of numerous banks across the country. Most hard-hit were rural banks that had financed agricultural loans, but banks in cities also faced great hardship. Continuous "runs" were being made, wherein customers, fearing an immediate collapse of their bank, lined up to ask for their money to be refunded. These difficulties led to the "bank holiday" of 1933, during which all U.S. banks were closed for four days to allow for an evaluation of remaining banks and to assure the public of their solvency (Klebaner 1990, p. 138).

The events stemming from the Depression led to the establishment of the Federal Deposit Insurance Corporation, which initially provided for $2500 in insurance for each depositor, in case the insured institution became insolvent. This limit was later increased to $100,000, until recently, when a temporary limit of $250,000 was established as a result of the nationwide financial turmoil of 2008. It is expected to be reduced to $100,000 again at the end of 2009. The Great Depression also brought about significantly more oversight by the regulating governmental agencies.

Another effect of the Great Depression was a change in the characteristic architectural style of American banks. Although the Depression did not end immediately, the remaining financial institutions eventually regained their viability and a new outlook in design began to prevail. One of the early modern banks was the 32-story Philadelphia Savings Fund Society building, built in 1932. It was designed by William Lescaze and George Howe and has been called America's first "truly modern skyscraper" (Belfoure, p. 227).

World War II and the Postwar Era

◀ *Manufacturer's Trust, New York City; SOM, 1954. This bank became a design pacesetter for the postwar years in the United States. Illustration by Dwain South.*

◀◀ *Philadelphia Savings Fund Building, 1932; Howe & Lescaze. The clean vertical lines and ribbon windows were well ahead of their time in this building, considered the first International Style high-rise project. It was placed on the National Historic Register in 1976. Historic American Buildings Survey.*

The National Credit Union Administration

In 1934 President Roosevelt signed into law the Federal Credit Union Act, which authorized the formation of federally chartered credit unions in all states. The National Credit Union Administration (NCAU) was established to charter and supervise the federal credit unions. Backed by the full faith and credit of the United States government, the NCAU operates the National Credit Union Share Insurance Fund (NCUSIF), which insures the account holders of the federal credit unions and many of the state-chartered credit unions.[3]

3. http://www.ncau.gov/AboutNCAU/Index.htm (accessed October 29, 2007).

WORLD WAR II AND THE POSTWAR ERA

American commerce and industry were completely dedicated to the war effort after the Pearl Harbor attack, and almost all bank construction was put on hold. The war years did provide bankers with an opportunity to reconsider the kind of bank that they wanted and their customers needed.

After the war, bankers were much less interested in the old classical influences. Of the immediate postwar banks the most dramatic was the Fifth Avenue branch of the Manufacturers' Trust designed by Skidmore, Owings & Merrill (SOM) in New York City in 1954 (Belfoure 2005, p. 248). An in-house competition was held over a weekend at SOM and the winner was Charles Evans Hughes III, who designed a four-story building with a glass curtain wall that featured the vault prominently visible from the street, a practice that is still favored by many bankers today.

FROM THE 1960s TO THE PRESENT
Over the last forty years, banking has undergone dramatic technological changes. Electronic banking, banking by phone, use of debit and credit cards, and the ubiquity of automated teller machines (ATMs) have revolutionized banking and financial institution buildings. Other, less visible innovations in planning, equipment, and the delivery of financial services have also been made, and these are featured in the following chapters.

The Bank Protection Act of 1968 and its amendment in 1991 have been significant to bankers and their architects alike, because it spelled out in great detail the security requirements for buildings and operations. The responsibilities it delegated to banks' boards of directors, and thereby the architects in their employ, became much greater as well. All agencies that regulate the financial industry in the United States are subject to these requirements. This legislation will be discussed in greater detail in later chapters.

Equally important were the regulatory changes brought about in 1999 by the Gramm-Leach-Bliley Act, which in essence overturned the strict banking laws enacted in 1933. The earlier legislation had precluded commercial banks from offering investment banking, insurance, and other services. It remains to be seen what the long-lasting effects of the 1999 act will be, given the credit difficulties lately seen, which stemmed from the subprime lending and other practices that followed its passage.

A most significant operational change was brought about in 2004 with the advent of Check Clearing for the 21st Century, called Check 21. This law allows a new negotiable instrument, called a substitute check, which permits a bank to truncate the original check and process the check information electronically. This has had an enormous impact on banking operations throughout the United States, with implications for the design of financial institutions.

The even more recent development of "remote deposit capture," which allows merchants to combine the processing and imaging of checks at the beginning of the payment cycle, rather than at the end, may have an even greater impact on banking and the bank's relationship with customers (Fisher 2006, p. 108). More will be presented in the following chapters about the physical requirements these changes have brought. (Chapter 9, for example, features a bank workroom that has been recently converted for use of the new Check 21 equipment.)

CHAPTER 2
THE STRUCTURE OF THE FINANCIAL SYSTEM

The financial structure of the United States is the focus of this work (with some discussion of parallel institutions in Canada). It is helpful for architects to understand the regulatory agencies and their responsibilities and relations to the various types of financial institutions, as well as the nature of these institutions and their consumer bases.

Chapter 1 described the establishment of the Office of the Comptroller of the Currency, which is the regulator of all national bank charters, and the Federal Reserve Bank, which is the central bank of the United States. This chapter considers these and other agencies and their duties and responsibilities, including the state regulatory agencies, and defines the institutions to be considered.

REGULATORY AGENCIES AND LEGISLATION

The Office of the Comptroller of the Currency (OCC)

As a bureau of the United States Department of the Treasury, the OCC is headed by the comptroller, who is appointed by the president to a five-year term, with the advice and consent of the Senate. The OCC office is comprised of a nationwide staff of examiners who conduct on-site reviews of national banks and provide sustained supervision of banking operations. It also issues rules and legal interpretations, and makes corporate decisions about banking, bank investments, bank community development, and other aspects of banking operations. The OCC has complete authority over the practices and procedures of national banks in the United States today, and all must comply with OCC regulations in order to obtain and retain their charters.[1]

In regulating national banks, the OCC has the power to[2]

- Examine the banks.
- Approve or deny applications for new charters, branches, capital, or other changes in corporate or banking structure.
- Take supervisory action against banks that do not comply with laws and regulations or otherwise engage in unsound banking practices. The agency can remove officers and directors, negotiate agreements to change banking practices, and issue cease and desist orders as well as civil monetary penalties.
- Issue rules and regulations governing bank investments, lending, and other practices.

The OCC's activities are predicated on four objectives that support the OCC's mission to ensure a stable and competitive national banking system. The four objectives are as follows:

- To ensure the safety and soundness of the national banking system.
- To foster competition by allowing banks to offer new products and services.

1 http://www.occ.gov (accessed October 21, 2007).
2 Ibid.

THE STRUCTURE OF THE FINANCIAL SYSTEM

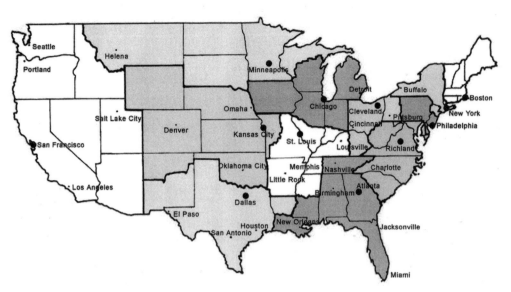

▶ The twelve Federal Reserve Districts of the United States. Alaska and Hawaii are part of the San Francisco district. Puerto Rico and the U.S. Virgin Islands are part of the New York district. There are additional branch offices within each district, as shown (see also appendix A).

- To improve the efficiency and effectiveness of OCC supervision, including reducing regulatory burden.
- To ensure fair and equal access to financial services for all Americans.

Office of Thrift Supervision (OTS)

The OTS is an agency of the United States Department of the Treasury that is the primary regulator of federal savings associations, or thrifts. These include both federal savings banks and federal savings and loans (S&Ls). The OTS is also responsible for supervising S&L holding companies (SLHCS) and some state-chartered institutions. Established by Congress in 1989 as a bureau of the Treasury Department, the OTS is entirely funded from the assessments paid by the institutions it regulates. As of this writing, however, Congress is giving serious consideration to merging the duties of the OTS into the OCC.

The mission of the OTS is "to supervise savings associations and their holding companies in order to maintain their safety and soundness and compliance with consumer laws, and to encourage a competitive industry that meets America's financial service needs."[3]

The Federal Reserve System

Created to provide the United States with a safer, more flexible, and stable monetary and financial system, the Federal Reserve, known also as the "Fed," is the nation's central bank, or the bank for all the other banks. It is a network of twelve Federal Reserve banks, each headquartered in a different region and with a number of branches, with oversight by a seven-member board of governors, a chairman, and a vice-chairman. Each member serves a fourteen-year term, except that the chairman and vice-chairman serve four-year renewable terms while serving their regular fourteen-year terms.

3 http://www.ots.treas.gov/?p=MissionGoal (accessed June 8, 2009).

Among other responsibilities, the Federal Reserve does the following:[4]

- It sets United States monetary policy and keeps consumer prices stable and interest rates relatively low.
- It supervises and regulates banks to ensure safe operations and protects consumer rights.
- It provides financial services to the depositing institutions, the government, and foreign central banks, including check clearing, processing electronic payments, and distributing coins and paper money to the nation's banks, credit unions, savings and loans, and savings banks.
- It conducts research on other financial matters.
- It distributes information about the national economy.[5]

The twelve Federal Reserve banks of the United States are headquartered in Boston, New York, Cleveland, Richmond, Atlanta, Chicago, Saint Louis, Minneapolis, Kansas City, Dallas, and San Francisco. The accompanying map indicates the Federal Reserve regions of the United States. (See Appendix A for specific locations and contact information.)

The Bank Protection Act

Enacted by Congress in 1968, with the latest revisions occurring in 1991, the Bank Protection Act (BPA) requires banks and other savings institutions to adopt appropriate security procedures to discourage bank robberies, burglaries, and larcenies. Originally enacted for national bank charters, the BPA has since been adopted for state charters and credit unions as well. Many of its provisions affect operations, and it is important for architects to understand the physical needs of the operational activities that drive their design decisions. Boards of directors now face much greater responsibilities, in complying with the BPA.[6]

The act includes provisions that every bank do the following:

1. Establish procedures for opening and closing for business and for the safekeeping of all currency, negotiable securities, and similar valuables at all times.
2. Establish procedures that will assist in identifying persons committing crimes against the institution and that will preserve evidence that may aid in their identification or conviction; such procedures may include, but are not limited to
    a. Using identification devices, such as prerecorded serial numbered bills or chemical and electronic devices.
    b. Maintaining a camera that records activity in the banking office.
    c. Retaining a record of any robbery, burglary, or larceny committed or attempted against a banking office.
3. Provide for initial and periodic training of employees in their responsibilities under the security program and in proper employee conduct during and after a robbery.
4. Provide for selecting, testing, operating, and maintaining appropriate security devices, as required.

---

4 "The 12 Federal Reserve Districts," http://www.federalreserve.gov/otherfrb.htm (accessed October 23, 2007).
5 Ibid.
6 http://www.occ.treas.gov/fr/cfrparts/12CFR21.htm (accessed November 18, 2008).

Each bank is required to have at a minimum the following devices:

1. A means of protecting cash or other liquid assets, such as a vault, safe, or other secure space.
2. A lighting system for illuminating, during the hours of darkness, the area around the vault if the vault is visible from outside the banking office.
3. Tamper-resistant locks on exterior doors, and on exterior windows if these are designed to be opened.
4. An alarm system or other appropriate device for promptly notifying the nearest responsible law enforcement officers of an attempted or perpetrated robbery, burglary, or larceny.
5. Such other devices as the bank's security officer determines to be appropriate, taking into consideration the following:
    a. The incidence of crimes against financial institutions in the area.
    b. The amount of currency or other valuables exposed to robbery, burglary, or larceny.
    c. The distance of the banking office from the nearest law enforcement officers and the time required for such law enforcement to arrive at the bank.
    d. The cost of the security devices.
    e. Other security measures in effect at the banking office.
    f. The physical characteristics of the banking office structure and its surroundings.

It should be noted that adequate lighting should also be provided for ATM facilities.

Federal Deposit Insurance Corporation (FDIC)

The FDIC was created as a result of the Glass-Steagall Act of 1933. It insures banks' and thrifts' checking and savings deposits against the threat of bank failure for each member institution. The insurance amount until year-end 2009 is $250,000 per depositor per bank, and the insured deposits are backed by the full faith and credit of the United States. This amount is scheduled to be reset to $100,000 beginning in 2010. A bank must be a member of the FDIC insurance program in order to obtain and keep a national charter. Many state charters also are insured by the FDIC.

State Bank Regulators

Each state has a state banking commission or agency that ensures that new banks have the necessary capital and management expertise to meet the public's financial needs. The charter grantor is the institution's primary regulator, with frontline duties to protect the public from unsafe or unsound banking practices.

Like the OCC, the states conduct on-site examinations to assess a bank's condition and monitor compliance with banking laws. They also issue regulations, take enforcement actions, and close banks if they fail.

It is now a requirement of all states that newly chartered state banks must join the FDIC and provide deposit insurance for their depositors.

The Dual Banking System

The continuous system of regulation in the United States at both the state and federal levels, depending on which charter an institution may hold, is known as the "dual banking system" and has been in effect for nearly two hundred years.

BANKING INSTITUTIONS

State-Chartered Banks

After the charter of the Second Bank of the United States was terminated in 1836 and until the Civil War, the majority of banking was done through state-chartered banks. These banks were given the right to issue banknotes. They were expected to lend money to state governments or to state-sponsored projects such as canal construction or railroad expansion. This began a movement toward "free banking," under which a bank charter was no longer a special favor of the state with each one requiring a special act of legislation. Instead, anyone meeting minimum requirements of honesty and capital could receive a charter from the state banking commissioner (Kohn 2004, p. 135). This system of state chartering has continued, although the charter itself now requires considerably more background information and substantiation.

There are three categories of state-chartered banks (Kohn 2004, p. 596):

1. Some state-chartered banks are members of the Federal Reserve System, and these are examined by the Fed and also sometimes by the state. They must be insured by the FDIC.
2. Some state-chartered banks are not members of the Fed but are insured by the FDIC. These are also examined by the FDIC.
3. Some state-chartered banks are not insured by the FDIC. These are examined by state regulators.

Nationally Chartered Banks

The National Bank Act of 1863 was passed in response to the difficulties of financing the Civil War. This act reinstated the power of the federal government to charter banks. The new national banks were given the exclusive right to issue banknotes that were used to purchase federal debt. When the state-chartered banks were deprived of their right to issue notes, they turned to deposits as their principal form of liability and soon recovered from the disadvantage (Kohn 2004, p. 135). The chartering of national banks has continued to this day and serves as one of the two parts of the dual banking system in the United States.

The OCC grants national charters, approves mergers, and new branches, examines these banks, and if necessary, closes them. All nationally chartered banks must be members of the Federal Reserve System, and they must be insured by the FDIC. They are thus subject to all federal laws and regulations (Kohn 2004, p. 595).

Commercial Banks

A commercial bank is an organization, usually a corporation chartered by a state or the federal government, that does most or all of the following: receives demand and time deposits; honors instruments drawn on them and pays interest on them; discounts notes; makes loans; invests in securities; collects checks, drafts, and notes; certifies depositors' checks; and issues drafts and cashier's checks.[7]

Such banks, if nationally chartered, are regulated by the Office of the Comptroller

---

[7] http://www.investorwords.com/featureadjumboros.html (accessed October 2, 2007).

THE STRUCTURE OF THE FINANCIAL SYSTEM

of the Currency and are subject to the rules of the Federal Reserve and the FDIC. If state chartered, they are regulated by state banking agencies but if covered by federal insurance, they are also subject to rules of the FDIC (Mayer 1987, p. 34). There are now also other, newer services and products being offered by some commercial banks; these will be discussed in chapter 7.

Investment Banks

These institutions purchase newly issued stocks and bonds from corporations and governments, then resell securities to investors in smaller quantities. They profit by selling these securities at a higher price than they pay for them. In the 1930s, they were prohibited by the government from engaging in investments while also accepting deposits and making loans, but by the 1980s large commercial banks were allowed to again buy and sell securities, within certain limits. By 1999 all barriers had been removed that separated investment banking from commercial banking.

Bank Holding Companies

A bank holding company is any entity that directly or indirectly owns, controls, or has the power to vote 25 percent or more of a class of securities of a United States bank. Bank holding companies are required to register with the Federal Reserve System, whose board has the responsibility for regulating and supervising bank holding company activities, such as the approval of mergers and acquisitions, and inspecting the operations of such companies.[8] This authority applies even where an institution is under the primary supervision of the OCC or FDIC.

Savings and Loan Associations

Also called thrifts or S&Ls, savings and loan associations are financial institutions, organized cooperatively or corporately, that hold the funds of their members or clients in interest-bearing accounts and certificates of deposit. They invest those funds chiefly in home mortgage loans, and many also offer other services (Mayer 1987, pp. 67–68). These were originally established to help people purchase homes, and for many years they were the main source of home mortgages. Now they have become diversified and offer a wide range of services that were formerly available only from banks, such as checking accounts, individual retirement accounts (IRAs), money market accounts, and now also consumer and business loans. Many former savings and loan institutions have become savings banks.

In the 1980s, because of deregulation and increasing unsecured investments in large-scale speculation, financial failures were rampant. More than five hundred thrift institutions were forced to close, so that by 1989 the FDIC was required to take over the responsibility for insurance from the previous Federal Savings and Loan Insurance Corporation (FSLIC) insurer, and the Office of Thrift Supervision (OTS), an agency of the United States Treasury Department, was established as the regulator.[9]

Savings Banks

Originally located in New England and New York, and now in other states, savings banks are also known as mutual savings banks. They are also considered thrifts, and they are regulated by the OTS but are

---

8 http://en.wikipedia.org/Bank_holding_company (accessed October 28, 2007).

9 http://www.infoplease.com/ce6/bus/A0843804.html (accessed October 9, 2007)

controlled by self-perpetuating boards of trustees. They offer savings and checking accounts and make personal or business loans. Their net earnings are paid out as interest to depositors, or are added to surplus as a cushion against losses. State-chartered institutions are regulated by state banking commissions, but are insured by the FDIC (Mayer 1987, p. 67).

Credit Unions

Credit unions are nonprofit cooperative financial institutions that are owned and controlled by their members; they are exempt from federal and state income taxes. They are organized to serve groups that share something in common, such as where they live, work, or worship. They provide services for savings and lending as well as other financial services for their members. Credit unions are chartered and supervised by the National Credit Union Association (NCUA), an independent federal agency that also administers the National Credit Union Share Insurance Fund (NCUSIF), a federal fund that insures the member credit unions.

CHAPTER 3
BRAND IDENTIFICATION

BRANDING

Unlike bankers and most other business professionals, who quickly learn the value of effective advertising, architects rarely have a fondness for it, and thus they usually go about including the required signage on or in their building designs with some trepidation. What they must learn now, however, is that a marketing philosophy is taking hold in banking that will require them not only to provide for signage, but also to implement a concept called "branding" within the entire scope of their projects.

Tom Asacker, a recipient of the George Land Innovator of the Year award, says in his best-selling *A Clear Eye for Branding* that branding is more than just a client's logo, a slogan, or a design scheme (2005, p. 5); rather, it may extend to the entire project concept, in ways that will require new ways of thinking about the fundamental design concept. Regarding branding for banks and other financial institutions, Asacker writes:

> A bank, like any other business today, is in the business of improving customer's lives. Given the choice in financial products, services, and information, today's banks must do more than offer competitive rates, services and product choice. They must also provide meaning and a sense of identity to their audience.[1]

In her book *Brain Tattoos*, Karen Post says:

> The word *brand* has many definitions from a variety of respected resources. I believe the brand is a mental imprint that is earned and belongs to a product, service, organization, individual, and/or event. It's the sum of all tangible and intangible characteristics of that entity. A brand is what an audience thinks and feels when it hears a name or sees a sign, a product, and/or a place of activity. It's what customers expect when they select an offering over a competing one. (2005, p. xv)

What does this mean to financial institutions and their designers? It means that they must go beyond their typical design endeavors and understand how the physical image they develop links up with or drives the overall brand expression, as delivered through all other channels—for example online banking; interior video messaging; merchandising; advertising; phone center operations; human resources and employee training; headquarters design; and subsidiary business integration.[2]

Post adds, "Branding is not merely the logo, some catchy tagline, or the creative pastime for the marketing department." It is now "a way of life," the "heart and soul of

---

1. Tom Asacker, e-mail to the author, Nov. 12, 2007.
2. Paul Seibert, conversation with the author, Oct 22, 2007.

an offering," and "should be woven into every important decision and resonate through every point of contact within a market's span" (2005, p. xv).

An effective approach to this encompassing conception of branding is to commission early in the process a wide-ranging study of the institution to determine the culture of its customer or member base. Such a cultural analysis should determine stakeholders' habits, pastime preferences, and vocational and occupational endeavors. A database of this information provides the brand consultant and architect with the basis to develop a thematic expression for a brand design. This may be extended to all channels that comprise the brand's presentation to its public.

One familiar method of identifying a building with a brand is, of course, the use of distinguishing architectural features, such as overhanging canopies or eaves, or a tower or other distinguishing vertical element, which might feature a clock, or the institutional logo, or both. (Many recent local regulations restrict the time-honored time-and-temperature pylon sign.) A multitude of materials and techniques can emphasize a particular image.

A number of banks and their architects are employing long-standing retail methods of display and photography, as well as newer flat-screen technology, which can showcase, in high-definition video and with high-fidelity sound, products and services offered by the institution. The customer path, from the entrance to the building through to the tellers, provides a significant opportunity to feature this technology.

CASE STUDIES

North Shore Credit Union

Paul Seibert, CMC, of EHS Design; Mark Weber, president of Weber Marketing; and their teams, including Atelier Pacific Architecture Inc., experts on financial institution design and branding applications, designed the North Shore Credit Union in Vancouver, British Columbia.[3] This project represents an effort to "translate the credit union's brand focus on 'member wellness' into a truly unique and dynamic retail branch environment that connected with its Vancouver-area target market's community and lifestyle," resulting in a concept called an "i-branch" by North Shore's management.[4]

Also termed a "West Coast financial spa," this project complements the many ways the institution seeks to improve the quality of its members' lives. A "concierge" greets and welcomes members and ensures they are directed to the most appropriate person, thereby creating a personal and intimate member experience. The new prototype branch "helps to support a local arts initiative—making for an unusual pairing of art and banking. A gallery-type exhibition space extends the ways the credit union gives back to the community and provides a unique showcase for local artists, on a rotating schedule. It links the way North Shore does business with the same activities its members deem important and valuable."[5]

3. http://www.ehs-design (accessed October 20, 2007).
4. Paul Seibert, message to the author (February 12, 2008).
5. Ibid.

Case Studies

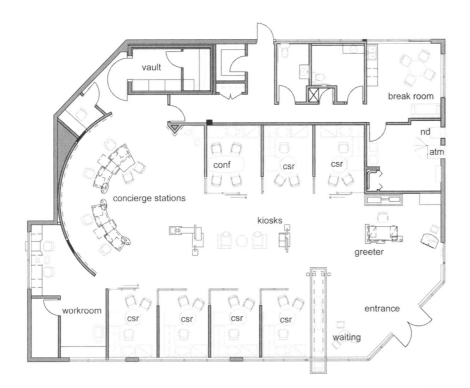

◀ Floor plan of the North Shore Credit Union, Vancouver, British Columbia; EHS Design. The new plan concept delivers a uniquely engineered member and staff experience that provides multiple development opportunities while ensuring a high degree of security through the application of "safe-catch" architecture, a system designed to discourage robbery. EHS Design Architects.

◀ Waiting area and entrance display, North Shore Credit Union, Vancouver, British Columbia; EHS Design. A highly branded multimedia "discovery wall" is presented in each branch lobby to communicate current and high-value messages. Roger Brooks Photography.

BRAND IDENTIFICATION

▶ *Member service and development lobby, North Shore Credit Union, Vancouver, British Columbia; EHS Design. Every member passes by the local artist display linking North Shore Credit Union to its target members' lifestyle interests. Teller pods (see chapter 7) are used to enhance member development and create opportunities to shake hands and introduce members to other staff. Roger Brooks Photography.*

"Throughout the branch, the native materials, colors, and artisan crafts, like Vancouver glass, make for a unique experience." These create a distinct brand image that reflects the local lifestyle. Traditional tellers were replaced with "teller pods" in front of a zen-inspired bamboo wall adorned with flat screens. According to Seibert, the new facility "provides the service quality of a spa combined with the ruggedness of the local environment for a truly different banking experience."[6]

Among the benefits created for the credit union members are "a fresh and vibrant concierge-style approach that helps bolster North Shore's standing as a premier boutique financial institution that delivers comprehensive and highly tailored financial solutions and advisory services." One North Shore's executive officers summed up the branch design as having "enhanced our members' experience by allowing us to address their financial needs at all levels, from daily transactions to investment advice, in an environment that is at once, innovative, imaginative, informative, and intimate."

Ascend Credit Union

A second noteworthy project to feature imaginative branding strategy in design is the Ascend Credit Union in Middle Tennessee, designed by NewGround. Originally named AEDC Federal Credit Union, the institution was established in 1961 to serve

6. Ibid.

Case Studies

◀ Ascend Federal Credit Union, Murfreesboro, Tennessee; NewGround. "Ascend's newly branded facilities now reflect who they are, where they're headed as an organization, and the companies and members they serve." © NewGround 2007.

◀ Interior of lobby, Ascend Federal Credit Union; NewGround. "The Ascend concept was incorporated into the interiors through the use of aircraft materials." The background wall surface was blue sky and white clouds, in keeping with the brand theme. © NewGround 2007.

BRAND IDENTIFICATION

▶ *E-Branch Center, Ascend Federal Credit Union; NewGround. The brand image is carried throughout the interior with colorful marketing opportunities and products-and-services displays.* ©NewGround 2007.

▶ *Ascend Credit Union teller pods; NewGround. Part of the new and dramatic brand image are these teller pods, described in detail in chapter 7.* © NewGround 2007.

Arnold Air Force Base. The client came to NewGround with a ten-year strategic growth plan for becoming the dominant credit union in Middle Tennessee. With thirteen branches in seven counties, they found their existing membership had little understanding of what the AEDC acronym meant; thus, it would have little impact on desired growth as they moved into the larger market. They therefore needed a new name, brand, and brand-infused branches to launch their action plan to fuel growth.

The branding solution was to leverage AEDC's aeronautical heritage. The new name selected was Ascend Federal Credit Union, with the striking theme of "taking flight," suggesting that Ascend could raise its members' hopes and possibilities and help them achieve their goals. The new brand was integrated into the retrofit of the credit union's existing branches, main offices, as well as into construction of a new facility in Murfreesboro, Tennessee.

NewGround also worked with Ascend to create and deliver a customized education program for all of its employees, explaining the new brand image and how it should be conveyed and demonstrated to Ascend's members.[7]

ING Direct

A third significant brand introduction is by the rapidly growing ING Direct organization. This now-famous brand features an orange ball to signify its emphasis on savings to its customers. The brainchild of Arkadi Kuhlmann and Bruce Philp, ING Direct has established numerous Internet "café banks"

7. From NewGround, "Ascend Federal Credit Union," http://www.newground.com/cs_ ascend.html (accessed October 30, 2008).

▲ ING Direct café bank, New York City; Gensler Architects. The well-known orange ball is the brand image of this fast-growing Internet banking operation that serves its customers from these "cafés" located in numerous major U.S. cities. The strong brand emphasis is carried out by the use of a three-part design image termed by the architects "cube, ribbon, and node." This concept was developed to accommodate the program requirements of serving counters, Internet and phone kiosks, graphic messaging walls, and merchandising displays.   Craig Duggan.

BRAND IDENTIFICATION

▲ North Fork Bank, Third Avenue, New York City; JRS Architects. The large LED sign is visible for several blocks, drawing attention to the new branch. Zweibel Photography.

in selected cities across the United States. The project shown here, designed by Gensler Architects, is in New York City. More about this innovative brand and the thinking that engendered it is presented in chapter 7.

North Fork Bank

Another new project that emphasizes its brand image with a high-profile advertising vehicle is the North Fork Bank's new Third Avenue branch in New York City, designed by JRS Architects. In this project, two giant LED screens are displayed inside the bank lobby. These can be seen from a great distance through the building's glass facade by all passersby. Comprised of 500 LED fixtures, the high-tech displays are controlled from a central computer system. At night this makes for a memorable brand attraction to the new branch.

THE USE AND FUTURE OF TECHNOLOGY IN BRANDING

Automated teller machines (ATMs) were among some of the early examples in the financial world to emphasize a brand image in promoting the institution. Although they are also now owned and operated by numerous nonbanking organizations, they are still used in this manner by banks and credit unions and still play an important role in brand image.

New products are constantly being used in the retail market that may have a place in the branding strategy of the financial industry. One is a "surface" computer by Microsoft that operates with touch commands, without a keyboard or a mouse. It can recognize the stored images in a digital or video camera or phone, and automatically reproduce those images and related data on the screen in a variety of ways; or it can recognize a credit card and automatically record a charge.[8] These and other technologies can

---

8. http://www.microsoft.com/surface (accessed October 9, 2007).

The Use and Future of Technology in Branding

present a brand image in a recurring manner, a very important attribute in the retention of a customer base. Architects and brand consultants must be able to incorporate such technologies, without having them detract from the design concept, in a way that combines design excellence with continuous customer attraction.

New developments in virtual reality, especially in three-dimensional graphics, are influencing how people react and adapt to such environments. There is a "virtual bank" in the increasingly popular Internet-based Second Life virtual world that uses "Linden" dollars, a virtual currency that has an exchange rate with real dollars.[9]

SmallBiz magazine reports that various individuals and businesses are using Second Life to explore real-world ideas at a much lower comparative cost, demonstrating one advantage of using virtual reality: "Virtual worlds, of which Second Life is the most populous, are becoming more than just [places] where Web surfers socialize, play games, or sell nonexistent products to imaginary people. Increasingly, tech-savvy businesses are using virtual worlds to design, create, and even test product concepts before they make their debut in the real world" (Tahmincioglu 2008). If, or exactly how, this might ultimately affect real banking in the United States or the world (there are now many Second Life participants throughout the world) is not known, but the possibilities are intriguing.

9. http://secondlife.com (accessed April 19, 2008).

◀ Typical through-wall walk-up automated teller machine. This ATM sign face features the institution's brand name and logo, one of the Aloha Pacific Federal Credit Union's ATMs named "Kalabash," from the Hawaiian word kala, meaning money.

CHAPTER 4
PROGRAMMING

One of the processes required in any architectural project is programming. Banks are no exception, and because they are the holders of the majority of the earnings of American consumers, it is even more critical that this phase of work is completed accurately and completely. Different methods are used to accomplish this important task, and most architects have their own system, but all must arrive at a progression that develops information to allow the project design to proceed.

After the important questions about brand image have been settled, architects or programming consultants should prepare a schedule for the following: client conferences, research for this phase of programming, schematic design, design development, construction documents (plans and specifications), bidding contracts or instruments, and construction administration. There may be some variation among these phases, but from the very beginning any work must have adequate and accurate programming.

Early discussions with an architect usually include the purpose of the building, its functional requirements, budget considerations, site conditions, and an overall description of client objectives. At this point there is probably nothing formally in writing, so it is the architects' responsibility to prepare the written architectural program. *Problem Seeking,* by William Peña, gives a good description of the five steps that should occur in architectural programming (1977, p. 12):

- Establish goals.
- Collect and analyze facts.
- Uncover and test concepts.
- Determine needs.
- State the problem.

What does a financial institution want to achieve, and how does that translate to the design goals? These program needs are sometimes easy to define, but usually they involve more than a simple list of spaces. How functions relate must be considered carefully at this stage in the process. Project goals are not concepts but are implemented through concepts. There are as many variations on bank design as there are banking industry members. The following programming guide checklist describes most of the interior spaces and equipment that may be considered in a new bank or credit union project, depending on the size and type of institution.

PROGRAMMING GUIDE CHECKLIST

Institutional type
1. Branch facility
   Drive-up (with or without island ATM)
   Island ATM
   Walk-up (store, mall, or airport, and urban core locations)
2. Headquarter facility (with or without drive-up or separate ATM)
3. Call center and/or data center
4. Building with tenant space (single or multistory)

PROGRAMMING

Note that chapter 6 includes information on site design and a separate checklist for that consideration.

Building space needs
(in larger facilities, many of the spaces listed may need to be in multiples.)
1. Customer entrance (vestibule)
   Circulation, stairs, escalator, or elevators
2. Lobby area (also see specialized equipment list)
   Waiting area(s)
   Coffee and beverage service, television (see marketing opportunities below)
3. Greeter or customer service representative
   Concierge station (see equipment list)
4. Marketing opportunities (kiosks, displays, video, and Internet)
5. Check stand or counter
6. Customer service greeter
7. Banking offices and departments (see sub-list of offices or departments)
   Files (lobby direct access)
   Office equipment
8. Manager or president's office or executive suite plan
   Secretarial and clerical
   Files and storage
   Conference room(s)
   Private restroom(s)
9. Board or conference room (if separate from an executive suite)
   Service counter and cabinets
10. Lobby teller area
    Teller line, pod locations, or remote teller machines (see specialized equipment list)
    Traffic control stanchions at teller line
11. Vault for safe deposit (see specialized equipment list)
    Cash vault
    Coupon booths
12. Drive-up tellers or remote teller room (see specialized equipment list)
13. Work room (see equipment list and chapter 9)
14. File room and or file cabinets (if separate room, type to be selected)
15. Break room or dining room
16. Kitchen or kitchenette
17. Public toilets
18. Mechanical rooms
19. Janitor rooms
20. Electrical, communications, and data equipment
21. LAN equipment room
22. Storage space
23. Security and alarm equipment needs and locations
24. Furniture, fixtures, and equipment
25. Interior design: color and finishes

Teller room equipment (also see specialized equipment list)
1. Teller counters
   End returns
   Back counters and storage
2. Under-counter equipment
   Stand-up or sit-down
   Security lockers
   Teller buses
3. Cash recycler or dispenser
4. Computer System
5. MICR printer
6. Coin counter
7. Proof machine
8. Security and alarm equipment needs and locations (see chapters 8, 9, and 10)
9. Furniture, fixtures, and other equipment
10. Bandit barriers

Programming Guide Checklist

Drive-up teller or remote teller room
(see chapters 9 and 10)
1. Teller counters
   Back counters and storage
   Undercounter equipment
2. Drive-up or remote system terminals
   (see specialized equipment list)
3. Night deposit and receiving safe
   (see specialized equipment)
4. Safe and teller lockers (see specialized equipment)
5. Cash recyclers or dispensers
6. Computer system
7. Security and alarm equipment and locations (see chapter 10)

Workroom equipment
(Check 21 operations; see chapter 9)
1. Cabinet and counter space and storage
2. Computer system
3. Check scanner and sorter, computer, and monitor
4. Temporary check storage cabinet
5. Auto folder
6. ATM control
7. Bill counter
8. Coin counter, sorter/wrapper
9. Credit card machine and printer
10. Camera system monitor
11. MICR printer
12. Shredder
13. Fax machine
14. Laser printer
15. LAN/server equipment (separate space)
16. Copy machines
17. File cabinets
18. Security and alarm equipment (see specialized equipment list and chapter 10)

Work room equipment
(before Check 21 implementation)
Add the following items to the preceding workroom equipment list, delete the check scanner:
1. Proof machine
2. Check encoder
3. Check protector
4. Microfilm machine
5. Power files for check storage

Bank department sublist
(usually in larger or regional banks)
1. Executive suite (multiple offices, secretarial, clerical, files, and conference)
   Possible multiple waiting areas in this and other departments
2. Commercial loan department
   Commercial real estate lending
3. Mortgage loan department
4. Consumer loan department
5. Agricultural loan department (or other specialty lending)
6. Trust department
7. Investment advisor
8. Bookkeeping department (accounting)
9. Loan processing department
10. Insurance department
11. Annuities department
12. Internal audit department
13. Human resources department
14. Collections department
15. Legal department
16. I.T. department
    Encoding offices
17. Network offices
18. Server room
19. Mail courier and sorting
20. Call center and or data center
    Special workstations and adjustable furniture

PROGRAMMING

Specialized bank equipment
(see chapter 10)
1. Pneumatic tube drive-up system
   Overhead, down-fed, direct buried, or culvert installation
   Customer units
   Terminals at teller room
2. CCTV and audio equipment for drive-up or remote tellers
3. Remote teller system
4. Interior teller undercounter equipment and security/alarm features
5. Drive-up windows and deal drawers
6. Vault system
   Modular or site-poured
7. Vault doors and day gates
8. Safe deposit boxes
9. Depositories
10. Safes and chests
    Composite safes
11. Teller lockers
12. Cash recyclers and dispensers
13. ATM facilities
    Walk-up or in-lobby
    Thru-wall lobby
    Thru-wall drive-up
    Island drive-up
14. Alarm systems and other security equipment
    Alarm terminals
    Security panels
    Security keypads and card readers and controls
    Hold-up devices (wireless)
    Motion sensors
    Door monitors
    Glass breakage monitors
    Camera systems, high performance and covert options
    Time-lapse VCRs
    Video surveillance and recording systems and software
    Color monitors
    VRS switcher controllers
    Height strip cameras
    Smoke detectors
    ATM alarm and security
15. Lane lights and signage
    Directional and wayfinding
    Informational
    Marketing

More will be presented about these spaces and equipment needs in the following chapters, but this list serves as a guide for establishing a project's program.

The programming facts are important and necessary if they are pertinent and appropriate. They may describe the site (see chapter 6), including physical, legal, climatic, and aesthetic aspects. Statistical projections, economic data, and user characteristics may be important as well, but only if they have a bearing on the project. A number of banks and credit unions have used outside consultants to help determine the programming requirements of a proposed project. In many projects, a team is assembled to provide programming direction, with the programming consultant as its leader.

From the question of whether a new facility is warranted, and if so where should it be located, to just what kind of financial service delivery method is suitable, are among the considerations that financial feasibility planning consultants often prepare. Bank owners or their key staff members, their architects and interior designers, and their equipment supplier or consultants should be important members of this team.

A client's desires are not always the same thing as a client's needs. It is difficult to make judgments of quality and adequacy of

Programming Guide Checklist

◀ *Community First Bank, Chicago, Illinois; Myefski Cook Architects. This project is an example of a complete and thorough program preparation. The 9,000 sq ft building is significant in its allusion to the Prairie style, evident in its program and planning.* Photo by Myefski Cook.

◀ *Dekalb State Bank, Tucker, Georgia; programmed and designed by Foreman Seeley Fountain Architects. This classic brick and hip-roofed bank was programmed to convey the surrounding character of the neighborhood and customer base.* Photo by Robert Wells, Foreman Seeley Fountain Architecture.

space without economic feasibility being soon brought into question.

Space requirements, construction quality, time constraints, sustainability, and, of course, the budget, all have a bearing on the final determination of needs. In most cases, a budget is not yet established when programming begins, and it is influenced by the information gleaned from the programming process. Owners and architects thus work together to establish the budget, and it should be a part of the program document. A professional cost estimator is often important to the effort to establish a realistic construction budget.

The program should state the salient points derived from the project analysis. It should outline the design goals in clear and concise statements. In larger, more complex projects, the program will be proportionally larger, but the process remains the same (Peña 1977, pp. 76–81). In some cases, a client will have at the outset a very good understanding of the programming needs of his or her facility. In others, this list may help uncover needs that have not been considered.

CHAPTER 5
DRIVE-UP BANKS

EARLY DRIVE-UP BANKS

When World War II ended, Americans were able to resume the pursuit of their hopes and dreams. The national economy grew at an unprecedented rate, and many Americans were finally able to purchase homes, automobiles, and other consumer goods. A middle-class relocation to the suburbs began. Financial institutions, interested in providing convenience to their existing customers and attracting new ones, joined the move to the new suburban communities. New branch banks were constructed, and it soon became popular to allow customers to access these new facilities while remaining in their cars. Busy housewives could go to their banks without dressing as for going out in public, and they could easily take their young children along (Belfoure 2005, p. 261).

There are differing accounts of the first "motor banks," one claiming the concept was pioneered as early as 1928 with an automobile-accessible window at a bank in Kansas City, Missouri, and another identifying the First National Bank in Nashville, Tennessee, in the late 1930s, as the original innovator. Further consideration to automobile access, however, was postponed until after the war. Most believe the first truly multiple in-car banking was introduced by the Exchange National Bank in Chicago in November 1946. That facility featured ten drive-up teller windows arranged in a line along the side of the bank building. In any case, the practice has remained popular since its advent, and only the methods of delivering financial services and the equipment have changed.

The early motor banks, or "drive-ups," as they were soon called, were designed with single or multiple windows and "deal" drawers, arranged so that customers could drive their cars to these windows, which were located in tandem along the building, sometimes in a sawtooth fashion, and often arranged on two or three sides of the bank. Obviously, the cars had to proceed in a counterclockwise flow so that the drivers were adjacent to the windows and drawers.[1]

The effect on the floor plan was that an irregular arrangement of teller locations was required, because of the placement of these decentralized drive-up windows. This led to the use of separate teller-occupied kiosks, much like tollbooths, that allowed the drive lanes to be located adjacent to each other and under a common canopy.

Separate tollbooth-style kiosks, with each housing a teller, were a short-lived experiment, as the inefficient use of personnel and insecure and inconvenient delivery of currency and other materials soon prompted implementation of a technology that had long been used in department stores, rail yards, and other commercial operations: pneumatic tubes.[2]

With the use of pneumatic tubes to deliver and receive currency and other items, motor banking in the mid 1960s finally achieved the goal of convenience and

---

1. "Drive-ins," *Architectural Record*, August 1950, 139.
2. Ibid.

DRIVE-UP BANKS

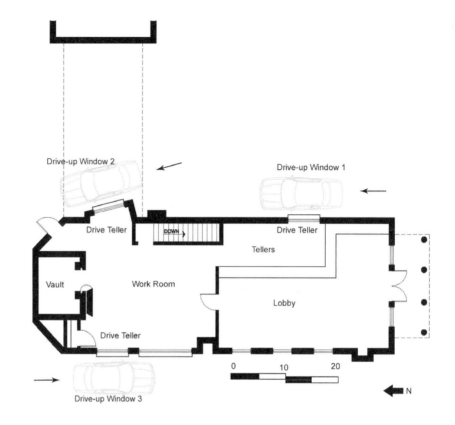

▸ Floor plan, Central National Bank's first branch drive-up, 1962, Junction City, Kansas; Ed Tanner, architect. In this early plan, the drive-up windows were arranged around the building to allow car access to multiple locations.

▸ Central National Bank's first drive-up, 1962, Junction City, Kansas; Ed Tanner, architect. The first window is placed squarely along the side of the bank, while the window at the far corner was set at an angle to allow the car to maneuver into the correct position and make the turn to the one-way exit lane. A window at the opposite side of the building accommodated cars continuing in a counter-clockwise direction.

Early Drive-Up Banks

security for both banks and their customers. The early tubes were installed in large culverts, usually of concrete, but sometimes in corrugated metal pipes (a practice still used). These reached the drive-up islands through poured-in-place concrete extensions, in which automatic receiver and delivery units (now called customer units) were located.

This improvement allowed customer access to multiple lanes, under protective canopies, and with all teller operations centrally located within the building, usually adjacent to the lobby tellers. The lobby tellers could thus double as drive-up tellers when needed. This configuration continued to require cars to proceed in a counterclockwise rotation around the building, and, in order for the tellers to maintain visual contact with the drivers, the lanes had to remain relatively close to the building. The early pneumatic equipment required close proximity as well.

The lane adjacent to the building continued to be served by a window and drawer. The remaining lanes, however, were served by tubes, which fed early kiosk-type receiver-delivery units that were located on the concrete islands. The kiosk units were each set forward in succeeding lanes, to allow visual contact between the tellers and customers (a practice also still used), and an audio link to each lane provided communication. The canopy was usually large enough to protect drivers from rain or snow.

The advantages of the system of pneumatic tubes in a buried culvert include the following:

- Once installed, the culvert allows other work on the islands to proceed unimpaired. Weather, scheduling of equipment, and canopy construction are not factors.
- Pneumatic tubes may be installed at any time.
- If the culvert is constructed for future expansion, additional tubes may be easily added.
- Drive-up equipment and tube sizes may be modified later with relative ease.
- Maintenance may be accomplished without disturbing other lanes or equipment.

The disadvantages are that culverts are expensive, whether concrete or steel, and a high water table may preclude their use in certain areas.

A later idea allowed for an overhead-fed tube system, which eliminated the costly culverts and simplified tube installation by

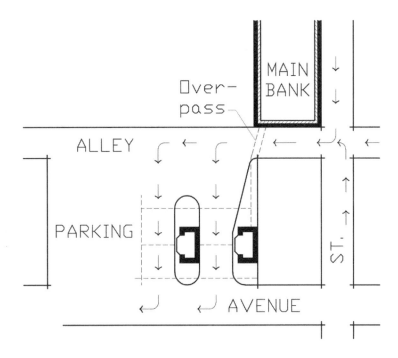

▲ Kiosk-style drive-up, First National Bank, 1950, Saint Petersburg, Florida; William B. Harvard, architect. This early drive-up, attached to the bank, placed a teller in each kiosk to provide service to each lane. Illustration by the author, from Architecture Record, August, 1950.

DRIVE-UP BANKS

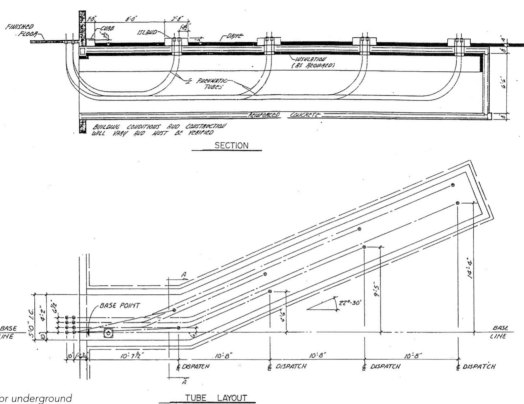

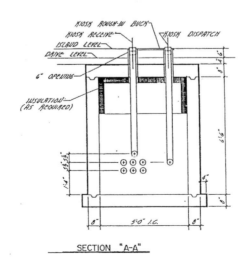

▶ Culvert for underground tube installation. Most early culverts were of concrete, but corrugated steel pipe was also used, and, although much improved, both methods are still in use today. Many equipment providers believe it is important to have the access to the tubes that such a culvert system affords. Great care must be taken to ensure that such systems are watertight.

placing the tubes in the drive canopy. This extended the tubes up from the interior teller area, through the canopy, and then down to the customer units at the islands. If a problem occurs, access to the tubes is less problematic, in that it does not require crawling through a culvert. The island configuration remained generally the same, and banks could avoid the costly construction of culverts. This method of pneumatic tube placement is still in use today, although the entire system is now much improved.

The advantages of an overhead pneumatic tube system include the following:

- It eliminates the need for trenches or culverts.
- It eliminates penetration of basements or floors.
- The system is easier to expand or modify, by simply extending the canopy.
- High water tables or poor soil conditions are not disadvantageous.
- Teller operator terminals can be counter-mounted and extended from above.
- The blower motors are easier to reach, via access doors in the canopies.
- The system does not have difficulty with overloaded carriers becoming stuck in an underground system.

The main disadvantages of an overhead system are that the drive-up canopy must be attached to the bank building, and although this arrangement provides better access to tubes and motors than some other systems, it is nevertheless sometimes necessary to remove parts of a canopy for repair and maintenance. More information about pneumatic tube systems in current drive-up design can be found in chapter 6, and the specialized equipment used is discussed in chapter 10.

CONTEMPORARY DRIVE-UP FACILITIES

Drive-ups are of course still being constructed, especially for branch facilities, as they offer the following advantages:[3]

- Lobby teller stations and space may be reduced because of the drive-up feature.
- The teller to customer ratio may be reduced from 1:1 to 2:3 or even 2:4.
- Security is increased because tellers are separated from customers by bullet-resistant glass, or by video communication.
- Customers may remain in car and do not need to park or enter the bank or queue in a teller line.
- Appearance and dress are not as important to customers, as they remain in their

3. © Diebold, Inc., 1994–2009. All rights reserved.

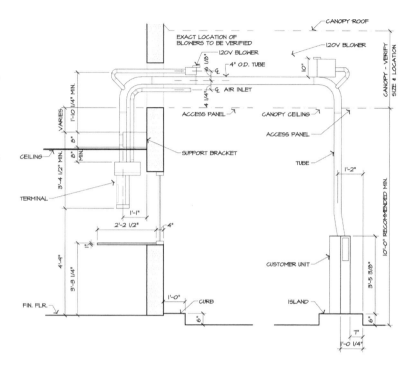

▲ Section of a typical overhead tube installation. As more lanes were added, requiring additional tellers, the vision windows were enlarged and installed in multiple units as well. Five or six lanes can be added in multiple drive-up arrangements, until the distance becomes difficult for conventional teller service. Tube blower motors are usually installed in the canopy, as shown.

cars, and it is easier for parents to manage children in the confines of their cars.
- Branches may extend hours without keeping an entire building open.
- Drive-up facilities open and improve the environment within the building, which in turn assists with cross-selling.
- "Cost" transactions at the drive-up are separated from the more income-generating transactions that can occur inside the building.

The factors for consideration in determining a location for a new branch or drive-up facility are discussed in chapter 6.

CHAPTER 6
SITE SELECTION AND PLANNING

PLANNING AND ZONING

A prominent banker once stated that "the best site for a new branch is on the right-hand side of a major route home from work, for the largest number of potential customers." This is perhaps an oversimplification, but it contains some truth.

The site requirements for a new bank depend on many factors. As the previous chapters described, branding strategies and the facilities program will determine the building space needs. For a new bank project, such factors as zoning, building setback requirements, type and location of planned drive-up facilities, and the car stacking space will determine the site size and configuration. Many other conditions and circumstances will have an impact on the site selection.

Thorough marketing and economic feasibility studies must be undertaken before a property is acquired. This kind of analysis is often performed by a consultant who specializes in assisting financial institutions in growth and expansion planning. The architect should be part of that team. Occasionally a banker will already have a site in mind, and it is the architect's task to see if it will work with the program as it has been articulated.

Site access, interior circulation, topography, and building orientation will be important, as will the state and use of adjacent properties. Prevailing winds and storm tracks are very important considerations when planning entrance locations. Year-round solar patterns and ambient lighting are critical to drive-up and ATM placement.

Most screens are difficult if not impossible to read when faced toward direct sunlight. Code-mandated requirements for open space—that is, the area not covered by building, parking, drives, and sidewalks—have steadily increased in many cities. Purchase costs are very important, but the costs of developing a parcel may be even greater by the time all required changes are made.

A fundamental question of security must be answered. For a large headquarters or multistory bank, it may be decided that all vehicular traffic be kept at some distance from the building. In that case, a drive-up, if provided, will be remote and served only by pneumatic tubes and televised teller assistance. It is now possible to place such facilities farther away from the building to lessen security risks. Other site features, such as bollards or planters, can be placed to prevent vehicular access at certain vulnerable points, such as large areas of glass. A recommended reference in this kind of security design is *Security and Site Design* by Hopper and Droge (2005).

Planting and landscape features may be important to the overall project success, and most cities now also require that a certain number of cars be able to stack in the lanes leading to the drive-up units. Parking space for both customers and employees will also need to be considered. An example of poor planning practice is when customer access to the building's main entrance crosses the drive-up lanes.

City planning and zoning departments now typically require an extensive checklist

SITE SELECTION AND PLANNING

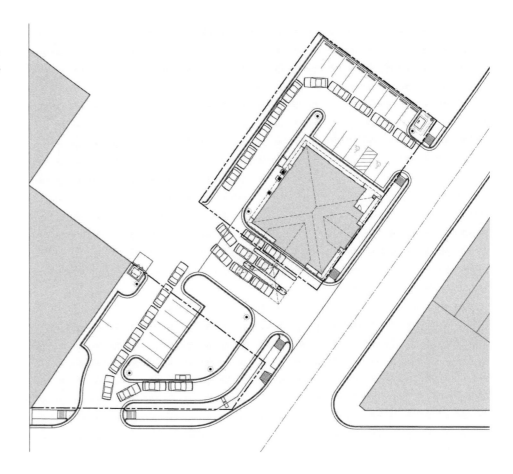

▶ Typical site plan, illustrating stacking and parking. This site plan allows stacking of six cars for each lane. An island ATM is located at lower left. The space between the tracts is a street that has since been vacated and is now used by the bank for the drive-up, ATM exit, and parking. Illustration by WSKF Architects.

of items to be fulfilled before a project can be realized. In many cases it will be several months before hearings can be scheduled, even when a project falls well within zoning requirements and no variance is being proposed. Every city department may have to sign off on a proposed plan for it to be finally approved. When a zoning variance is needed, considerably more time may be required. This occasionally creates the need for a zoning consultant to represent the owner in this matter.

The first important item of business after a site has been chosen is a topographic survey. This should include important matters such as a legal description, property boundaries, and any easements or other physical conditions relative to the site. A study of the "lay of the land," depicted by the contours or point-elevations, is essential to establish proper drainage and appropriate grades. The existing utilities are also extremely important. Sometimes sites lack sufficient sanitary sewer, water, or storm sewer services. It is necessary to know whether natural gas is available and, if not, what other energy source may be used. Electric service must be available, and a three-phase service is usually preferred.

The zoning usually describes the amount of space that is usable, as well as the setback

Planning and Zoning

distances from property lines. More communities are now also requiring a landscape plan to be submitted with any construction permit application. A qualified landscape architect can provide this service. Before any meaningful planning can start, however, an accurate survey is a must; this can usually be obtained only from a licensed land surveyor. Architects and engineers will be able to prepare the needed design documents after they have the building program and the site survey, and most are able to assist bankers in determining if a certain site is suitable.

Equally important is information about soils at the site. The structural engineer will need a subsurface soils report to determine site suitability and appropriate foundation design. More often than not, a study will be required of the site drainage. There have been numerous legal entanglements resulting from the runoff onto an adjacent site or parcel. Such a circumstance can be avoided with adequate knowledge of the site. A seemingly good site, also, may become economically unfeasible because of a subsurface condition, such as unseen rock that would be too costly to remove.

A good reference for selecting a branch or drive-up facility site is the Diebold, Inc., *Drive-up Banking Applications, Concepts and Strategies Guide* (n.d.), which lists the following types of suitable locations:

- Near highways and main routes of a car-commuting workforce. There should be relatively easy access on the way to or returning from work for drive-in (ingress) and drive-away (egress). Sites adjacent to industrial parks, business centers, and at off ramps to expressways may be good prospects.
- Boundary areas of readily visible public shopping malls. Such branches should remain open during hours convenient to customers. In-mall operations are particularly impacted by the mall's opening and closing times.
- Where there are high numbers of demand-deposit and passbook savings accounts, high check-cashing volume, and collection of monthly payments (utilities, loans, etc.), and where there would be an expected high transaction activity.

The following checklist describes much of the information that will be needed for the site planning and selection of a typical new branch facility:

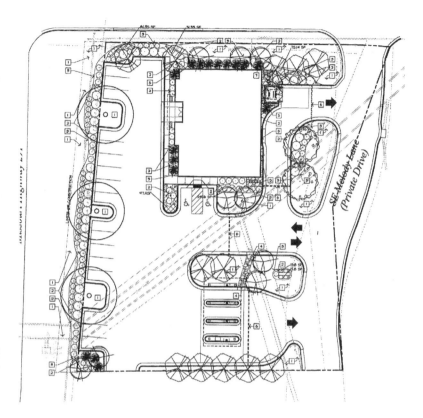

▲ *Typical landscape plan. Most cities require extensive landscaping, as this project illustrates. Some require plants of a certain height when planted. This plan, because of extensive underground drainage easements, requires cars entering from the east to circle back to face the opposite way to enter the drive-up. Illustration by WSKF Architects.*

SITE SELECTION AND PLANNING

Site checklist
- Is a current topographic and land survey with legal description available?
- What are the site's adjacent street access and type?
- Is existing soil suitable? Are tests available to determine subsurface conditions?
- Is impact of cut or fill to or from the site suitable?
- Is zoning suitable or can a variance be granted?
- Have existing structures or other site demolition requirements been assessed?
- Are utilities available and accessible (sanitary, storm, water, gas, and electric)?
- Are the types of energy source, electric service, and telephone service suitable?
- Will off-site or on-site transportation improvements be required?
- Is the site, or any portion thereof, in a floodplain?
- Will storm runoff need to be retained?
- What are current setback requirements?
- What is the maximum floor/area site density required?
- What are parking requirements for customers and employees?
- What are stacking requirements per drive-up lane?
- What are soil conditions relative to pneumatic tube placement?
- What are refuse containment and access requirements?
- What are landscaping or screening requirements?
- Will existing trees or other landscape features be retained?
- Will a traffic study be required?
- What are the local signage regulations?
- Is there fire and police protection? (This impacts insurance rates.)
- Are there wetland areas or other environmental issues?
- Is an environmental impact statement required?
- Can temporary banking facilities be used while construction is underway?

If the project is a renovation or addition to an existing building, many of these items may still be needed, together with detailed plans of the existing structures. Where an operation is to continue while the building process occurs, even greater detail will be needed and a construction phasing plan must be established.

TEMPORARY FACILITIES

Banks often acquire a site that is ready for development but need a temporary facility in order to get a head start or stay in business while a new building is being constructed. Prefabricated trailer units set up to be banks are readily available, if the site will accommodate them and allow for the new facility construction to take place at the same time. It will be necessary to provide for the construction area of the new building, the equipment and storage space, the staging area, a construction office, and allow for deliveries, while also accommodating the temporary bank-trailer and its parking and drives, all on the same site. Most prefab bank trailers have a drive-up window and deal drawer, so provision for that access must be provided as well. Some may even provide a canopy and tube system for a second drive-up lane.

The selection of a temporary facility must be made, and it is necessary to have pertinent information about it, such as the floor plan and utility connection requirements. It is helpful if the utility connections can be extended later to the new building, without constructing completely new lines, but this is not always possible.

Temporary Facilities

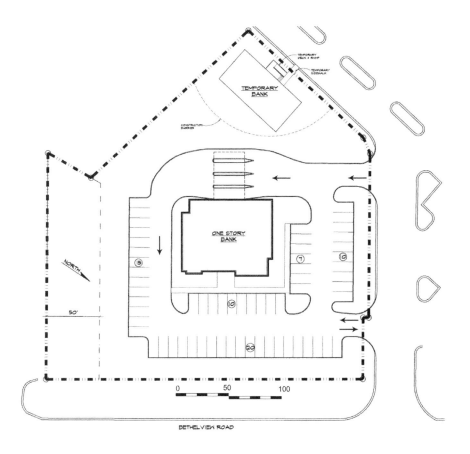

◀ *Mountain State Bank, Cumming, Georgia; Foreman Seeley Fountain Architects. This site plan shows a typical doublewide temporary bank unit used while the permanent bank was being constructed. The temporary facility allowed the bank to get a head start in business operations. There are various plan arrangements available. The figure below shows a typical single-width unit. Illustration by Foreman Seeley Fountain Architecture.*

▼ *Typical temporary mobile bank unit plan. Double-width units are also available in various plan configurations.*

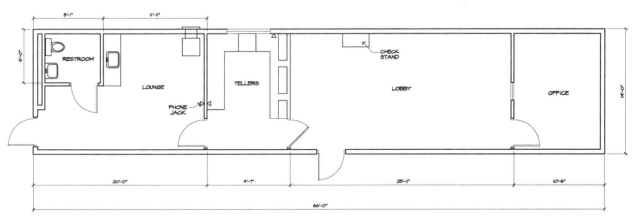

TYPICAL TEMPORARY (MOBILE) BANK FACILITY

SITE SELECTION AND PLANNING

▶ *Conventional drive-up bank site plan, Quantum National Bank, Suwannee, Georgia; Foreman Seeley Fountain, architect. The cars move in a counterclockwise direction to proceed through the drive-up, while parking is on the east and south sides of the bank building. Illustration by Foreman Seeley Fountain Architecture.*

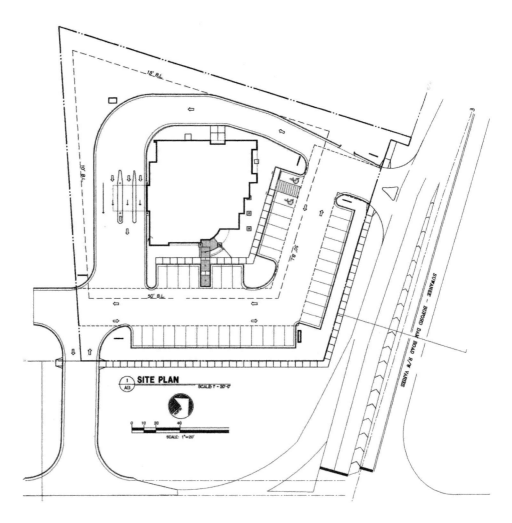

As soon as the new building is completed, the temporary facility is removed, and the site work is completed. Suppliers of temporary bank facilities are listed in appendix C.

CONVENTIONAL DRIVE-UP

A conventional drive-up with cars traveling in a counterclockwise rotation will feature a window at the building—the size of which depends on the number of lanes it serves—an automatic drawer, and an audio system at the first lane. Other lanes will be at islands with customer units served by pneumatic tubes, fed from above or below. These customer units may be equipped with a video monitor or simply with an audio connection to the tellers, who remain in line-of-sight with the customer. With the use of video monitors and audio units, many banks have eliminated the teller windows and in so doing allow the cars to proceed in either a clockwise or counterclockwise direction.

Conventional Drive-Up

◀ *Floor plan, Quantum National Bank, Suwannee, Georgia. The corner lot provided an ideal arrangement for the entrance to be oriented toward parking and the busy surrounding streets. Access to the upper floor is with a stair and elevator that can be locked off from the bank itself when needed. Illustration by Foreman Seeley Fountain Architecture.*

The customer units are then placed accordingly. In these examples, all of the lanes are served with closed circuit television–equipped units. Placement of the television screen is important, because glare from direct sunlight may cause it to be unreadable. These customer units will be described in greater detail in chapter 10.

The island design usually is arranged with concrete platforms raised 6 in. above the pavement and usually a minimum of 2 ft wide for typical customer units. At the drive-up itself, the grade must remain reasonably level in relation to the building. The length of the islands is variable but is usually determined by the need to align the cars and provide for canopy-supporting columns. Steel bollards or other appropriate barriers are used to prevent damage to customer units and ATMs, as well as to the support columns, depending on their design. The number of lanes also determines the length needed for the islands. An important consideration is canopy drainage, which must not become a problem below, at the islands, or adjacent to drive lanes. Canopy design is discussed later in this chapter.

Lanes are normally a minimum of 8'6" wide, and provision for stacking of five or six cars is usually required for each lane.

SITE SELECTION AND PLANNING

▶ *Exterior, Quantum National Bank, Suwannee, Georgia. The main entrance is clearly defined in this well-planned modern bank.* Foreman Seeley Fountain Architecture.

Some cities, however, now require as many as ten car spaces for stacking. City planning departments now typically stipulate the stacking spaces required along with other pertinent site-use requirements.

Careful consideration must be given to the traffic merging both to and from the drive-up islands. Some bankers prefer wider lanes, but it has been shown that if they are too wide, drivers occasionally become positioned too far from the customer units, and when multiple cars are waiting behind, it is almost impossible for a driver to back up and attempt to realign his or her car correctly. Thus, the narrower lanes help bring about the correct car placement relative to the customer units. This is also true of free-standing ATM island design. Diebold Inc. has provided a guide for the suggested turning radius approach to a drive-up.

Some ATM units are available in self-contained enclosures and may be installed over a narrower island width. Other ATM and customer units, however, require wider islands, so it is essential to know exactly what unit is to be used.

Bankers usually have a preference for the location of an ATM facility; often, this is the last drive-up island, requiring that this island be wider, with a 3 ft minimum (some newer units require 3 ft 6 in.). The design of the canopy support will also determine island width, as adequate clearance must be provided to protect the structure.

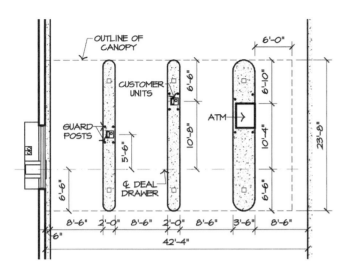

◀ *Typical drive-up dimensions. This plan is based on an overhead tube system. The ATM is housed in a premanufactured enclosure. The dimensions may vary depending on the specific equipment selected. Some customer units require wider islands, and many new ATM units are freestanding at the island (see chapter 10). Illustration by WSKF.*

▼ *Recommended turning radius approaches for drive-ups. There is a wide variation in vehicle sizes across the United States. This is based on an average passenger car. Illustration by Diebold, Inc.*

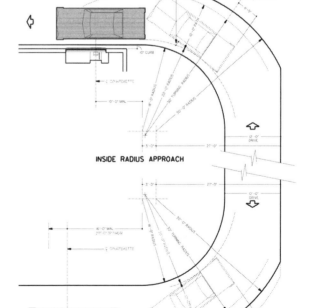

Experience also has shown that a bypass lane is helpful beyond the last island lane, so that when a customer needs to skip the transaction, for whatever reason, that can be accomplished up to a point in the car queuing process; many cities now require these to be provided. More about ATM siting can be found later in this chapter, and the units are described in detail in chapter 10.

Some bankers are exploring the idea of a multiple-use facility that may offer more amenities than just banking, such as the Freestar Bank of Downs, Illinois, by BE Design. In addition to a bank, this new facility has a coffee shop and a dry cleaner (see page 157).

FACE-UP LANES

Multiple lanes of five or more, in a conventional drive-up arrangement (that is, adjacent and connected to the building), result in considerable distance between the tellers and farthest cars. This has brought about the idea of a "face-up" drive-up configuration, in which all lanes face, and are more

SITE SELECTION AND PLANNING

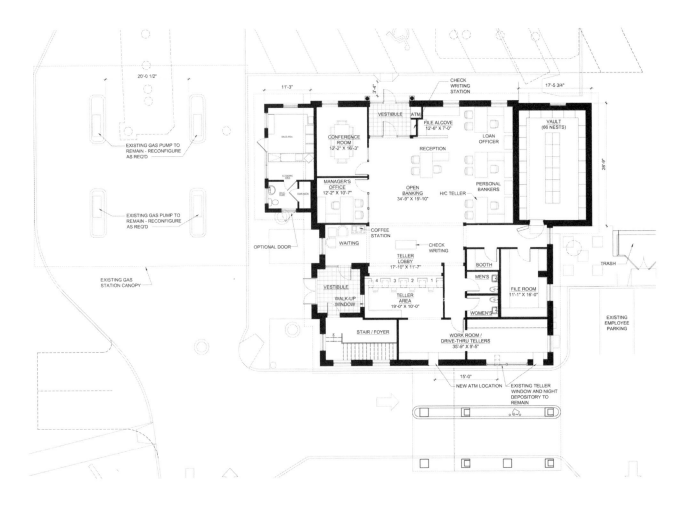

▲ Combination bank/gas station, Glencoe, Illinois; Myefski Cook Architects. The gas station is to the left of the building and the bank drive-up is at the lower right. Illustration by Myefski Cook Architects.

or less equidistant from, the tellers. Ample maneuvering and stacking space is required.

In some cases, the drive canopy may be connected to the building, providing for overhead tube placement, but in other cases the drive-up is served by an underground tube arrangement, as described later in this chapter. The islands may be wider than the 2 ft minimum, depending on the number of lanes; however, the length is usually only one car length, as all cars are aligned in a row at the same distance from the building.

These may be perpendicular to the building or set at an angle. The minimum canopy dimension is usually not greater than approximately 25 ft.

Another important factor in the planning of face-up facilities is the provision of an adequate turning radius for the departing cars. The illustration presented indicates dimensions often used. In another face-up example, the elevation of the islands may be different from the teller or building elevation. In the case of more distant islands, the

Face-Up Lanes

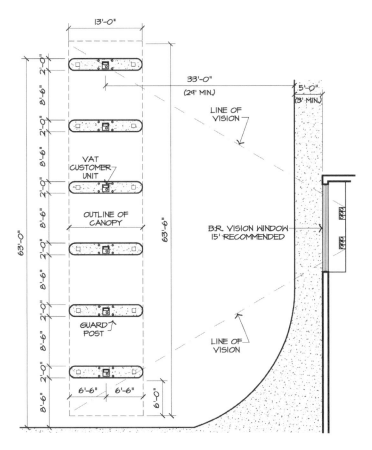

◀ *Typical face-up drive-up plan. This indicates an arrangement based on the Diebold Inc. VAT 23 system using direct-bury pneumatic tubes. This system may be equipped with closed circuit TV as well. Where the drive-up canopy may be attached to the bank building, overhead delivery of the tube system is possible. A careful analysis of the equipment to be used is important, because most systems do not allow for a down-loaded (underground) tube system for a commercial lane (which will carry a heavier load). In that case, a commercial window is usually placed at the bank building. Illustration by WSKF.*

◀ *Typical multiple-lane face-up drive-up, by ComCo Systems Inc. The two-way audio/video-equipped customer units allow for an almost unlimited number of additional lanes. This installation features a down-loaded (underground) tube system. Photo by ComCo Systems Inc.*

SITE SELECTION AND PLANNING

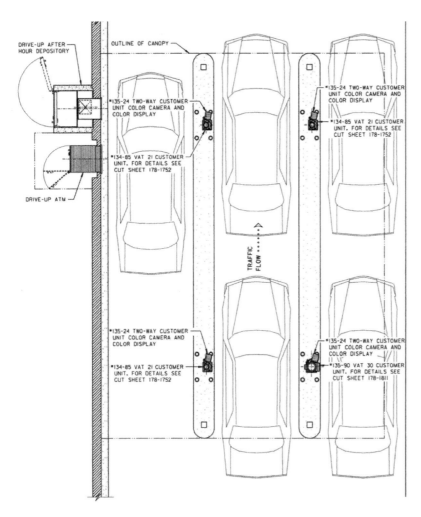

▲ Plan of reconfigured tandem drive-up. This system allows existing drive-up lanes to be converted to allow for two new customer positions, served by the existing drive-up tellers. To minimize customers' impatience, it is important for tellers to hold completion of a transaction for the rear car until service to the front car has been completed, and in some cases the customer in the front car may be required to advance and park and complete the transaction inside the building, so as to not subject the customer in the second car to a lengthy wait. Carefully selected CCTV and audio equipment providing for teller transaction privacy is important as well. Diebold Inc.

elevation difference may be greater yet.

While the face-up idea allowed more lanes to be served from a common teller area in the building, it also resulted in a problem when conveying heavier carrier loads from commercial customers. Equipment manufacturers soon developed a larger-capacity customer unit and overhead tube system to accommodate them. Chapter 10 describes the larger units and tubes now available.

Another factor that is sometimes a problem is that during short winter days, the face-up car headlamps are aimed directly at the tellers. Aside from simply asking the drivers to dim or turn off their lights, this problem can be lessened by placing the face-up islands at a slight angle from the direct line to the tellers.

Tellers may also be located above the drive-up islands on a second floor. This can be made to work as long as the canopies are designed to provide visual access from tellers to customers. A CCTV and audio system will provide for visual needs for the transactions in this circumstance.

TANDEM ISLAND CUSTOMER UNITS

Another design idea that has allowed for nearly simultaneous customer service from the same lane is that of tandem island customer units. With this system it is possible to retrofit the drive-up customer units within existing facilities. (Some cities, however, have restricted this tandem vehicle configuration.) It may be necessary to lengthen the island and also to extend the canopy to accommodate the second active customer. This configuration can be controlled by a conventional teller or by a modified teller system using a CCTV system from an updated teller area (see chapter 7).

DIRECT-BURY AND TRENCH INSTALLATIONS FOR REMOTE LANES

In the mid-1970s, the development of direct-bury pneumatic tubes and better blower motors enabled banks to locate drive-up lanes much farther away from the bank building. This capability, however, has required that a much-improved audio and television system as well. Several equipment manufacturers now offer these improved customer units, complete with higher-definition television and better audio systems. See chapter 10 for a detailed description of these new customer units.

When tubes are direct-bury or trench installations, it is absolutely necessary to have them installed in a watertight manner. This system is possible where a culvert could not be installed because of a high water table or unfavorable soil conditions. If the tubes are installed in a trench, it is equally necessary to have them watertight, but the trench is filled with sand, and this must be done in strict accordance with the equipment supplier requirements. Since electrical conduit is usually installed within the same trench, care must be given to ensure that this is also wrapped in a watertight manner. The trench should extend below the frost line. Some soil conditions can cause electrolysis, so it is prudent to test the soil where contact may be made with a direct-buried system.

It is now possible to locate a drive-up as far as 600 ft from the building and still have a reasonably quick turnaround of carriers between customers and tellers. (In some other industrial uses, pneumatic tubes are extended much greater distances.) The majority of new drive-up facilities where the canopy cannot be connected with the bank building are now equipped with direct-buried or trench-installed pneumatic tubes.

The following advantages come with a direct-buried or trench-installed tube system:

- It can be used in a high–water table circumstance if installed properly, where a culvert cannot.
- It is a less expensive method of customer service where the facility may be temporary.
- It can be used in poor soil if added surrounding sand is kept intact.
- Perhaps most important, the drive-up itself may be located at a greater distance from the building by use of remote customer units equipped with CCTV.

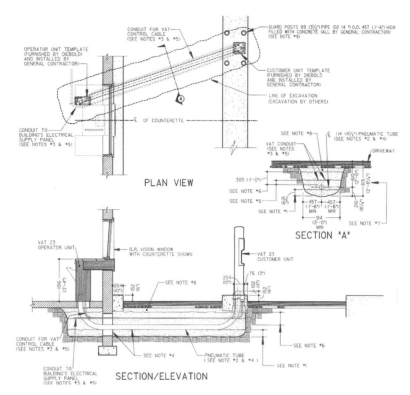

▲ Typical direct-buried tube installation. This plan and section depict the Diebold VAT 23 System. Multiple customer units may now be located much farther from the bank, with several tubes combined in a single trench. Great care must be taken in installing such a system to avoid moisture buildup and to protect the tubes from heavy vehicle loads from above. Diebold Inc.

SITE SELECTION AND PLANNING

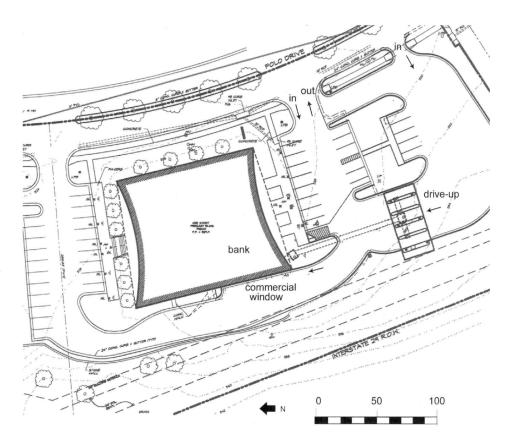

▶ *Face-up drive-up and separate commercial lane at the bank building, First Bank of Missouri, Kansas City, Missouri. This face-up system is located to the right of the building and uses five lanes served by an underground tube system installed in a concrete culvert. The commercial window is at the building with a separate drive-up location. The bank itself occupies one-fourth of the office building on the lower right side.* Illustration by WRS Architects.

Disadvantages include the inaccessibility of the tubes, and the possibility of electrolysis. When a carrier is overloaded, it may become stuck in the underground tube and be very difficult to remove.

COMMERCIAL LANES

As has been mentioned, heavier carrier loads have created a need for larger commercial-lane equipment, particularly at remote drive-ups. There are now units available that will transport loads of 25 lb in larger (usually overhead) tubes. An argument against using these is the heavy lifting needed to load or unload the carrier by the customers and tellers (a bag of coins can weigh 25 lb).

Some bankers therefore prefer to simply have these items brought directly into the bank for deposit. Other arrangements make use of a single commercial lane immediately adjacent to the building, similar to conventional drive-ups.

Yet another arrangement has the commercial window located at the drive-up tellers, but in front of the face-up lanes. A drawback of this idea is that while the commercial window is in use, the other cars cannot be seen by the tellers. A separate commercial lane requires greater use of space to accommodate the drive lane and its access, and it also can require a floor plan arrangement with a separate commercial

ATM Facilities

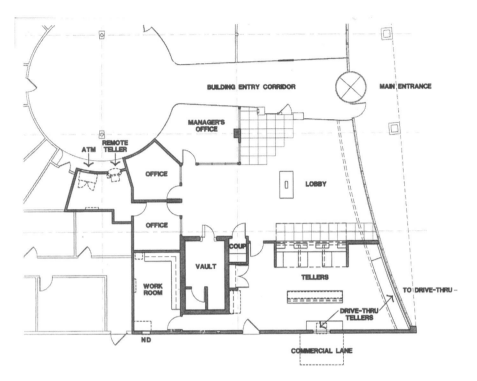

◀ *Floor plan showing separate commercial lane at building. Although the drive tellers are able to see the cars, they are too distant to use conventional equipment and instead use a remote televised system. These tellers are also able to serve the commercial lane with a conventional window and drawer. Note the center lobby remote teller machine and ATM.* Illustration by WRS Architects.

teller location in the building. This requirement is further discussed in chapter 7.

ATM FACILITIES

The ATM, or automated teller machine, was first used in England in 1967, and after a series of improvements it has become a mainstay in almost all financial institutions worldwide. In addition to their use at the buildings or on the grounds of banks, ATMs have also been placed in countless other commercial locations.

At first, these units were located inside bank buildings and were accessible by customers from either inside or out, depending on the desired use. Many bankers still prefer the units to be located inside the building in order to service and replenish them, an arrangement that creates less of a security issue.

Later, self-contained units were manufactured that could be placed outside the building, and these often were located at the last drive-up island. This practice is also still popular, although it was not uncommon for thieves to attempt to rob them, sometimes by trying to take the entire machine. One remedy is to have the ATM unit housed in a building structure, often of a similar design theme as the bank building, thereby minimizing the threat of theft but increasing the security risk while replenishing. Bankers soon discovered that ATMs were not only popular with their customers, but also had become a well-advertised brand destination for the wider public.

SITE SELECTION AND PLANNING

▶ *Separate ATM lane with through-wall service from inside the building, Farmers Bank of North Missouri, Saint Joseph, Missouri; WSKF Architects. The ATM is at the right and the main drive-up canopy is seen at the far left. Photo by Paul Brokering.*

▼ *Island ATM enclosed in a building structure. A security drawback is that this ATM must be replenished regularly by personnel going outside the bank building. Many banks hire private security firms to perform that task.*

Freestanding island ATM facilities are now used not only at remote locations throughout a city or town; bankers often place them in a prominent location at a main bank or branch site as a well-lighted advertisement, set apart from the building or drive-up. Diebold Inc. provides a suggested guide to the approach and exiting for freestanding ATM units.

Many banks with multiple ATM locations have developed prototypical designs that identify their brand, as they have done with their branch locations. The drawback of remote, island, or exterior units is that the constant replenishing is a security issue, and many banks are delegating that task to independant security agencies. The advantages of ATM facilities are:

- They can extend the hours of operation to 24 hours a day, 7 days a week.

Canopy Design

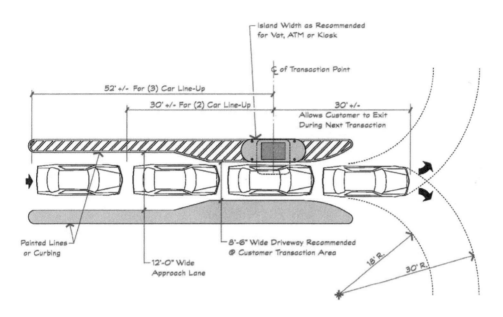

◀ *Recommended vehicle approach to island ATM. Note that the lane narrows at the ATM itself, providing for the correct alignment of the car with the ATM. The canopy extends to protect the driver. Diebold Inc.*

- They increase the transaction volume of customers and attract new ones.
- They expand the institutional delivery system to off-premises locations.

See chapter 10 for a detailed description of ATM units.

CANOPY DESIGN

There are as many different canopy design ideas as there are architects. Some are quite disparate, but all should have a relationship to the building design, and there are a few important considerations to keep in mind. Since there is increasing tourist traffic in many locations, it is prudent to consider the height of their vehicles. They often have large buses, vans, or recreational vehicles; because of this, the canopy should be high enough to provide the needed clearance. Jumbo pickup trucks with campers or stock racks are also taller than other vehicles, and air-conditioning units on top of camper shells increase the heights even more. In short, plan for the height needed. Canopy heights of 12 or even 14 ft are often used, although equipment suppliers sometimes suggest lower heights based on the average passenger car. Diebold Inc. has provided a guide to suggested passenger car clearances and areas of coverage for drive-up canopies and ATM facilities.

Direct sunlight on the customer units should be avoided. These should be higher if campers, trucks, or other recreational vehicles will be using them. Careful consideration should be given to the particular institution and its customer base when establishing the canopy height.

Another design strategy sometimes used effectively is to extend the building over the drive-up lanes when a 2-story building is planned. In this case, the building's second floor becomes the canopy. Care must be

SITE SELECTION AND PLANNING

▶ Typical canopy design, Midland Bank, Liberty, Missouri; WRS Architects. The staggered canopy is an extension of the wide fascia of the building and covers the five-lane conventional drive-up facility.

▶ Recommended plan of canopy coverage for conventional drive-up. Some sources recommend an 8' minimum driveway width; others suggest 2' 6" island widths. It is important to verify the specific equipment to be used early in the design process. Diebold Inc.

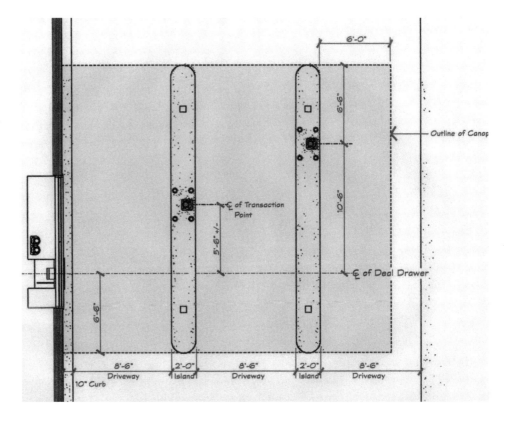

Canopy Design

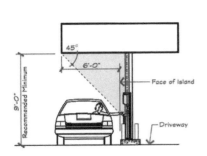
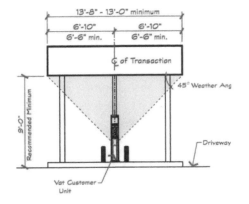

◀ Recommended minimum island canopy clearances. These are adequate for passenger cars, but should be increased for trucks and SUVs. Direct sunlight on a monitor or screen may also be a problem. Diebold Inc.

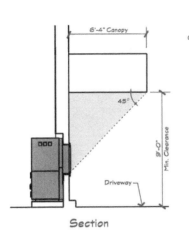
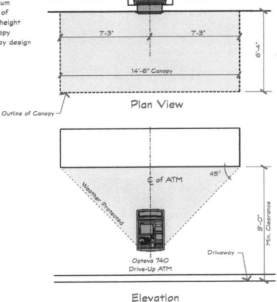

◀ Recommended ATM canopy clearances for through-wall installations. These should be increased to accommodate large trucks or SUVs. Diebold Inc.

SITE SELECTION AND PLANNING

▶ *Second floor above the drive-up. This project makes an effective and attractive use of a limited site by building two stories and extending additional floor space over the drive-up. When offices or other occupied spaces are placed over the drive lanes, it is important to ensure that the blower motors do not cause excessive noise. Photo by Myefski Cook Architects.*

▶ *Recommended radius bend clearance for canopy design. The equipment pictured on the left is a Diebold VAT 30 commercial unit with larger tubes, requiring a 42" tube radius bend. The unit on the right is a VAT 21 standard unit with a 4.5" tube and a 20" tube radius bend. A drive-up ATM and night depository are also shown. Diebold Inc.*

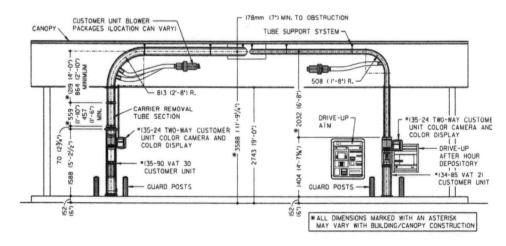

given to provide the necessary clearances in this case as well. An example of this planning is the North Shore Community Bank & Trust in the Sauganash region of Chicago by Myfeski Cook Architects.

Canopy drainage is very important. Water must be channeled down and away from islands or lane surfaces (usually under them) in order to prevent freezing in colder climates. Surface water is still a nuisance even in warmer locations, but good design practices should prevent it becoming a problem.

Where overhead pneumatic tubes are installed in the drive-up canopy, consideration must also be given to allow for the radius bends to clear the canopy structure. Diebold Inc. (n.d.) has also developed a guide to the suggested tube placement.

Another frequently used feature provides lane lights or signs on the canopy surface to signal drivers as to when to proceed. These are described in chapter 10. Most bankers prefer to have well-lighted canopies that also have signage on one or more sides of the canopy structure.

SITE SIGNAGE

As more communities enact stricter signage regulations, the familiar time-and-temperature pylon featuring a large lighted sign is seen less and less. Most regulations now limit the size, number, and configuration of signs, as well as the type and intensity of the lighting used. A separate sign application is often required that shows the complete design and specifications of proposed signage. Some areas allow only low-profile signs that cannot be more than 3 ft above the ground, and these cannot have letters larger than 1 ft in height.

▲ Low-profile sign at Norlarco Credit Union, Fort Collins, Colorado; EHS Design. This sign design is in keeping with the building's architectural theme. Many cities now limit site signage to this low-profile type, and the associated lighting is often restricted to avoid glare to surrounding property. Time Frame Photography.

SITE SELECTION AND PLANNING

The orientation of the building often requires signs on more than one side, but regulations limit the number and size of these as well. Consideration for sign identification at the drive-up canopies and at island ATMs is also warranted. Numerous other signs may be needed for traffic control, parking, or other directional messages, and these are usually part of the special banking equipment for a particular building project. They are discussed in chapter 10.

It is a constant struggle between sign companies, owners, and community authorities to arrive at a signage result that satisfies all parties. It is advisable for owners and designers to find out well ahead of the permit application time exactly what the sign regulations will allow, and if the branding strategy of the institution is, or can be, in sync with those regulations.

CHAPTER 7
BUILDING DESIGN

THE FLOOR PLAN

After the site information is received, programming requirements established, and fundamental brand identification strategy settled on, it is time to set a design direction. Early on, it is necessary to establish the institution's method of service delivery. If the delivery of services will be conventional, then a plan will follow that provides for bringing customers into the facility, usually through an entrance vestibule, past a reception area that may double as a marketing opportunity, and then to the lobby area. Adjacent to this will be the teller area. Many variations are possible, but, as discussed in chapter 3, it has been shown that "showcasing" products or services along this path is an effective marketing tactic. Tools may include flat-screen video monitors and literature displays in bright recesses. Very good examples are shown in the Norlarco Credit Union, Fort Collins, Colorado, by EHS Design; the Pilot Bank, Tampa, Florida, by NewGround; and the River Bank, Osceola, Wisconsin, by BKV Architects.

Depending on the program, numerous other spaces and uses may be placed adjacent to the lobby. Basic questions of configuration, such as whether two or more stories or a basement are needed, will be settled by site conditions and the program. If such are to be included, it is then necessary to consider their ingress/egress and circulation requirements. If a vault is to be part of operations, it will be located where it can be easily seen, and may also have one or two coupon booths nearby. Many floor-plan concepts will place the workroom near the teller areas, so that it is directly accessible to them, and perhaps via an exterior entry hall as well.

A bank workroom will be used for many important activities, and its layout will depend on whether the facility is a main or branch office, what kind of operation is planned, and how checks are cleared by the banking operation.

Check Clearing

It may be helpful to define the activity of check clearing, as follows:

> The movement of a check from the depository institution at which it was deposited, back to the institution on which it was written; the movement of funds in the opposite direction and the corresponding credit and debit to the involved accounts. The Federal Reserve operates a nationwide check-clearing system.[1]

The following describes the usual process for the clearing of conventional paper checks:

1. You go shopping and write a check from an account you have with your financial institution.
2. The store, or merchant, deposits the check with its bank. The store, bank, or the Fed places a magnetic ink code for

---

[1] http://www.advfn.com/money-words_term_6468_check_clearing.html (accessed January 23, 2008).

the dollar amount in the lower right-hand corner of the check.
3. The store or merchant's bank sends the check to a private bank, called a "correspondent bank." (The Federal Reserve clears about one-third of all checks written in the United States.)
4. The Federal Reserve runs the check through its sorting machines.
5. After processing your check, a credit and the check are presented back to the depositing financial institution. The institution then credits or debits the appropriate store or customer account.[2]

For a single banking operation that has in-house accounting and uses the conventional method of check clearing, more workroom equipment is needed than would be required for a branch that simply forwards checks to a central clearing house by electronic means. As mentioned in chapter 1, the Check 21 Act has brought about innovations in the payment system and has enhanced its efficiency by removing some of the legal impediments to check truncation. In short, the bank makes an electronic copy of a check and then holds the original check for a limited time before destroying it. The electronic copy is promptly sent to the clearinghouse and follows the same clearing process as for paper checks. Workroom space needs are significantly reduced. Fewer and fewer banks are using the old system of paper check-clearing. (This process of using electronic copies, called "Remote Deposit Capture," has also become directly available to bank customers.)

[2] "The Life of a Check," http://www.federalreserveeducation.org/fre_director/print.cfm? (accessed February 2, 2008).

Other Floor-Plan Considerations

Bankers and their architects must have complete mutual understanding about how the workroom should operate, what items of equipment are needed, and what activities will take place within the space. Specific workroom needs and specialized equipment are listed in chapter 9.

A break room and employee toilet rooms will often be near the teller area. Sometimes a separate photocopy room is needed. Mechanical equipment, computer servers, and separate utility room or rooms are also needed. It is not recommended to have the server or LAN equipment located in a janitor's room where there are also plumbing lines or fixtures. Fundamental decisions about offices—for example, whether private, open, or a combination—must be made. Is there a conference or boardroom? Where will loan closings take place? These and other questions will be considered in detail later in this chapter.

In some locations, institutions have chosen to use automated teller machines or PC stations for online banking in the banking lobby. A decision must be made as to the advisability of providing real-time machines that offer audiovisual service with pneumatic conveyance instead of traditional face-to-face teller service. Another possibility is to use a "concierge" pod with a personal service representative. We will consider the pros and cons of the conventional teller system, remote teller units, and pod stations in more detail later in the chapter. In any financial institution operating within the United States, important security requirements are required by the Bank Protection Act (see chapter 2).

The Floor Plan

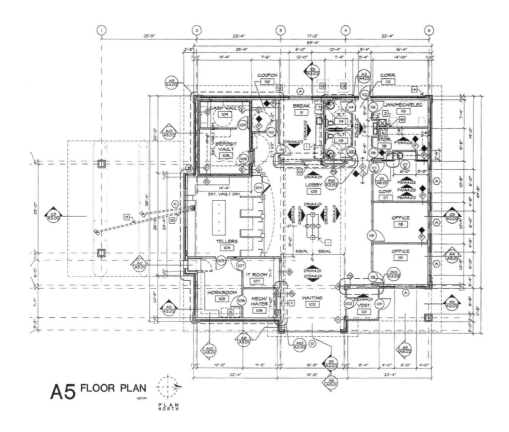

◀ *Typical branch bank floor-plan construction document. This working-drawing floor plan is for a new branch with a conventional three-teller-line lobby and a three-lane drive-up. The bank uses Check 21 processing and has a safe deposit vault. A separate island ATM is located away from the building but on site.* WSKF Architects.

Conventional Teller Stations

The single most important reason to use a conventional teller counter is that most customers are familiar and comfortable with this way of conducting their banking. Most bankers, also, do not wish to depart from tried-and-true methods of operation. Even so, the typical bank of 1970 or earlier, with its plentiful supply of lobby tellers and long lines of waiting customers, is forever gone. Another significant development is the requirement for accommodations for disabled customers and employees. Some banks simply provide a seated teller arrangement that easily serves customers in wheelchairs. Others add a lowered teller station at the teller line. Either way, it is important for bankers and architects to provide for such ADA requirements.

The era of ten or twelve teller lines inside a moderately sized suburban bank is, for the most part, over. The establishment of scattered branch facilities with drive-up banking, ATM facilities, debit cards, and personal computers has brought about this change. Most new branch facilities, however, still have two to four lobby tellers; and many also provide a seated teller area to serve handicapped customers. A new headquarters building, or even a branch in a dense metropolitan area, may need more lobby tellers, but that is exceptional and will

BUILDING DESIGN

▲ Conventional teller counter, First Bank of Missouri, Kansas City. The three teller stations serve lobby customers and also provide teller service to a remote drive-up installation and a separate commercial window. Photo by Mike Sinclair.

depend entirely on a particular bank's clientele. The teller stations will usually follow an architectural design concept, but they most likely will conform to some common dimensional standards.

Check Stands

From the earliest banks in the United States, check stands have been provided for the many needs of customers or members. These may be large or small and can be designed in an infinite variety of ways. Usually placed near or in front of the teller counters, they can also be designed as counters and may be placed against a wall; they may also even be installed with wheels, for portability. Check stands are also available from suppliers who specialize in the manufacture of teller counters and other bank casework. Consideration must be given to ADA access as well.

Cash Dispensing and Cash Recycling

Relatively new inventions in the supply of currency to teller stations are cash dispensing and cash recycling machines. These provide the redistribution of bills as needed by mechanical and electronic means, and they are said to provide additional benefits:

- They boost productivity by eliminating teller time to count or recount cash, which allows for up to twice as many customers to be served per hour.
- They increase security by reducing opportunities for internal fraud and safeguarding funds in the event of a robbery.
- They increase transaction speed and volume in teller lines and drive-up lanes, containing costs.
- They reduce teller cash setup at the start of the day and time to balance at day's end.
- They streamline cash handling and shorten drive-up lines.
- Each machine serves two tellers and holds up to 10,000 notes.

Countless design variations are possible. Personal ideas about security will influence a resulting concept, such as the use of bullet-resistant glass surrounding the teller area. Others may feel that a more open concept is appropriate, but where there are

The Floor Plan

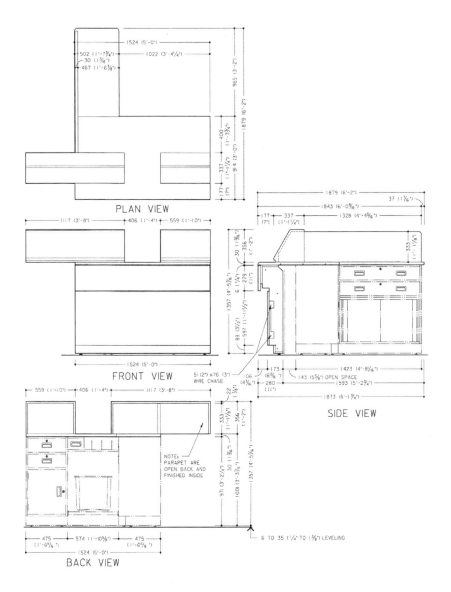

◀ Typical dimensions of casework for tellers. Most architects prefer to custom design the outside components of casework for each project, but the under-counter metal assemblies are usually provided by a specialty equipment supplier. Diebold Inc.

human tellers in plain sight, this arrangement is undoubtedly less secure than a lobby with a series of remote teller machines. In the end, it will fall on the owner-client to decide which of these methods will be used. It is not recommended to use a combination of remote teller machines and conventional tellers in the same location, because customers tend to line up for the traditional tellers if they are available and feel slighted if directed to a remote teller in the same location.

Where the customers are older and accustomed to live, face-to-face service, bank facilities are likely to have a conventional teller system or perhaps a concierge system (see below). As time passes, however, these facilities may consider a retrofit to accommodate

BUILDING DESIGN

▶ Typical check stand. This stand is open on two sides, while some are open on all four sides. Others use a counter arrangement along a wall or adjacent to another item of casework. KKE Architects.

remote teller systems. Time will tell if and when Americans accept these inventions as readily as they have, say, self-serve gasoline stations.

Conventional Drive-Up Teller Counters

Theses paces are usually adjacent to the lobby tellers, for ease of cross-service. A teller counter is usually located at a drive-up window with a drawer serving the first lane, and a back counter is also sometimes provided. Other lanes use pneumatic tubes and direct visual access to the customers along with an audio system for the customer drive-up

▶ Typical check stand details. An infinite variety of design ideas are used for check stands; designs usually complement the teller counter or other interior design theme. WSKF Architects.

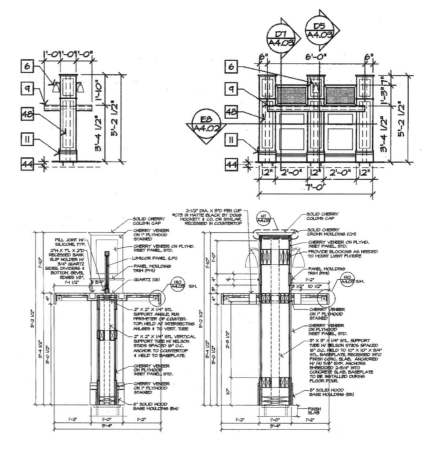

The Floor Plan

units. The tubes can be fed overhead or from below. If customer units are equipped with a televised system, a different configuration will be advantageous, as shown below.

Teller Pod Stations

Washington Mutual Bank, in concert with equipment suppliers, was an early developer of a new concept of teller delivery kiosks, or "pods." Rather than offering services from behind a long, secured counter, teller pods allow tellers increased customer contact, as there are no barriers between staff and customers. Inclusion of PC terminals and cash dispensers and recyclers brings advanced technology, customer service techniques, and security to the pod concept.

Many banks copied the concept, some successfully and others not. Success seems to have depended on a change in the business model, with corresponding changes in the training and expectations of the staff, so that the pod concept might function properly and allow for the advantages of new staff-to-customer relationships, cross-selling, and reduced staffing requirements. Teller pods can be a powerful customer tool but only if properly designed and located and operated by well-trained staff.

Teller pods promote the elevation of staff, through cross-training, from mere teller functions to customer service and sales. Staff now have more time to focus on customers and thereby create stronger relationships by attending to and promoting their interests and needs. This provides for a much richer customer experience, due to the open environment and the reduced time required for cash handling. Additionally, teller pods support a more secure design, as they permit staff to walk away from a potential robbery situation.

◀ Cash recycling machine. These are sometimes needed more at drive-up teller locations than at the lobby because of the shorter transaction time resulting from the drive-up service. Remote teller machine terminals, however, also operate with shorter transaction times, and the recycling need is greater there as well.

▲ Conventional drive-up teller counter and vision window. The system pictured here is a Diebold VAT 21 ("vacuum air tube") overhead pneumatic tube system and vision window. This counter design is the standard 40" height. When a handicapped-accessible counter design is needed, it should be set at a 34" height and provide operator knee space under the counter. Diebold Inc.

67

BUILDING DESIGN

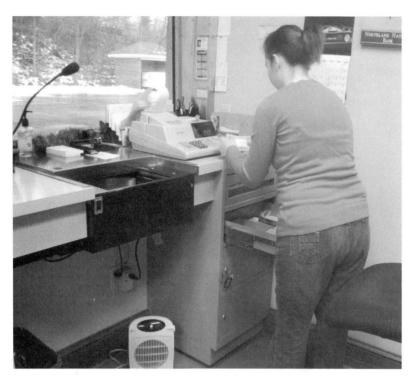

▲ Drive-up teller counter with under-counter and deal drawer. Note the small electric heater under the counter; such devices need to be included with the original HVAC design. The deal drawer is usually equipped with a built-in heater.

▶ Teller video module (voice system with CCTV teller screen). This device provides for secure communication between the teller and drive-up customer. It may be configured to allow video of both the customer and teller or just the customer. ComCo Systems.

A very good example of the use of teller pods is in the Ascend Credit Union in Murfreesboro, Tennessee, by NewGround, (see p. 22).

Concierge Station

Greeter stations have been an element of large branches for many years. A drawback of many greeter stations is that the greeters often answer the phone, type letters, and complete loan processing while occasionally greeting customers. The greeter station has lately evolved into a concierge station, a position of high hospitality and service responsibility delivering more than just occasional recognition. The station design features more of a retail appearance, and its proponents believe it enables an institution to provide greater service with fewer staff.

The concierge now manages branch traffic and facilitates staff-to-customer interaction. This position is no longer assigned to lower-paid branch staff. Like Starbucks staff, the concierge is expected to have the knowledge, appearance, attitude, and energy to relate directly with customers at each branch. He or she must be able to explain the bank's brand and how that branch supports the brand as well as to relate the basic facts about all products and service offerings. The concierge must know where to find the answers. The concierge is the host, the person most responsible for creating the first impression and making customers feel welcome, important, and intelligent. The development of these stations has produced several insights about their use and the duties of the service representatives who man them.[3]

---

3 Paul Seibert of EHS Design, communication to author, October 23, 2007.

- The stations work well in larger branches where the concierge is an active position and full-time staffing can be afforded. They must be well-positioned in the engineered customer path with trained personnel to provide multiple services.
- In smaller branches, the concierge function can be provided by a customer service staff member positioned at a multifunctional station that allows both standing and seated interaction.
- Concierge service representatives must focus on the customer 100 percent of the time. They are the first point of customer contact and should not be expected to perform secretarial or phone reception duties.
- The stations should be elevated to allow staff to provide eye-level customer contact.
- Concierges must have thorough knowledge of all products and services and must be able to cross-sell.
- They must understand and perform established security procedures, and they are usually the first point of contact in a robbery attempt.
- The concierge position must be strategically located to greet everyone entering and leaving. It must have full visibility of the retail area of each branch.
- In facilities with remote teller systems or automated cash transactions, concierges serve as hosts or hostesses and must create a warm, friendly, and professional environment for their customers. They are the human link between technology and people, both staff and customers.
- They must be able to communicate the rationale behind the brand image and deliver the brand experience through every action.[4]

Concierge station, North Shore Credit Union, Vancouver, British Columbia; EHS Design. Greeters are positioned at the entrance of every branch. They are highly knowledgeable hospitality workers who must understand all products and services of the institution. They manage the lobby, promote the brand, and provide high member recognition. (The floor plan of this facility is shown on p. 19.) Roger Brooks Photography.

Two examples of the concierge system are the North Shore Credit Union, Vancouver, British Columbia, by EHS Design, and the Frandsen Bank & Trust in Forest Lake, Minnesota, by HTG Architects. This system is promoted by HTG as part of their trademarked "Evobank" (for "evolving bank").[5]

The Remote Teller System

This is a system that makes use of personal teller machines, also called "RTS," which function much like an ATM except that a live teller is available—a televised one who, coupled with a pneumatic tube delivery system and an audio sound system, can perform all the services of a conventional teller. Teller and customer are even face-to-

4 Ibid.

5 http://www.htg-architects.com (accessed October 27, 2007).

BUILDING DESIGN

▶ "Evobank" concierge station; HTG Architects. These stations permit a trained bank or credit union employee to provide usual teller services, but they are able to offer much more assistance and can cross-sell other important products and services, and to more customers or members. (The floor plan of this facility is shown on p. 171.) HTG Architects.

face, albeit via the video link. Manufacturers of RTS machines claim they have several advantages:

- They improve efficiency by reducing transaction time for the tellers.
- Fewer tellers can serve more customers.
- They greatly increase security, because the tellers and currency are somewhere else—perhaps not even in the same building.
- It is possible to optimize staffing for peak and off hours.
- They provide increased marketing opportunities, with integrated graphics and video.
- Business hours may be extended.

In some cases, new integrated teller centers have replaced traditional teller operations with tellers in a secure remote room that can serve twice as many customers by using remote teller units in a reconfigured lobby. One example is the ASI Federal Credit Union in West Wego, Louisiana. In this project, ASI built a new branch adjacent

The Floor Plan

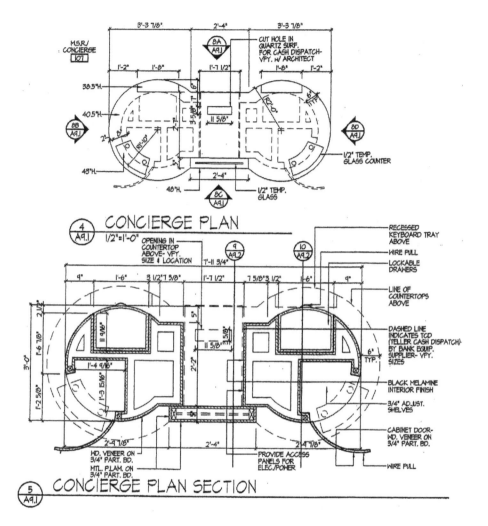

◀ Evobank station plan and section; HTG Architects. HTG Architects.

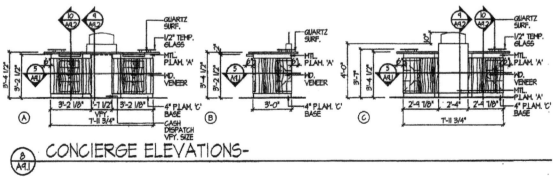

▼ Evobank concierge elevations; HTG Architects. HTG Architects.

BUILDING DESIGN

▲ Remote teller system. The customer is able to receive complete teller services at a secure kiosk via phone, television monitor, and pneumatic carrier. Diebold Inc.

to an existing building. ASI decided to incorporate a total "tellerless" lobby and move the tellers to a new integrated teller center, equipped with teller units and teller workroom equipment by ComCo Systems.[6] ComCo has also developed a new tube system that is made of an eco-friendly Plexiglas that will contribute to the green or LEED rating in any new or retrofit application.

Tellers that previously staffed a six-position walk-up teller line now serve twelve lobby teller units, while comfortably seated in the new secure and efficient teller center.

With all teller units easily within reach and serviceable from two sides, plus the use of cash dispensers, the same six tellers are able to process transactions from the twelve customer units in the same amount of time. "Where there used to be lines of members waiting in the old building, members now have very little wait-time to be served."[7]

These are all good reasons for considering these machines, but the question of customer acceptance should be considered. There is a consensus that where these have been installed they are successful.[8] A good example of the measure of customer acceptance is the experience of Aloha Pacific Credit Union in Honolulu, Hawaii; president and CEO Wallace Watanabe states that it "took about a year for customers to readily accept the new units, but by that time they were being used without hesitation."

EXISTING BRANCH TRANSFORMATION

Any effort to upgrade facilities will confront questions of how best to modify an existing bank plan to accommodate the new methods of customer service. Diebold Inc. has developed a suggested transformation, as shown at right.

The first construction phase is to convert the existing drive-up islands to a tandem arrangement, allowing two customers to be served by each lane. These may be served by the drive-up tellers while other modifications are made. The second phase is to modify the teller area to accommodate the CCTV system and a new pneumatic tube system serving new tandem drive-up units.

The third phase provides for modifications to the workroom and development of the 24-

6 http://www.comcosystems.com (accessed December 12, 2007).

7 Ibid.
8 ComCo Systems (2007).

Existing Branch Transformation

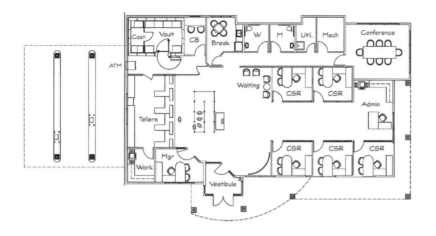

◁ *Branch prior to transformation. The plan is of a typical branch bank with a conventional four-teller line, a manager's office, five other private offices, an administrative open desk, a safe deposit vault with cash room and a coupon booth, a conference room, a break room, utility, toilets, and a three-lane conventional drive-up. Diebold Inc.*

◁ *Potential areas for transformation. Diebold Inc.*

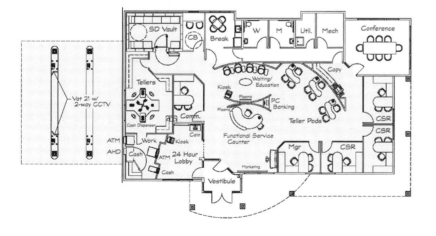

◁ *Transformed branch plan. The complete remodeled and transformed branch plan, with features allowing for phased construction, so that the bank might remain open during the process. Diebold Inc.*

BUILDING DESIGN

▶ Cut section plan of existing branch. The three-dimensional drawing indicates the existing space usage and original permanent or full-height walls. Diebold Inc.

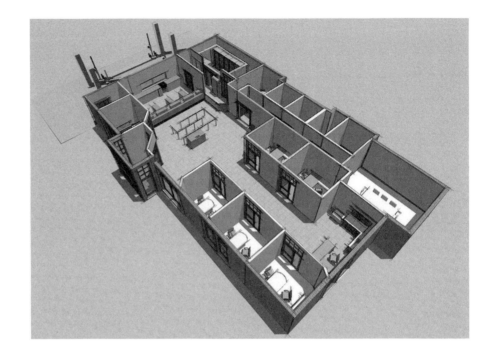

▶ First phase cut section of plan. This shows the new tandem drive-up configuration that adds two more customer units to the existing drive-up lanes at upper left (see also p. 50). Diebold Inc.

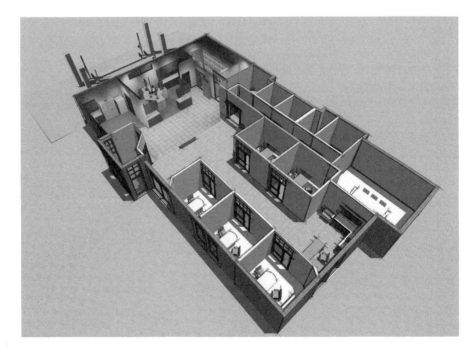

Existing Branch Transformation

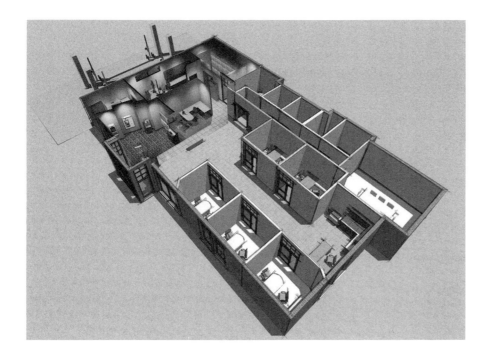

◂ Second phase cut section of the plan. The former teller room is reconfigured for remote teller operations accommodating the added drive-up spaces and the use of cash recyclers. A drive-up ATM is added, along with the night depository, which is equipped with a larger cash safe as well. This allows the safe deposit vault to be modified for removal of the cash room to a separate space, and provides for more safe deposit boxes. Diebold Inc.

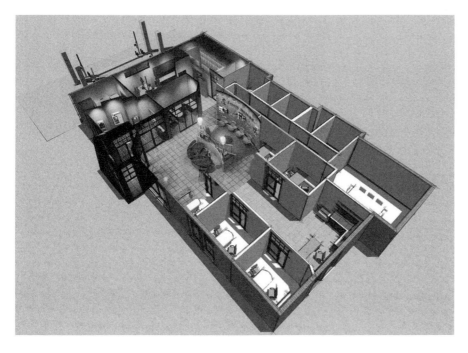

◂ Third phase cut section plan. A new 24-hour lobby is added, with an ATM, a cash dispenser, a remote teller machine, and a coin machine. A commercial lending office is placed in front of the new teller room. The lobby is modified to add a functional service counter, plasma screen and product displays, a PC banking station, a customer kiosk, and a new waiting/education area. Glass-lined walls and new flooring, ceiling surfaces, and lighting are also added adjacent to the other renovated spaces. Diebold Inc.

BUILDING DESIGN

▶ *Fourth phase cut section plan. This completes the renovation of the lobby, adding the four teller pods, a manager's office, three customer service representative offices, and a copy center. Diebold Inc.*

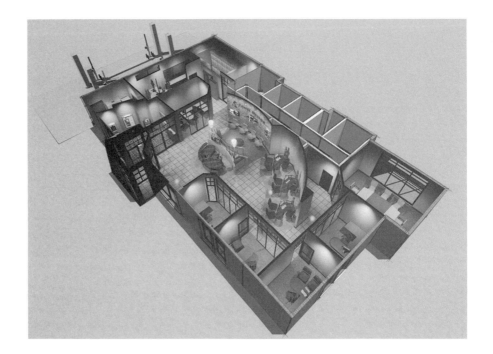

▶ *Cut section plan of remodeled and transformed branch. The final phase renovates the exterior and main entrance. Diebold Inc.*

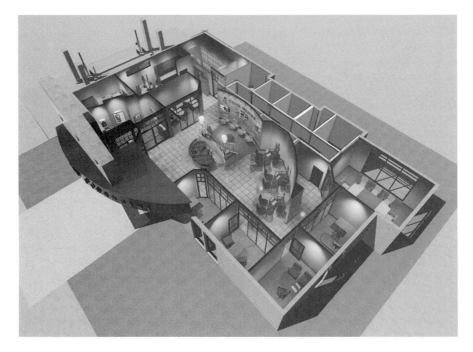

Existing Branch Transformation

hour lobby, as well as other changes, which may include changes to the main lobby, including a functional service counter, a PC banking station, and various marketing features, including flat screens and a new waiting and educational area.

The fourth phase of interior transformation adds the new teller pods, a copy center, and newly configured offices for the manager and customer service representatives.

Drive-Up and Remote Teller Room.

Diebold Inc. has also developed an improved arrangement for the new equipment available for the televised drive-up units and for remote customer units. This allows for a central teller console with the tube terminals

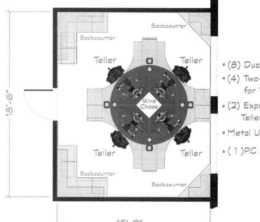

▲ Floor plan of new teller room concept. The layout depicted here will allow the four remote tellers to handle as many as eight drive-up lanes or remote teller machines. Diebold Inc.

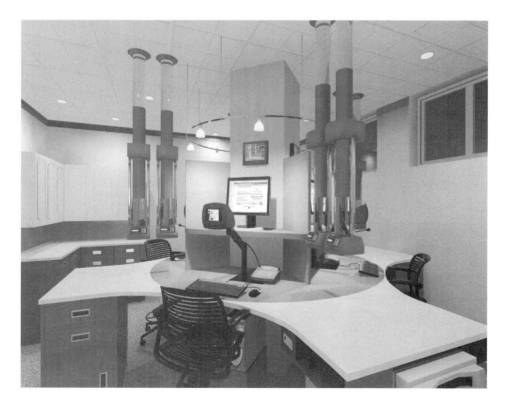

◀ View of new teller room concept by Diebold Inc. The teller is able to serve two or more lanes with the CCTV and pneumatic system. A cash recycler is placed between two tellers and can just be seen at the lower right. Another is placed at the opposite side of the console between the other two tellers. Diebold Inc.

BUILDING DESIGN

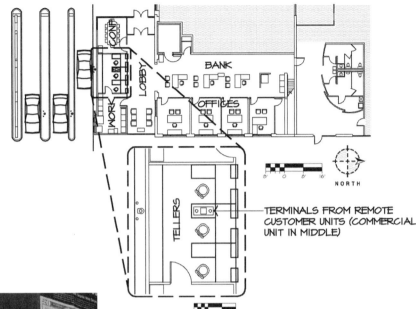

▶ Floor plan of lobby teller remote terminal for Premier Bank North Kansas City, Missouri; WSKF Architects. This was a complete renovation of an existing industrial building. The garage bays were used for a three-lane remote teller drive-up system that allows the lobby tellers to serve drive-up and lobby customers from the same location. WSKF Architects.

placed around the center between the tellers. The illustrations at left and above show how this equipment may be arranged. The use of the cash dispensing and cash recycling machines has greatly improved the supplying of currency to these tellers. These machines are described in more detail in chapter 9.

Combined Lobby/Remote Teller Service

Another way to service remote teller units is through a feature that connects the terminals of the drive tubes directly to the lobby teller counter returns. The obvious benefit is to allow lobby tellers ready access to the terminals without moving to a separate location and without the need for separate drive-up tellers. A televised system keeps the tellers at their stations for dual lobby/drive-up service.

THE BOUTIQUE BANK/SHOP

Some new banks have very little resemblance to conventional banks, as they are being built with an informal coffee-shop or boutique theme. An example is a facility designed by Gensler Architects for ING Direct in New York City (see also p. 23). The bank's objective was to attract new customers while serving their existing ones. The upbeat design provides for Internet banking in a café with a street presence. ING, a Netherlands-based company with banking operations in fifty countries, has had remarkable growth in the United States, with "cafés" serving customers via electronic access in six major cities. The now well-known orange "code" is the brainchild of ING's founding CEO, Arkadi Kuhlman, and partner Bruce Philp, of GWP Brand Engineering. By the end of 2007, ING had achieved in one decade phenomenal growth, of nearly 7.4 million accounts and 80 billion dollars in assets (Kuhlman and Philp 2009, p. 234).

In ING Direct's New York City café bank, the bank's colors are featured in bands of tile on floors, walls, and ceilings. Other uses of perforated metal, frosted acrylic, Corian, plastic laminates, and routed wood inlay add to the desired impression. The existing building facade was kept intact except for the bank logo and a canopy that extends over the sidewalk. The design reflects the desired integration of architecture, graphic design, retail design, and high-tech media (flat-screen video, food menus, sound system, and Internet kiosks).

◂◂ Pneumatic tube terminals at lobby teller counter return. The lobby tellers have access to the tube terminals from both sides of the end-return cabinet, which allows them to provide service to the drive-up or the lobby customers from the same location. The CCTV monitor and audio control are shown at left, above the teller pedestal.

▴ ING Direct café bank, New York City; Gensler Architects. The usual bank atmosphere is completely absent, in favor of a more relaxed, customer-friendly, Internet-oriented operation. Photo by Craig Duggan.

BUILDING DESIGN

PROTOTYPICAL DESIGN

Almost all large financial institutions that have numerous branches, or that operate regionally or nationally, have prototypical branch facilities. Some have more than one prototype, and often when they seek to open a facility in another part of the country, they find that a prototype must be modified significantly. Differences in climate and weather account for some of these modifications, but there are also different style preferences in different regions of the country. The Spanish Mission style of the American Southwest, for example, does not fit well with the colonial image of Williamsburg, Virginia. When a prototype is modified for site-specific conditions alone, there are frequently major adjustments that must be made. Moreover, certain architectural styles and finishes are now mandated in particular locations because of zoning or developmental regulations.

Certainly there are successful prototypes being used regionally or even nationally, but while the buildings may appear similar, there may have been hundreds of plan variations necessary to accommodate differences in location. Fast-food chains are particularly adept at achieving similar-looking facilities. (See page 177 for an example of a bank branch built from a prototype.)

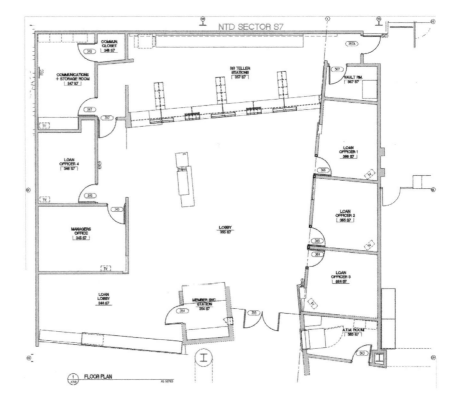

▶ American Airlines Credit Union floor plan; McHarry Architects. The unusual configuration allows for a spacious, upscale appearance. Note the separate ATM accessible from the main corridor for 24-hour use. McHarry Architects.

MALLS, AIRPORTS, AND IN-STORE LOCATIONS

There are advantages to locating new branch facilities in malls, airports, supermarkets, large discount retailers, and other such interior locations. These usually have high customer traffic, adequate parking, and—because they are inside existing structures—relatively low start-up costs. It is also usually easier to move from such locations when market conditions require a relocation or discontinuation of operations. It is just as important as with freestanding banks, however, to consider design and brand image.

CALL CENTERS

Call center design is a topic unto itself, but it intersects with bank design, because in recent years numerous financial institutions have included call centers as part of their customer-service operations. Watermark Credit Union includes a call center in its newly renovated headquarters office in Seattle, Washington, designed by IA Interior Architects (see following page and pp. 184–186). Among the design concerns particular to a call center are ergonomically correct furniture and equipment, including adjustable chairs, keyboards, and monitors.

◂ American Airlines Credit Union at the Miami International Airport, Florida; McHarry Architects. The airport location offers a very high traffic count, and parking is automatically provided. Photo by Dan Forer.

BUILDING DESIGN

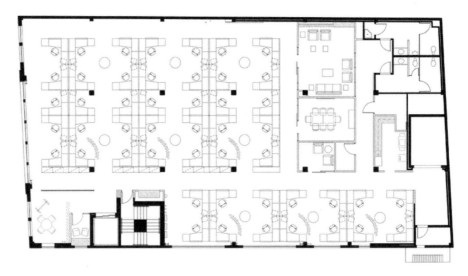

▸ Fifth-floor plan, call center of the Watermark Credit Union, Seattle, Washington; IA Interior Architects. Creation of the call center was integrated with the renovation of the entire building for the headquarters of Watermark Credit Union. IA Interior Architects.

▸▸ Plan modified to include online tellers. Note the single drive-up lane and the night depository integrated with a safe. The electronic tellers, located adjacent to the drive-up tellers, who were established for home-mortgage assistance, also field telephone calls. The meeting room was included for banking staff and customer education use. WRS Architects.

One size definitely does not fit all. It is also important to have modules that are adequate in size and that feature concealed power and data cabling, so as to avoid the visible "spaghetti" tangle of cords and cables that otherwise occurs. Another possibility is the placement of all cabling in overhead trellises that feed down to work stations. Adequate and well-defined pathways should be provided to such amenities as conference rooms, restrooms, cafeterias, and break rooms. Some designers are using modules based on 120-degree workstations placed in clusters, instead of the usual 90-degree rectangular grid.

ONLINE BANKING AND TELLERS

Electronic banking has introduced a new category of bank employee, the electronic teller. Many larger banks are now centralizing these new tellers in data-center facilities that bear almost no resemblance to a bank. They are in office buildings and are usually arrangements of cubicles without permanent walls. These tellers work online and seldom, if ever, meet customers face-to-face. These are usually not the tellers who operate the remote teller system; they are instead responsible for online banking operations. With Internet use ever more ubiquitous, especially among young consumers, more and more banks and credit unions will be offering basic teller services through this method of delivery.

A quick survey of the rapidly increasing use of social networks such as Facebook, Twitter, Plaxco, and LinkedIn makes it easy to see how banking will be added to that method of communication, and the likely resulting sales volume. It is estimated that as of this writing Facebook has 200 million users, with Plaxco at 40 million, LinkedIn at 35 million, and the newer Twitter already 18 million. The formidable RE/MAX real estate group has counted 2.3 million unique visitors online every month since its entry into this marketing sector.[9] Banks and credit unions will most certainly enter this market group in some form.

The ING Direct café bank shown on

---

[9] From Dan Vick, ReMax Real Estate, Kansas City, MO; June 4, 2009.

page 79 features customer access via the Internet, while some other institutions are operating without any physical facilities except a headquarters building or main office. An example is Bank of the Internet, based in San Diego, California, which started business in 2001 and has seen its assets grow by 800 percent in eight years.[10] Except for an office floor with a data center and a lobby ATM, it has no other traditional brick-and-mortar bank-related features, but instead serves its customers exclusively by the Internet.

The floor plans of these spaces provide for a typical office atmosphere complete with the normally required amenities. A cubicle space for the online teller is commonplace

Modification to Include Online Banking Tellers

The facility shown at right was converted to accommodate a modest lobby clientele with two tellers who also serve a single drive-up lane, but the significant new feature was provision for seven additional electronic banking tellers arranged in cubicles.

SELECT-MARKET BANKS

Some banks are now limiting their customer base to privately held businesses, wealthy families, and individuals who have a high net worth. They offer complete banking and trust services to those clients and are said to provide a much higher level of personalized assistance. One of these is Private Bank, a publicly traded company based in Chicago with banking offices in numerous other cities.[11] This kind of banking operation

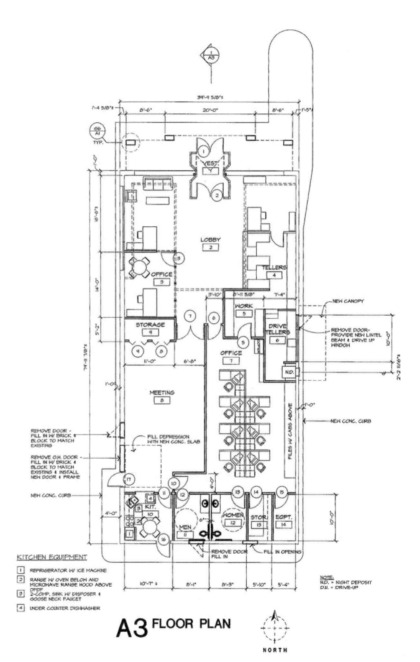

10 http://www.bankofinternet.com (accessed October 28, 2007).
11 http://www.theprivatebank.com (accessed October 29, 2007).

BUILDING DESIGN

▲ The Private Bank, Kansas City, Missouri. This view of the reception desk shows little resemblance to a traditional bank. Financial services are offered to select clients in the modern setting of a sixth-floor office.

often includes an ATM as one of the few commonly recognizable features of a bank. It often takes the form of upscale business offices, with all financial service operations, including teller services, occurring in an office suite.

NEW PRODUCTS AND SERVICES

The relaxation of federal laws that precluded banks from certain lending and investment practices has resulted in numerous new services and "products" being offered, for example, insurance, annuities, securities, real-estate services, and others. A careful analysis of space needs and relationships must be made in order to provide for these new operations. In some cases, the operations must be clearly separated from the main bank area. Because of occasional changes in regulatory guidelines, it is prudent to check with the appropriate agency before determining the exact location and configuration for these spaces.

SINGLE- OR MULTIFLOOR

Depending on the program and the site limitations, a project may need to have more than one story. If a bank is projected to grow and needs additional space in the future, it may be wise to build the additional space at the outset. The space may be subleased to a tenant until needed by the bank. Or the bank may determine that additional revenue from the leased space contributes sufficiently to its profitability and may therefore continue to rent out the space. If a public meeting room is part of the program, that space might also be on either a lower or an upper level. Circulation must be carefully considered, as stairs and elevators are expensive, but necessary in any multiple-floor arrangement.

Great Northern Bank, Saint Michael, Minnesota, designed by KKE Architects, is in a new 21,000 sq ft, 2-story building that has been designed for the bank and for lease space on both floors. On a 2-acre site, it has been planned to accommodate a future 10,000 sq ft addition as well. The design goal was a building that would recall the historic character of the community in a warm, old-time atmosphere, but also have the latest features in technology to serve its 2,500 customers.

The main entrance opens to the building lobby, which in turn leads to the bank or to the other suites on the first floor, in addition to a community meeting room. Two sets of stairs, an elevator, and public restrooms are accessible from the main building corridor. A janitor's closet and a sprinkler service room are off the main corridor.

The bank lobby is configured with a customer service desk near the entrance, a waiting area surrounding a working fireplace, and the traditional teller counter. The three

Single- or Multifloor

◀ First-floor plan, Great Northern Bank, St. Michael, Minnesota; KKE Architects. The building's main entrance provides access to the bank, at left, and the other tenant spaces, in addition to a community room and lockable corridor to the elevator, public toilets, and stair. The bank has its own internal open stair for its second-floor access. A second fire stair at the rear provides direct access to the second-floor tenant spaces. The dashed lines at the right indicate a future building addition. KKE Architects.

◀ Second-floor plan, Great Northern Bank, St. Michael, Minnesota; KKE Architects. The bank's open atrium provides a visual connection between the banking floors. The shaded area is lease space and can be expanded in the future as indicated by the dashed line to the right. KKE Architects.

stand-up tellers are adjacent to the drive-up tellers who operate the five conventional lanes beyond. A lowered portion of the lobby teller counter accommodates handicapped customers. A workroom and the safe deposit vault are to one side of the tellers. An antique gilded vault doorframe has been reused to highlight the new vault.

Five private offices, two conference rooms, and a break room are grouped around the bank lobby, and a separate interior stair leads to the second floor of the

BUILDING DESIGN

▶ Exterior view of main entrance elevation, Great Northern Bank, St. Michael, Minnesota; KKE Architects. The building's main entrance clearly defines the bank at left and the tenant space at the right. The light-colored stone face and darker masonry are separated by even lighter-colored horizontal bands between the windows and wall areas. Philip Prouse Photography.

bank. The bank's second floor is comprised of office suites placed around an open 2-story space that looks down to the bank lobby and tellers. Another conference room and a room for the computer server equipment are also located on the second floor.

The balance of the building's second floor consists of two separate suites for lease, the two main stairs, an elevator, and additional public restrooms.

THE COMMUNITY MEETING ROOM

In smaller communities throughout the country, many banks include a public meeting space in their buildings. These are usually made available at no cost, as a public service. The idea is that the bank will profit by the goodwill that the use of the space generates. These are often located in a basement area but sometimes on a second floor. The advent of the Americans with Disabilities Act (ADA) in the late 1980s has required all public facilities to be accessible by anyone, without regard to physical handicap. This has resulted in the need to provide an elevator for those uses when they are not on the ground floor.

Since these meeting rooms are not often used during business hours, they require a separate access that can bypass the entrance to the institution, but allow use of toilet and kitchen facilities.

Building codes also often require a second stair for life safety exiting or access. Designers therefore must plan for these needs, and the resulting costs must also be considered.

Operational Space Needs

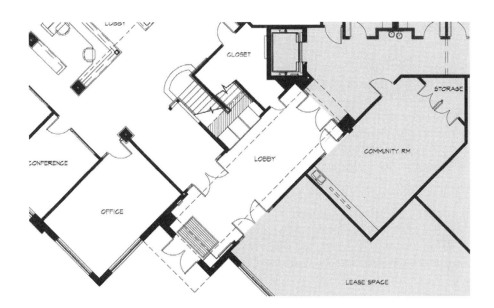

◀ Community room. This room, unlike many that are located on a basement level, is on the main level of this multitenant 2-story bank. KKE Architects.

OPERATIONAL SPACE NEEDS

Whether a headquarters, branch, or other financial service provider, most banking facilities will have space for a lobby, teller areas for inside service and drive-ups, offices, meeting rooms, workrooms, break rooms, and many other areas dedicated to the facility's particular mode of operation and service delivery. The following descriptions will define such particular space needs.

Lobby and Waiting

A vestibule entrance is recommended, especially for areas of the country with temperature extremes and in the cases of multiple-tenant or multistory buildings, where it will also provide access to a separate stair and elevator lobby. The appropriate ADA clearances and door swings must be provided. The bank lobby should be designed for the expected traffic and accessibility. It is necessary to determine if open desks and other furniture and equipment will be used and where they will be located. File space is commonly needed adjacent to the bank offices; depending on the size of the institution, this may be accomplished with standard file cabinets or with a separate file room off the lobby. File storage types are discussed in chapter 10.

A check stand will usually be placed in this area, and clearance for it as well as for teller access should also be maintained. Many other options and amenities may be located in or near the lobby, such as a coffee bar, fireplace, waiting-area furniture, and perhaps an Internet banking station. All of these needs should be determined in the branding and programming phases. The plan of a project featured in chapter 11, the River Bank in Osceola, Wisconsin, by BKV Group Architects, demonstrates a very good arrangement of these spaces along the customer path (see p. 166).

BUILDING DESIGN

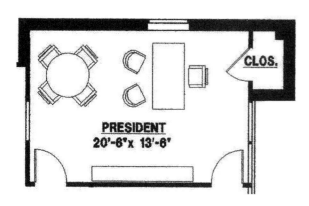

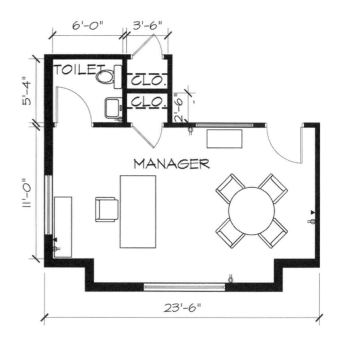

▲ *President's office, Quantum National Bank, Suwannee, Georgia; Foreman Seeley Fountain Architects. There are countless variations on office plan concepts; the building program should establish each specific requirement. Foreman Seeley Fountain Architecture.*

◀ *President's or manager's office with private toilet and closet. The office has a small conference table as well. The electrical outlets and phone connections are shown. Data and security components must also be provided; these are discussed in chapter 8. Foreman Seeley Fountain Architects.*

Offices

Successful banks have been built with very few offices, and others operate equally well with private offices for every key employee. The decision whether to have private offices, an open desk arrangement, or a combination depends on the style of operation desired by the owner-client and should be defined in the program. In general, offices are located adjacent to the banking lobby, with glass facing the lobby and teller area so that officers can observe the activities taking place. In larger headquarters banks, offices may be much more extensive, in separate departments, and perhaps on separate floors.

Manager or executive offices may have a separate conference area in addition to the normal office furniture, and some will also have access to a private bathroom. The president's office may also have a direct access to an adjoining conference or boardroom, and other offices may require a secondary exit

Conference, Boardrooms, and Closing Rooms

In a headquarters bank, the boardroom is designed to accommodate board members, executive staff, and any anticipated guests. The size will depend on what activities are expected and the overall size of the facility. The program should determine the dimensions. Provisions for service and equipment, such as audiovisual equipment and Internet access, will also be needed. Cabinets may also be included, as well as a sink and refrigerator. Many facilities have adjacent private bathrooms. Larger banks will usually have additional conference and closing rooms of varying sizes, placed according to the activity and need.

In many branch banks, the boardroom will also serve as a conference room, and depending on the branch size, it is often placed adjacent to the banking lobby, along with private offices or officer spaces. Loan

Operational Space Needs

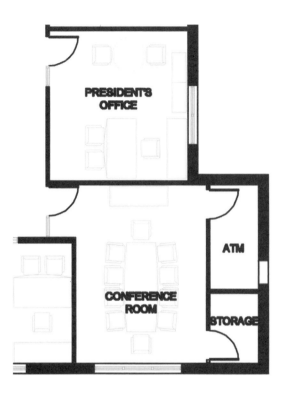

◀ President's office and adjacent conference room. Note the ATM room off the conference room, with a through-wall ATM for drive-up customers. (Regular service and replenishment to the ATM is more secure because of this feature, although access through the conference room is less desirable.) Conference rooms may need to be larger, depending on the activities planned and the size of the facility. The rooms depicted here are in a Midwestern bank of 4,500 sq ft. WRS Architects.

◀ Typical boardroom. This new boardroom is equipped with the latest technological amenities and has a view of the outside as well as the adjacent lobby area.

BUILDING DESIGN

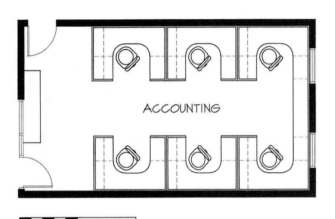

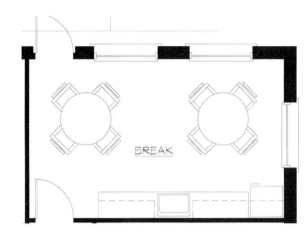

▲ Typical in-house accounting department. This plan suggests cubicles, although more elaborate suites are sometimes used. KKE Architects.

▼ Typical break room. These usually include a small kitchenette with a refrigerator, dishwasher, and a cooktop or oven and microwave. The sink is usually equipped with a garbage disposal. Larger facilities may have a full kitchen, depending on their needs. Foreman Seeley Fountain Architecture.

closings are also often held in these rooms (they are also frequently used by examiners). These are not usually as large as headquarters bank's boardrooms and are sometimes made a part of a manager's office. Many are equipped with power screens and projectors and other computer-related technologies.

In headquarters banks, the offices and office suites may be much larger and may require several conference rooms, separate closing rooms, and much larger boardrooms. Other examples of these are shown in the case studies in chapter 11.

Workrooms

A bank workroom will need numerous items of equipment, depending on how it operates and whether the new Check 21 process has been implemented. These are considered in much greater detail in chapter 9.

Vaults and Vault Doors

Many new branch banks have eliminated costly walk-in safe deposit vaults in favor of smaller safes or chests that are both secure and fireproof. In such facilities, armed car services are regularly dispatched to transport currency and other valuables as needed so that the large vaults are not required. Others still feature the larger vaults, and many are now using the prefabricated modular systems that are available, while fewer are being constructed with poured-in-place concrete. The reduced profit from safe deposit box rentals versus the cost of new vault construction is one reason for this trend. Some facilities, however, are still being designed and constructed with site-poured concrete vaults. The prefabricated vault systems and vault doors that are available are shown in chapter 10. Manufacturers are listed in appendix C.

Accounting

The accounting for most branch facilities is undertaken at a headquarters facility or home office of the institution, and much is outsourced. Where the institution does have an in-house accounting department, the size and configuration of the department depends on each institution. In some cases an arrangement of workstation modules may be used as depicted above, or an office with open desks may be used.

Building Codes

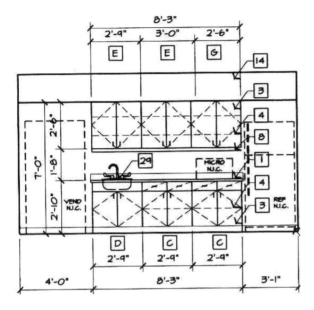

▲ Break room cabinets. Break rooms are sometimes equipped with small premanufactured kitchen units, while others have full kitchens with extensive cabinets and appliances. WSKF Architects

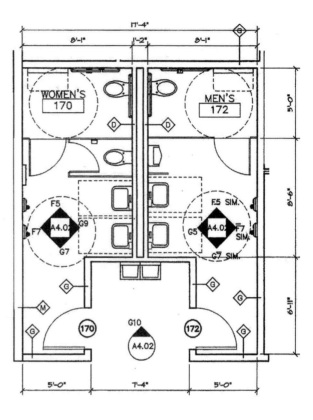

▲ Typical restroom plan. Most new branch facilities have simple but adequate restrooms, and all must be designed for ADA compliance. The drinking fountains in this illustration require the space for handicap access in the extended corridor. A janitor's closet is sometimes placed between or adjacent to the restrooms. WSKF Architects.

Other Spaces

Other spaces typically needed include break rooms and, of course, toilet facilities.

BUILDING CODES

The new International Building Code has replaced many of the codes formerly used throughout the United States, but many local and state jurisdictions still maintain their own added requirements. It is the responsibility of the architects and engineers to design for the appropriate building code and life safety provisions for their projects.

In various parts of the country, projects have sometimes been constructed that have failed to comply with basic life safety and other code requirements. These are generally projects that have been undertaken without the services of licensed architects or engineers. Some owners, in attempting avoid the expense of professional architectural or engineering fees by using unlicensed designers and construction firms, discover later that they have inherited a costly code violation that could have been prevented. The code provisions or standards for each item of equipment are discussed in chapters 9 and 10.

ADA Provisions

The general requirements for compliance with this act are well known to most architects and engineers, but several provisions relevant to financial institutions are important

BUILDING DESIGN

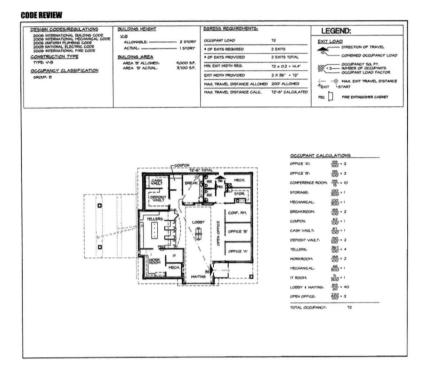

▲ Typical code review for a new branch bank building. Most cities require a graphic and written code review similar to this to be included in the construction documents. WSKF Architects.

to note. One of these provisions concerns vault design; a disabled person must be able to gain access to both vault and coupon booth in a wheelchair. The same provisions must be made for turning and maneuvering a wheelchair as are required for toilets. The law provides for accessibility by disabled employees and customers alike, so it is important to consider the design of workplace features to accommodate handicapped employees as well as customers.

Another location of concern in a bank or credit union is the main teller line. A disabled person must have access to teller services by having a segment of counter, or a separate counter, designed for wheelchair use. Where employees are disabled, they must have provisions for accessibility as well, with lowered teller counters that provide for knee space, for example.

Other well-known areas of concern are improper ramps, inadequate toilet facilities, and inaccessible drinking fountains. It is essential to eliminate barriers. ADA provisions are now important in planning for parking and access to the building as well. These requirements are listed by the Federal Register and other sources, as follows:

- U.S. Department of Justice, for technical assistance relative to the applicability of the ADA title III and legal interpretations regarding enforcement: 800-514-0301; www.ada.gov
- U.S. Architectural and Transportation Barriers Compliance Board (ACCESS Board): 800-USA-ABLE or 202-272-5434; www.access-board.gov
- Job Accommodation Network (offers advice to employers on methods of making accommodations accessible), 800-232-9675; http://janweb.icdi.wvu.edu
- Regional Disability and Business Technical Assistance Center (offers local technical assistance relative to any aspect of the ADA), 800-949-4232

Another important ruling, regarding tax credit provisions for costs incurred in making ADA improvements in a building, is available from the IRS:

- Internal Revenue Service, 800-829-1040; www.irs.gov

For projects in California, Title 24 requirements must be met as well.

Building Codes

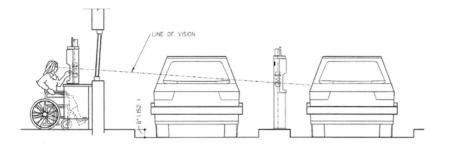

◀ ADA accessible drive-up teller station. This illustrates the importance of providing accommodation for employees as well as customers. Diebold Inc.

◀ Plan and elevation of ADA-compliant drive-up teller station. This indicates the maneuvering requirements for a wheelchair and illustrates a cash dispenser to the left of the ADA station. It is suggested that a screen be placed behind the tellers for better visual effect with the televised system. Diebold Inc.

BUILDING DESIGN

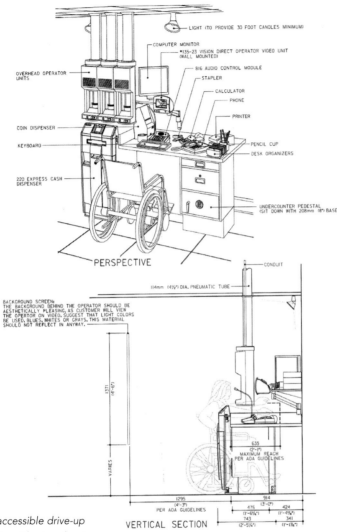

▲ ADA accessible drive-up teller station. The top drawing depicts the typical arrangement of teller amenities for ADA compliance; the bottom drawing indicates the horizontal dimensions at the station and the suggested vertical dimensions of the screen. Diebold Inc.

UTILITIES

As mentioned in chapter 6, the site must have, or be able to obtain, necessary utilities. The architect, engineers, and/or land surveyors should verify that these utilities are accessible and adequate for the building contemplated. Various parts of the country offer different services, and plans should reflect the available connections. A heating system should obviously not be designed for natural gas where natural gas is not available. The electrical service is very important in any financial institution, as so many items of equipment rely on a specific power requirement. In some areas, transformers may be required in order to obtain the proper power or suitable electrical phase needed. Chapter 8 discusses mechanical, electrical, and plumbing needs.

Sewage disposal is also a common problem where a public system is not available. Engineers are usually able to offer alternatives such as septic systems or even small individual package disposal systems. Allowance for proper disposal of runoff and storm water must be made to protect the property of both the owner and neighbors. Provisions for the temporary on-site storage of excessive storm water are commonly required.

CONSTRUCTION COST COMPARISONS

The shelf life on cost information is very short, so this information should be rechecked regularly. The source for the data given here is R. S. Means Co.'s *Means Square Foot Costs 2009* (30th ed.). Variations occur throughout the country, depending on the availability of materials, and shipping and labor costs. Numerous factors have an impact on a final cost, a detailed survey of which is beyond the scope of this work.

The size of a project is another important factor. Square-foot costs are greater in smaller projects than large ones. The economies of scale have a direct bearing on project costs.

An example is an analysis is given by Means for the square-foot cost of a 1-story branch bank of 4,100 sq ft. The building is to be constructed with a steel frame and a lightweight concrete block and face-brick exterior wall. This example has 256 linear ft of perimeter wall, and the average cost per sq ft in the United States is $225.00. It should be noted that a wide range is given for this example, from $127.50 to $313.80 per sq ft. (Means lists many other examples of construction types and their relative costs.)

As similarly constructed projects increase in square footage, the respective costs are $220.35 per sq ft for a 4,800 sq ft building; $216.65 per sq ft for a 5,500 sq ft building; $212.40 per sq ft for a 6,200 sq ft building; and $207.80 per sq ft for a 7,600 sq ft building. The Means guide provides a good method of estimating approximate square-foot costs when its system is carefully followed, but there are also wide variations by region of the country, and some are significantly higher than the Means guide may suggest. It is therefore advisable to obtain the services of a professional cost estimator or contractor who is familiar with local market conditions and can provide detailed estimates.[12]

SUSTAINABILITY

There are numerous sources for and works about green design and sustainability, and it is not the intent of this work to provide detailed consideration, but with most of us spending more than 80 percent of our time indoors, sustainable design is the healthy choice for better living. In traditional construction, the indoor environment is often more polluted than outdoors. This is due to building materials, poor lighting, and other factors.

[12] Editors of R. S. Means Co., *2009 Square Foot Costs* (Kingston, MA: R. S. Means Co.), 88–89.

"Green buildings are sited, designed, constructed, and operated to enhance the well-being of their occupants and to minimize the negative impact on the community and natural environment" (Freed 2007). Our buildings consume 40 percent of the world's energy, 25 percent of its wood harvest, and 16 percent of its water. Our society cannot continue to build using wasteful traditional methods. It is a matter of time before we run out of resources, so the sooner we change our habits and building methods, the better. Geothermal systems for heating and cooling are described in chapter 8, and several banks have already installed such systems, which use no fossil fuels and emit no harmful gases.

The first question that seems to come up in relation to sustainable design is cost. In practice, it has been shown that while a first effort to go green is usually more costly, the second project and those that follow are carried out more smoothly and at less cost. Moreover, the life-cycle operational costs are much less, and this should of course be considered, as such savings soon eclipse the added costs of construction. A project discussed in chapter 11, the Banner Bank in Boise, Idaho, was one of only 20 Leadership in Energy and Environmental Design (LEED) Platinum–certified projects in the world at its completion and is reported to have cost no more than a conventional project and to have taken a comparable time to complete.

PNC Bank has received a 2.0 Silver rating for its new 647,000 sq ft building in downtown Pittsburg, Pennsylvania, making it one of the largest LEED-rated buildings in the country. PNC has at present "more buildings LEED-certified—27—than any company in the world, with more than 40 others already designed and built to USGBC (United States Green Building Council) standards" (Streeter 2007, p. 29). The tradeoffs include a building with lower operating costs. Wainwright Bank, Boston, has two LEED-certified branches, and the green cost differential payback time for these is estimated to be ten years or less, with a prediction that it will soon drop to three or four years (Streeter 2007, p. 29). A video presentation of the Banner Bank and its LEED Platinum certification was the recipient of an Academy Award for a documentary and is available from its producers.[13]

It follows that banks and credit unions must consider construction of certified projects from an operational standpoint when such paybacks are available, even if the initial cost is as much as 25 percent greater. The increased initial costs are expected to drop as more financial institutions build in this way, and with careful planning sustainable design and construction may even be had at no greater cost. Architects and engineers who are LEED-certified are able to assist in achieving rated projects. Perhaps we should take a Native American proverb into account when we consider the question of sustainability:

> We do not inherit the earth from our ancestors, we borrow it from our children (Sustainable Design Forum 2008).

13 Ben Shedd, http://www.deepgreen.tv.

◀ Main entrance facade at dusk, Norlarco Credit Union, Fort Collins, Colorado; EHS Design. The community cultural and lifestyle preferences are expressed in the design. Time Frame Photography.

▼ The lobby of the Norlarco Credit Union, Fort Collins, Colorado; EHS Design. It surrounds members with engaged staff. Climbing ropes hold up banners, and toboggans back high-impact merchandising, while an abstract flock of geese fly over the teller line. Time Frame Photography.

▲ Exterior view to main south entrance, Farmers Bank of North Missouri, St. Joseph, Missouri; WRS Architects. The aluminum-clad canopy for the drive-up extends up and over the teller lobby and is reflected in the lower ATM canopy at the far right. Paul Brokering Photography.

◄ Interior of lobby, Farmers Bank of North Missouri, Saint Joseph, Missouri; WRS Architects. The clerestory glass is effective in illuminating the entire lobby area with natural light, while the metal trim at the check stand and teller counters matches the exterior canopy face. The teller line is shown at the right, with seating provided at the last station. Open desks for banking officers are at the left. Paul Brokering Photography.

▶ Exterior view at main entrance, FreeStar Bank, Downs, Illinois; Bailey Edward Architecture, Ellen B. Dickson, AIA. The clean modern lines of the exterior reflect the cutting-edge architectural concept of the bank and retail facility. Focus Photography.

◀ Detail at skylight, FreeStar Bank, Downs, Illinois; Bailey Edward Architecture, Ellen B. Dickson, AIA. The skylight is reminiscent of the central atrium spaces of older, classic banks. Focus Photography.

▼ Interior view of main lobby, Hyde Park Bank, Chicago, Illinois; Florian Architects. The tellers are located to the left, beyond the monumental open stair. The new lighting is also very important to the grand hall's continued use in the award-winning building renovation. Photo by Barbara Karant/Karant+Associates.

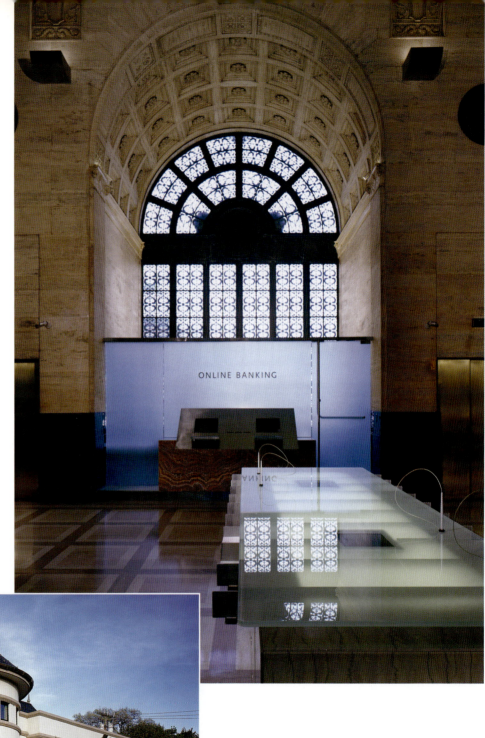

▶ Check stand with online banking station beyond, Hyde Park Bank, Chicago, Illinois; Florian Architects. The sensitive use of modern features, along with the renovated historic building materials, provides a very effective architectural result, as seen in the unlikely pairing of online banking in front of the classic window and coffered arch. Photo by Barbara Karant/Karant+ Associates.

▼ Exterior view of the entrance turret, Madison National Bank, Signature Branch, Merrick, New York; JRS Architect, P.C. Exterior materials of brick, stone, and contrasting trim are reminiscent of the Richardson style. The architectural character reflects the brand image. Bausch Photography.

◁ Interior view toward the main entrance and fireplace waiting area, Madison National Bank, Signature Branch, Merrick, New York; JRS Architect, P.C. The open desks and surrounding chairs are all part of the historic style. Bausch Photography.

▼ Exterior facade, Pilot Bank, Tampa, Florida; NewGround. The attractive front elevation and its main entrance are well-lighted and easily found. Photo by NewGround.

▶ Interior at teller counter, Pilot Bank, Tampa, Florida; NewGround. Customers may be seated at the teller line and may receive online service as well. Meeting rooms instead of dedicated private offices provide areas for consultation with bank officers and employees. Photo by NewGround.

◀ Exterior view toward main entrance, Old National Bancorp Headquarters, Evansville, Indiana; HOK, design architects, and VPS Architecture, principal architects. The 8-story elliptical-shaped building and windows provide a noteworthy view from every direction, and with the use of their mini-optical light shelves, actually save a significant amount of energy. Photo by Sam Fentress.

▶ Interior view across the atrium, Old National Bancorp Headquarters, Evansville, Indiana; HOK, design architects, and VPS Architecture, principal architects. The light, open interior is shown by this view across the atrium and illustrates the fact that a well-designed project may also be significant in energy conservation. Photo by Sam Fentress.

▲ Main entrance south facade, River Bank, Osceola, Wisconsin; BKV Group Architects. The 2-story brick and cut-stone structure features a corner entrance that is also a 2-story-high portal. At the far corner is a similar structural form that provides a fitting frame for the sloped roof and ribbon windows between. Photo by Steve Bergerson.

◀ Lobby interior from the main stair, River Bank, Osceola, Wisconsin; BKV Group Architects. This view of the lower lobby seen from the stair landing shows the significant customer service facilities offered by the bank—from the greeter at the left and the waiting area at the right, to the Internet banking station along the path to the tellers. The interior color palette was chosen to reflect the river valley's natural materials by the use of cherry wood and river slate, brightened by the clerestory natural light. Photo by Steve Bergerson.

▶ Facade of main entrance, Mountain State Bank, Cumming, Georgia; Foreman Seeley Fountain Architects. The multicolored stone, stucco, wood trim, and roof support brackets used for the new bank reflect the surrounding countryside and are well suited for the Arts and Crafts style as well. Photo by Jeff Seeley, © FSF Architects.

▼ Lobby view to the teller counter, Mountain State Bank, Cumming, Georgia; Foreman Seeley Fountain Architects. The coffered ceiling of dark-stained wood beams reflects the colored tile floor and blends well with the wood-lined columns and matching teller counters. Photo by Jeff Seeley, © FSF Architects.

▲ Exterior showing main entrance and clock tower, Rock Springs National Bank, Rock Springs, Wyoming; NewGround. The clock tower is a popular feature and brand image for the new bank. Photo by NewGround.

◀ Interior at fireplace waiting area, Rock Springs National Bank, Rock Springs, Wyoming; NewGround. Large easy chairs, grouped around the fireplace with its large flat-screen television monitor, provide a welcome waiting area for the bank's customers. Photo by NewGround.

▶ Interior showing teller area, Rock Springs National Bank, Rock Springs, Wyoming; NewGround. Customers may be seated on one side of the check stand, or use a computer for online connection as well as the usual stand-up counter on the opposite side. The stainless steel vault door is seen beyond. Photo by NewGround.

▲▲ Main entrance facade, Frandsen Bank & Trust, Forest Lake, Minnesota; HTG Architects. The overhanging eaves, hip roof, and stonework add a more residential character to the building design. Photo by HTG Architects.

▲ Exterior view, Home State Bank, Willmar, Minnesota; KKE Architects. The large, open lobby atrium receives natural light from the glass wall on two sides. Photo by Scott Gilbertson.

◀ Interior view of waiting area, Home State Bank, Willmar, Minnesota; KKE Architects. The 2-story glass wall provides a wide view from the lobby waiting area. Photo by Scott Gilbertson.

◀ Aerial view of model, Colonial Bank, Anthem Branch, Henderson, Nevada; Dr. Robert A. Fielden, FAIA, architect. The model shows how the building was designed to appear as a much larger project. The narrow site was carefully planned to accommodate the bank, the drive-up, and required parking. Illustration by RAFI Architects.

▼ Interior of bank lobby, Colonial Bank, Anthem Branch, Henderson, Nevada; Dr. Robert A. Fielden, FAIA, architect. The high ceiling adds to the impression of a much larger building, one of the owner's goals for the project. New accounts are at the left, with the seated teller counter beyond. Product and services displays are on both sides of the lobby. Photo by RAFI Architects.

▲ Night view of the entrance facade, Wachovia Bank at Eagles Landing Financial Center, Stockbridge, Georgia; Gensler Architects. The extended canopies and walls also provide an ideal location for Colonial's brand logo and signage. The main entrance is framed by the well-lighted lobby and surrounding glazing. This curved roof elevation is a branding icon for the prototype. Photo by David Joseph.

▶ Interior view of lobby, Wachovia Bank at Eagles Landing Financial Center, Stockbridge, Georgia; Gensler Architects. The unobstructed lobby provides for ready access to the check stand, financial counseling, or orderly queuing to the teller line. Both natural light and light fixtures inject an abundance of light to the entire lobby area. Photo by David Joseph.

◀ Concierge station, St. Cloud Federal Credit Union, Sartell, Minnesota; HTG Architects. The brand and marketing images on the wall immediately behind the concierge stations describe the products and services that are offered to credit union members. Photo by HTG Architects.

▼ Lobby interior, St. Cloud Federal Credit Union, Sartell, Minnesota; HTG Architects. The rounded lobby is well defined for the member functions, and it also provides for significant marketing opportunities. Photo by HTG Architects.

▶ Exterior "after" view, night scene from southeast, North Fork Bank, Long Beach Branch, Long Beach, New York; JRS Architect. The exterior now exhibits an entirely new image. The modifications to the roof and extensions on each side of the front, together with the clerestory above, creates an inviting vestibule for the bank. A new drive-up canopy is behind and to the left in the photograph. Zweibel Photography.

▼ Interior "after" view of teller lobby, North Fork Bank, Long Beach Branch, Long Beach, New York; JRS Architect. The striking new bank interior bears no resemblance to the former restaurant and uses the limited space very effectively. Zweibel Photography.

▶ New exterior looking southwest, Aloha Pacific Credit Union, Honolulu, Hawaii. The new main entrance to the credit union is clearly visible from the street or the courtyard. Photo courtesy of Aloha Pacific Credit Union.

▼ Exterior at entrance, Watermark Credit Union Headquarters Facility, Seattle, Washington; IA Interior Architects. The backlit Watermark signage is easily noticed in the night photograph. Photo by Nick Merrick/Hedrich Blessing.

▼ Large boardroom, Watermark Credit Union Headquarters Facility, Seattle, Washington; IA Interior Architects. While flexibility and a plan that fosters collaboration were essential for the overall space, another priority was a high-end boardroom. The design team worked with the owner's board of directors to conceive this space. The stone and wood boardroom table was custom designed by IA. Metal ceiling and pendant lighting add to the aesthetic. The room is configured for wireless technology and video. Photo by Nick Merrick/Hedrich Blessing.

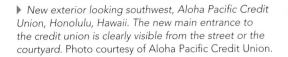
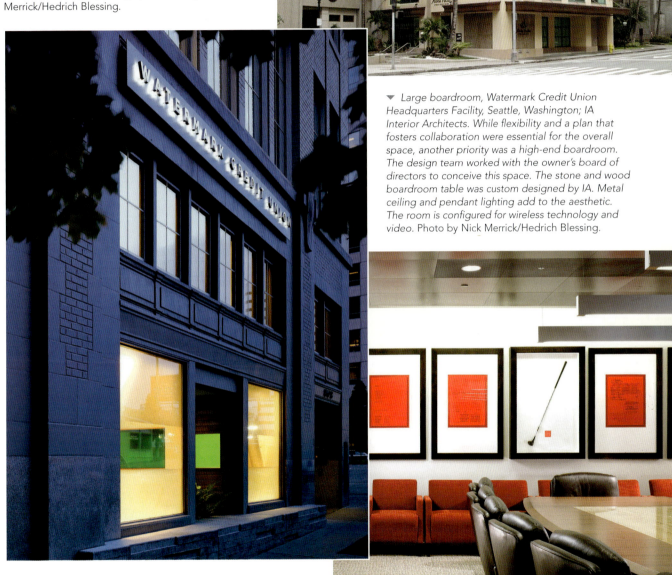

▶ Interior view of member service center, FivePoint Credit Union, Bridge City, Texas; NewGround. The bold red face of the member service center energizes the space, along with the other colorful decor. Photo by NewGround.

◀ Exterior view to northeast, Banner Bank, Boise, Idaho; HDR Architects, with The Architects Office (Price, Sanders, Cooper and Rhees) and Cornerstone Design, interior design. The new 11-story building occupies a former brownfield site, giving new life to downtown Boise. Constructed of nearly 42 percent recycled material, it was one of only 20 LEED Platinum buildings in the country when completed. Alpha Image; photo by Guiseppe Siatta.

▼ Interior of lobby, Banner Bank, Boise, Idaho; HDR Architects, with The Architects Office (Price, Sanders, Cooper and Rhees) and Cornerstone Design, interior design. The attractive circular teller counter is reflected in the dropped ceiling and check stand in the spacious lobby. Photo by Mitch York.

CHAPTER 8
MECHANICAL, ELECTRICAL, AND PLUMBING SYSTEMS

Any contemporary structure in the United States should be designed to provide a comfortable working environment for customers and employees. Banking presents some additional requirements, such as the minimization of noise from air-moving systems and the need to keep computers and LAN systems within an optimal range of temperature and humidity. Numerous kinds of heating and cooling systems are used throughout the country. Energy sources vary as well. Where natural gas is available it is often the choice for heating. Cooling is most often provided with electrical energy. There are now other exchange methods in use as well, such as the increasingly popular ground-source systems for heating and cooling.

Occasionally engineers design systems that are so complicated that full-time service people or professional engineers are needed to operate them. Such systems also usually have high installation costs. A balance needs to be struck between system design and overall budget, and the long-term costs must also be considered. Power requirements are part of the engineers' design criteria, so it is very important to provide them with accurate equipment information from the suppliers and manufacturers. The following guidelines, by Kurt Ewert, PE, of Hoss and Brown Engineers, pertain to the mechanical, electrical, and plumbing systems for banks and credit unions.[1]

HVAC SYSTEMS

Code Review
Before the schematic process begins and during each phase of design, it is necessary to consult the pertinent building codes to verify compliance.

Architectural and structural coordination
Many new banks or credit unions are lightly constructed, often framed with a truss roof structure that affords limited space in which to conceal ductwork, piping, and other mechanical or electrical components. Early planning is critical to ensure that adequate space is made for such systems. It is also important to know applicable fire ratings for structural systems, walls, floors, or ceilings. It is necessary to follow various rules and code provisions that dictate the use of ductwork and if and how it may penetrate a rated surface or component.

Where piping or ductwork requires a wall or other surface to be thickened for a chase, it should be identified and coordinated with the architects and other design professionals as early as possible, so that it can be included in all architectural or engineering construction documents. When equipment is to be mounted on a roof or suspended from a structure, it is also important to coordinate such information with the project's structural engineer early in the design process.

Design temperatures
There will be a seasonal difference in the designed temperature comfort range,

---

[1] Kurt Ewert, PE, of Hoss and Brown Engineers, communication to the author, December 31, 2008.

MECHANICAL, ELECTRICAL, AND PLUMBING SYSTEMS

depending on where the project is located. One rule is to have interior spaces maintain 75°F during cooling months, with a relative humidity of 55 percent. The same space should be designed to maintain 72°F during heating months. The national movement to lower energy costs will certainly impact such ranges, and each owner, together with their architects and engineers, should consider the question in relation to their particular facility.

Conditioning zones

Between the various spaces within a financial institution can be a great variation in heating and cooling loads, given the different exposures that affect them. These variations can be quite challenging to the design process of establishing conditioning zones. Conference rooms and lobbies are randomly occupied throughout the day, while offices and teller areas are more predictably used. The zoning design must accommodate such differences. Wherever possible, conference rooms and lobbies should have individual temperature controls. Offices may often be grouped, if they share a common exposure. A design with more zones will deliver greater comfort but at an increased cost, so it is important to optimize the number in keeping with the proposed budget.

Ventilation

Mechanical codes provide for the minimum quantity of outdoor air required for a bank. In general, however, the lobby and vault require 15 cu ft per minute (cfm) per person, and other spaces, such as offices, conference rooms, workrooms, teller areas, and break rooms, require 20 cfm per person. Consult the appropriate codes for other specific areas.

Because the number of occupants varies greatly through the workday, the engineer may wish to consider varying the amount of ventilation according to the amount of CO_2 in a space. This often results in a significant energy savings as well as an improvement in humidity control.

Where mechanical equipment is located inside the building, outdoor air intakes will be needed. These may take the form of louvers in exterior walls or a weatherproof intake mounted on the roof. The size and location of these items should be closely coordinated with the architect to minimize their aesthetic impact. It is also important to keep louvers away from the drive-up lanes, to avoid drawing in car exhaust.

Indoor air quality

While ventilation is very important to good indoor air quality, it is also important to consider other factors, such as air filtration and humidity control. Standard dust filtration will assist in reducing particulates, but it is sometimes necessary to use more aggressive filtration if the building is located in an area with high levels of pollutants. These filters may include ultraviolet C (UVC) radiation, electrostatic, charcoal, or higher-efficiency particulate filters. In areas with higher humidity it is critical to control moisture levels, to reduce the potential for mold and other spore growth; desired humidity is typically within the range of 45–55 percent. In drier climates or during winter months, it is necessary to add moisture to the air for human comfort.

HVAC system options

Selection of a mechanical system is usually governed by an owner's budget; however, it is very important that an owner be made fully aware of both short- and long-term costs of a particular system. Short-term

HVAC Systems

◀ *Typical forced-air furnace. This is a natural gas–fired forced-air furnace with a ducted return-air feed extended from a ceiling space. Note the small hot water heater at the upper right, to provide water to the break-room kitchen.*

savings may be far offset by the long-term costs. It is prudent to conduct a life-cycle analysis that takes into account not only initial costs but also projected maintenance and replacement costs. Such analyses are often based on a 20-year span but can be calculated according to any period of lesser duration. A accurate longer-term analysis is difficult, because of the many unforeseeable factors that come into play.

Small- to medium-size branch banks usually do not have an extensive maintenance staff. In order to balance quality, reliability, and simplicity, it is important to select a system that can be operated by a staff with general knowledge of the equipment and not require an on-site engineer. Adjustments and minor repairs should be quick and relatively easy. For more complex service, an owner will usually hire an

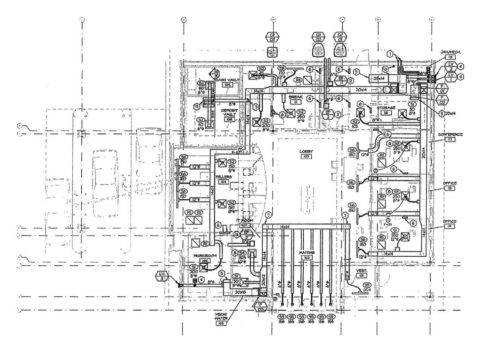

◀ *Typical duct system for a new branch bank. The system is zoned to accommodate different activities and locations.* Hoss & Brown.

outside specialist, who is often also the original installer.

Adequate zoning of a system will help ensure comfort, as has been mentioned, but it also affects costs. As a general rule, for smaller projects, split systems or rooftops are typically used. For larger facilities, variable air volume systems may be more cost effective.

HVAC systems efficiency

These systems offer one of the most significant possibilities for reducing energy usage in buildings. Most existing buildings with aged equipment operate far less efficiently than current codes require. HVAC systems are now available that can operate with as little as half the energy usage required by code. To realize such savings, however, it is necessary to couple these high-quality, high-efficiency systems with other properly designed building assemblies. Another possibility is to use a ground-source heat pump system. These are discussed later in this chapter.

To maximize building efficiency, a well-insulated building shell and high-efficiency lighting must be installed. The wall and roof insulation should exceed the energy code by at least 35 percent. Windows should have an R-value of at least 2 and shading coefficient no greater than 0.25. Lighting should be T-5 or T-8 fluorescent, LED, or other high-efficiency source. Incandescent lighting should be kept to a minimum.

HVAC system use during construction

Contractors often use a newly installed HVAC system for heating or cooling while a project is being completed. Engineers should specify requirements, proper filtration, and protection of these systems during such use. Dust from construction can collect in ductwork, causing mold and bacteria to form at a later point. It can also deposit on heating or cooling coils, reducing capacity and efficiency.

Geothermal systems

An increasing number of buildings are being conditioned with geothermal systems, also known as ground-source systems. These are comprised of three components: a heat pump, usually installed inside the building; an underground closed-loop field for a heat exchanger, comprised of holes that allow a continuous pipe to extend down and up in a series of loops to and from the heat pump; and a distribution system, normally a duct system, for the conditioned air.[2]

The first question usually asked is how long it will take for the operating savings to overtake the initial cost. The cost of grid energy is constantly increasing, and directly affects payback time. Some payback times have been reported to have been as low as 4–5 years. One engineer's estimate based on current conditions is an average of 10–15 years; another's is 20 or more years. It is obviously very important for owners and designers to have as accurate an estimate as possible, but in considering this question it is important to compare total life-cycle costs. These include initial cost, energy cost, maintenance cost, and equipment life. Reputable sources maintain that a geothermal system may be the lowest-cost option based upon these comparisons.

One rule of thumb for the installation cost of a geothermal system is that it will add $3,000 per ton; approximately 350 sq ft

---

2 Vanderford Associates, Smithville, Missouri.

per ton of conditioned area is an average requirement. On that basis, it can be estimated that the initial cost is increased by $9 per sq ft. Other estimates place the initial cost increase at $18–20 per sq ft, including controls and electrical. Another rule of thumb is that one well is required for each ton of conditioning; thus, a 2,500 sq ft building would require 13 tons and 13 separate wells. Note also that each well may be 250–400 ft deep.

There are significant benefits to these systems in terms of sustainability and lowered operating costs. The systems use no fossil fuels and do not emit any gases or other particles into the atmosphere. Three Midwestern banks that have recently installed geothermal systems are the Bank of Versailles, Versailles, Missouri; the Laurie Bank, Laurie, Missouri; and the O'Bannon Bank, Buffalo, Missouri.

Ceiling space

A typical ceiling space may contain ductwork, plumbing and piping, electrical wiring and lighting, sprinkler piping, and telephone and data wiring, as well as structural elements. For all of these needs it is important again to coordinate the systems with the architectural planning. A preliminary duct system design will be very helpful in preventing a later redesign.

Mechanical room

HVAC should be coordinated with architectural planning for many reasons. One is to minimize mechanical system noise. This equipment should not be installed immediately adjacent to a lobby, conference room, private offices, or other sound-sensitive areas. Outdoor condensation units or chillers should be kept away from operable win-

◀ *Typical heat pump for a geothermal system.* Photo by Vanderford Associates.

dows, although many new banks are constructed without such, for security. Rooftop equipment should also be located above less sound-sensitive spaces, such as toilets or break rooms, wherever possible. Sound-absorbing support diaphragms may also be used.

It is important to consider all other equipment that may be included in this room. Items such as water heaters, janitor's sink, backflow prevention devices, and fire sprinkler equipment may be included. Electrical, telephone, and computer equipment are best placed elsewhere, if possible.

MECHANICAL, ELECTRICAL, AND PLUMBING SYSTEMS

▶ Typical electric service panel system. This service is extremely important to the operations of all equipment, especially sensitive and complex security and alarm systems.

Temperature controls

It is imperative to have a high-quality, complementary temperature control installed along with a high-quality HVAC system. This may be as simple as wall-mounted thermostats or as complex as complete building automation. With preset hours of operation, simple programmable thermostats can provide significant energy savings and meet any reasonable budget. Larger buildings and some remote branch offices may be more suitable for controls that can be monitored remotely. Owners, architects, and engineers should discuss this question early in the design process.

SPECIAL INTERIOR CONDITIONS

Open Lobby Desks

A common practice is to have multiple open desks and waiting areas in bank or credit union lobbies. These are sometimes near an entry and so are subject to infiltration. Warm summer or cold winter air can cause these spaces to be quite uncomfortable when doors are constantly being opened. To offset this effect, engineers should design the system to bring in more outside air than is allowed to escape, by about 0.08 to 0.10 cfm per sq ft, to ensure that the building is under positive pressure.

Architects can also help mitigate infiltration by designing vestibule entrances with double doors or, in much larger projects, even revolving doors. Consideration, however, should also be given to adding individually controlled heating elements under the desks of workers that are located in places susceptible to inordinate infiltration, such as at drive-up teller counters.

Radiant Effect

Concrete slab-on-grade floors so often used in new financial buildings, together with large expanses of glass, present a particular problem: cold surfaces during the winter months, even when the surrounding space is heated to normal temperatures. Carpeting or other surface applications can help insulate occupants but still do not completely solve the problem, especially under desks or teller counters, where warm air does not reach the floor. Heated slabs are an ideal solution but are usually too costly.

Where large windows are used, a good strategy is baseboard heating directly below the glass. If these are sized properly, the warm air rising from the heater will offset the cold air falling from the window surface. In many locations the solution is to supply air directly at the window, but for large glazed areas that also introduces cold drafts. A drive-up teller deal drawer is also a location for cold infiltration, and although most are supplied with built-in heaters, it is helpful to add baseboard heating there as well, if space allows. (Electrical, data, and telephone outlets take priority for space, so it is often difficult to accommodate baseboard heaters here.)

Sound Control

In conference rooms, private offices, and spaces such as coupon booths, it is very important to prevent sound migration, to protect private conversations.

Any penetration, such as electrical or duct connections should be examined for this possibility and insulated properly. Supply and return ducts should be arranged to eliminate sound from these spaces. Acoustically lined ductwork is very effective in reducing sound, but where that is not used the duct may be designed with at least three turns from one space to the next, to mitigate sound transmission. Another preventative measure is to introduce a level of "white noise" from air diffusers into a space, to help mask conversations.

Vault Ventilation

Vaults must be ventilated by code, and manufacturers of prefabricated vaults provide built-in vents in vault doors. Where site-poured vaults are used, they may be ventilated by the same means. The selection of vaults, doors, and other specialized equipment should be made early to allow for coordination with all HVAC, electrical, and data connections.

Technology Rooms

In rooms such as data centers that are designed for LAN computer servers and other important data or electronic equipment there is often an increased heat output, which must be considered in the design of the cooling system. These rooms often need cooling even in the winter months and should therefore have a stand-alone system to provide for that need. Larger and more complex banks have used raised floor systems for this installation, as in the Banner Bank in Boise, Idaho, by HDR Architects (see p. 188).

PLUMBING

Fixtures

Plumbing fixtures for banks are similar to those used in any office building, and include public and private toilets, drinking fountains, coffee bar sinks, break room sinks (usually with garbage disposers), and sometimes complete kitchens with dishwashers and icemakers. In large banks, these are also often included in or located adjacent to boardrooms. Care should be taken to insulate sound from toilets that may adjoin offices or conference rooms. It is also very important to consider ADA provisions in the design of these facilities.

Water Use Reduction

New low-flow plumbing fixtures are available that can greatly reduce water use in a building. Newer faucets can be effective at

MECHANICAL, ELECTRICAL, AND PLUMBING SYSTEMS

0.5 gallons per minute (gpm), whereas older models use as much as 2.5 gpm. Dual-flush water closets offer an option of flushing with half the normal water usage. Urinals are now available in no-flow or ultra-low-flow models. Almost all newer plumbing fixtures will reduce water use.

Another increasingly used method of reducing water consumption is collection of storm water for irrigation or a gray water system. This approach may require a supply pump and water treatment system. The savings realized can be estimated through life-cycle cost calculations.

Lawn Sprinkler Systems

Depending on the region, most new banks and credit unions have a sprinkler system installed to treat their landscape plantings and lawns, especially during the hot, dry seasons. These can be extensive and expensive and should be designed by a specialist.

Fire Sprinkler Systems

Where a project is large enough or the building code requires, a sprinkler system must be provided. An engineer who specializes in these systems should be consulted, and most suppliers of such systems will have the expertise in-house. Insurance coverage may also be dependent upon the provision of such a system. Special attention should be given to larger projects in colder climates where a building space may be located above a drive-up and any sprinklers below must be a dry system.

ELECTRICAL

Lighting

Adequate lighting is a must in a financial institution, not only because of the need to read and write documents but also because it is critical to the architectural character. Adequate lighting levels must be maintained at teller counters, desktops, conference tables, and any surface where the financial business is conducted. Public spaces and pathways must be clearly seen by young and old. Illumination engineers and experts should coordinate with owners and architects to ensure that design objectives are clearly defined and achieved.

General illumination

General lighting should make wayfinding and circulation easy and convenient. Lighting styles and fixtures should conform to the architectural style of the building. Where softer light is desired, indirect lighting that reflects off ceilings or walls may be appropriate. It may also offer a more diffused and evenly distributed illumination.

Task lighting

Numerous areas of a bank will require task lighting, including not only the areas mentioned above but also check stands, coupon booths, safe deposit vaults, workrooms, accounting offices, and similar spaces. The task fixtures may be recessed or pendants that are focused on a surface. Such lighting is usually permanently installed but may also be free standing. Care must be taken to avoid glare from a fixture, especially where a surface is highly reflective.

Specialty lighting

Many signs used in a bank or credit union are illuminated from the inside; however, where they are not, it is important to plan for their illumination from without. Wayfinding signage should be illuminated on the fixture face.

Electrical

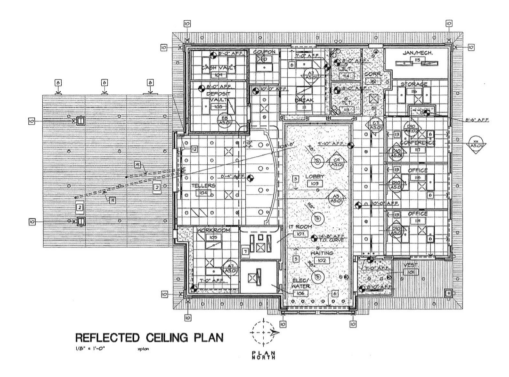

◀ *Typical reflected ceiling plan. The center lobby ceiling is a curved vault that uses recessed can lighting. A large glazed area also allows natural light to enter the area. WSKF.*

For security purposes, several fixtures should be chosen for interior night lighting. These should provide a clear view of interior spaces for drive-by security personnel.

Drive-up lighting

The drive-up lanes must have illumination adequate for security and for the transaction. Customers must read and write small text while remaining in their cars. Additional light may be added to the face of the drive-up customer units, but care must also be given to minimize shadows from the vehicles. All of the fixtures under the canopy should be located to avoid glare at the teller window, and in a conventional drive-up it is necessary that the teller and customer have a clear view of one another. Even in remote drive-up locations, the cameras and monitors must have adequate lighting.

Exterior lighting

Adequate illumination is equally important for the security of parking areas and sidewalks, for customers and employees alike. Lighting should clearly mark the path to the building entrance. Surrounding vehicles and landscaping should also be clearly seen. ATM facilities, whether walk-up or drive-up, should also be well lighted. Most municipalities do not allow excessive light to affect adjacent property, so the designer must implement this control in the basic lighting design. Many cities now require a lighting plan that projects illumination levels for an entire building site to ensure that lighting is appropriate and not invasive.

The enhancements of a well-designed building by a creative lighting scheme are considerable. At the least, fixtures should be selected to coordinate with the building and landscaping design.

MECHANICAL, ELECTRICAL, AND PLUMBING SYSTEMS

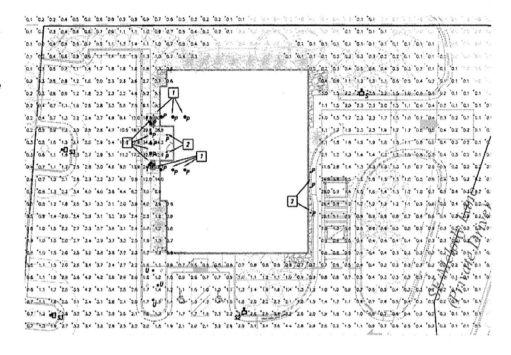

▶ *Typical site lighting plan. Many cities now require such a plan to be submitted for approval, to ensure that lighting levels are appropriate and do not adversely affect adjacent properties. PKMR Engineers.*

Recommended light levels
Recommended lighting levels for financial facilities are as follows:

Interior spaces:

- Teller counters: 60–80 footcandles (fc)
- Drive-up tellers: 30–50 fc
- General circulation: 20–40 fc
- Workrooms: 40–50 fc
- Safe deposit vault: 30–50 fc
- Offices and conference rooms: 30–50 fc
- Lobby areas: 20–30 fc (check stand: 40–50 fc)
- General: 10–20 fc

Exterior suggested levels:

- Building façade: 5 fc (increase where emphasis is needed)
- Signs: 3 fc (depends on integral sign illumination)
- Drive-up canopy: 5–10 fc
- ATM: 10 fc
- Parking: .5–2 fc
- Egress from site: 1 fc

Lamp color index
When lighting sources other than incandescent lamps or bulbs are specified, the color rendering index (CRI) should be considered. Each light source provides varying levels of light from each part of the color spectrum. The selection of a lamp color should be coordinated with the architects or interior designers to ensure that the colors of materials in the building or furnishings are enhanced by the lighting. Failure to consider the CRI can result in distorted colors and make artwork, for example, appear dull or washed out.

Lighting controls

In projects that make use of large expanses of glass in exterior walls, whether windows, skylights, or clerestories, interior lighting controls that will respond to ambient light levels should be considered. These can reduce general lighting automatically when it is not needed and thereby reduce energy consumption. Another possibility is to add multiple levels of illumination to offices and conference rooms or other areas so that individuals may have their preferences regarding lighting levels. Providing multiple switches in each space allows occupants to select for their preference.

Exterior lighting should be controlled with a combination of photocells and time switches. An adequate amount of illumination must be provided around a building for security. Other lighting may be turned off during evening hours or when the building is unoccupied, such as some remote parking lot fixtures. The combined use of a photocell and time switch allows this flexibility.

Efficiency

High-efficiency lighting design can result in significant energy savings. By also using automated lighting controls, savings may be increased even more. Relatively simple controls, such as motion sensors, photo cells, and timers can be used to ensure that lighting is turned off when not needed.

Motion sensors in offices, break rooms, file rooms, toilets, and other spaces that have intermittent occupancy will turn lights on or off as people enter or leave. Photo cells can be used to turn lighting off when natural light reaches proper illumination levels. Timers can be used to turn lighting off during unoccupied hours.

Power

In determining the source for general power, owners, architects, and engineers must weigh the initial costs and operating costs. In some cases there may be only one choice. The choice of a source—electric, gas, or other—will have a great impact on an operating budget. Electric heat, for example, will also have a significant effect on the electrical service required. One purpose of estimating the electrical load for a project is to help determine the amount of space required for the electrical equipment.

Some banks, especially in headquarters facilities, may require emergency power. An emergency generator can provide power to all or part of a building when normal power is lost. Computer servers, telephone systems, security and alarm systems, and other critical equipment are often connected to an uninterruptible power supply (UPS). A UPS consists of batteries that can provide power immediately upon loss of normal power. They typically are not needed longer than 30–60 minutes at a time and are often coupled with a generator.

Communications

Banks today, like many other new buildings, are highly reliant on technological systems, including basic computer networks, bank equipment, voice communications, and intra-branch communications. Highly reliable low-voltage distribution systems and hardware are thus critical to the successful operation of the financial institution. Because technology is constantly changing and improving, it is important to provide flexibility and expandability in a system design.

MECHANICAL, ELECTRICAL, AND PLUMBING SYSTEMS

Cabling
The cable system infrastructure should be installed during construction. It is important to provide outlets for all equipment and allow for future equipment needs as well. For an average branch bank or larger headquarters facilities, cable tray should be considered. Tray allows for easy organization of the numerous cables as well as for quick access in making future changes. Small banks and credit unions will easily have more than 100 cables between voice and data systems. Large institutions may have thousands. Various sizes of tray will handle the large quantities.

SPECIALIZED BANK EQUIPMENT
Chapters 9 and 10 describe most of the equipment that will be used in a new building, including drive-up, remote tellers, teller under-counter, vaults and doors, safes, night deposits, ATMs, and many other items of equipment. Most of these items require multiple connections, which may include power, data, voice communication, and alarm/security.

Early selections of these items will aid greatly in the coordination needed for successful installation. Many items require infrastructure to be installed below grade or below concrete or asphalt drives. For those installations it is prudent to increase the conduit by one size, providing an extra conduit for future use and at a minimal first cost.

Data
Data systems are critical to the success of nearly any modern building, and with global ATM and Internet access to accounts,

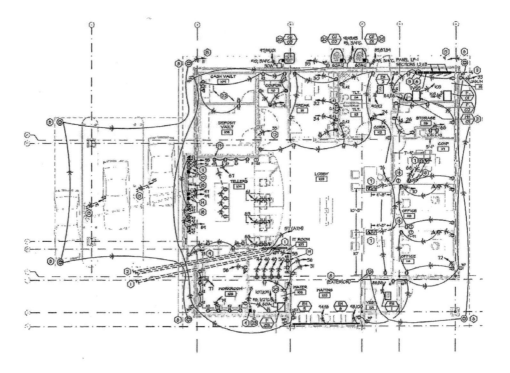

▶ Typical power plan for a new branch bank. Hoss & Brown.

financial institutions require very fast, reliable, and accurate transaction communications. Data systems must employ extremely high security measures to protect institutional and customer assets.

Multiple systems may be required to maintain banking data separate and secure from basic file-sharing and email servers. Coordination between owners and their information technology staff and the system designers and engineers during the design process is absolutely essential, given the level of sophistication of these systems.

Voice
Telephone systems may be wired through direct cabling to a central phone panel. Many new phone systems use the data infrastructure for communications with the central phone panel instead of a dedicated voice cable system. The data-based systems are called voice over Internet protocol (VoIP). VoIP phone systems are increasingly popular because of the simple installation and flexibility for very large systems. Since the phone systems use Internet protocol, individual phones can be installed remotely in home offices or faraway job sites and communicate seamlessly with the main telephone system. With the vast differences in available phone systems, exact requirements must be coordinated with the owner, vendor, and design engineers to ensure that all system components are provided.

Security
Cameras, alarms, motion sensors, door monitors, magnetic locks, glass breakage sensors, horns, strobes, and other items are all possible components of a financial institution's security system. Such systems may be local only or remotely monitored. Remotely monitored systems require a data or phone connection or both. Each accessory in the security system may be powered from the central security panel through the low-voltage cable or may also require 120-volt power. Security system requirements should be coordinated with the designer and engineers to ensure that all infrastructure and components are installed during construction.

BUILDING COMMISSIONING AND VERIFICATION
In almost every new building there are systems and pieces of equipment that do not work as planned. Commissioning is a process whereby equipment and systems are verified to ensure they are working as designed and manufactured. An item of equipment may be rated at 90 percent efficient but may require adjustment to reach the suggested performance.

Owners, architects, and engineers should insist that the installation contractors, suppliers, and testing and balancing contractors certify that the equipment is operational, but the commissioning agent is brought in to verify that the systems are operational and offer the best possible performance.

Verification means checking systems periodically to ensure they continue to work as intended and with optimum energy efficiency. This should be done at least annually, and ideally at the outset of each heating or cooling season.

CHAPTER 9
TELLER ROOMS, WORKROOMS, AND ASSOCIATED EQUIPMENT

This chapter addresses typical lobby teller areas, drive-up and remote teller rooms, workrooms that are usually adjacent to them, and the equipment normally used within them. The workroom plan shown on page 115 is in a facility that has recently converted to Check 21 check clearing (see chapter 6). Fewer and fewer financial institutions continue to forward actual paper checks, choosing the easier Check 21 electronic system. See chapter 10 for equipment for remote teller operations.

TELLER AREAS

Under-Counter Equipment
Under-counter equipment is manufactured by numerous concerns (see appendix C) and is available in several sizes and with several options. The standard height for stand-up counters is 38¼" with adjustable leveling legs. The sit-down models are 28½" in height. The following features are usually offered:

- Lockable drawers and cash drawers with movable/removable core locks.
- Lockable file drawers.
- Teller lockers with electronic combination locks. These locks can be opened by keying in six-digit combinations and are UL-listed as group 1 by passing a 20-hour expert manipulation test.
- Locker doors of ½" exterior metal with three-point locker bolts.
- Bottom drawer equipped with automatic bill-trap, with alarm connection upon removal.
- Accessories including removable cash trays, currency and coin trays, and adjustable filing inserts.
- Movable under-counter buses as an option.

Most manufacturers have standardized modules that may be placed under customized cabinets, and many manufacture the casework as well. Some banks chose to

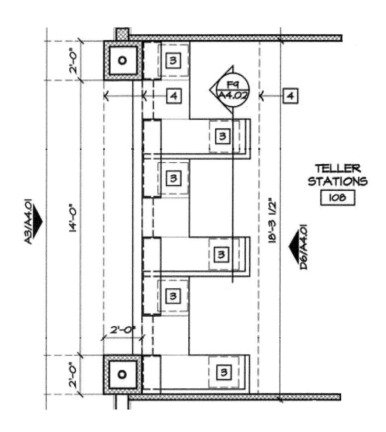

▼ *Typical lobby teller area floor plan. This plan indicates a three-unit stand-up teller counter with end returns. The under-counter metal equipment fits precisely behind and under these counters. WSKF Architects.*

TELLER ROOMS, WORKROOMS, AND ASSOCIATED EQUIPMENT

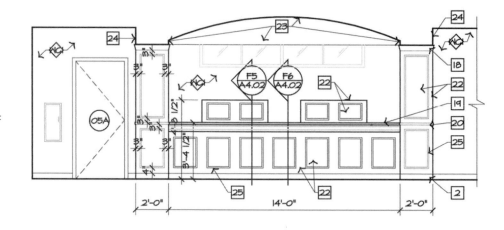

▶ Elevation of teller counter. Three teller positions for standing customers are shown; some prefer an adjacent sit-down counter to serve wheelchair-bound customers or members. WSKF Architects.

 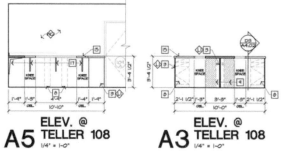 

▲ Lobby teller room casework elevations. These views are from inside the teller room and depict the counters and end returns. WSKF Architects.

▶ Teller counter casework sections. The casework provides an enclosure for the metal under-counter equipment used by the tellers. WSKF Architects.

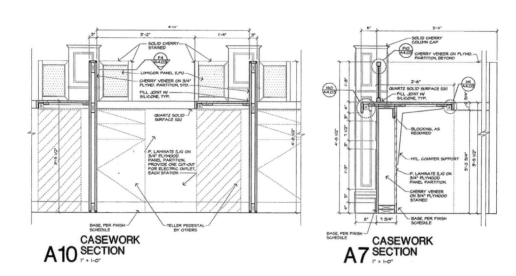

Teller Areas

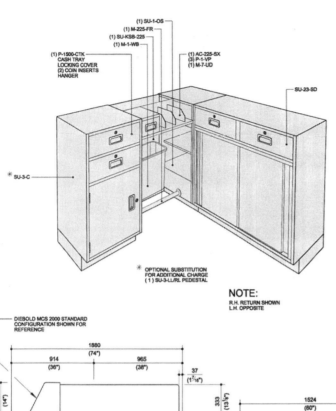

◁ Standard under-counter teller equipment. Depicted here is the Diebold under-counter system, with the teller return cabinet between teller positions. Diebold Inc.

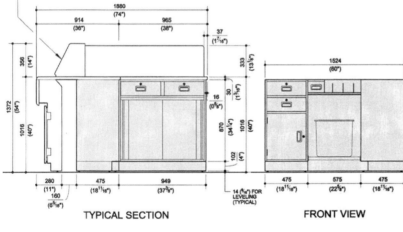

have the entire system made by a local millwork shop. Very attractive and functional results may be obtained from either source; however, the alarm system, locks, and other security features are included with the modular equipment. Plastic laminate tops and sides are still commonly used, but owners and designers have learned that these soon become worn or outdated, and more permanent materials have replaced them in many locations.

Cash dispensing and recycling machines
These machines, described in chapter 7, are increasingly used by lobby tellers and drive-up tellers, in concierge pods, and in remote teller workroom locations. See appendix C for manufacturers.

TELLER ROOMS, WORKROOMS, AND ASSOCIATED EQUIPMENT

▶ Cash recycling machine. This model is by Diebold Inc. and has the same security rating as a UL 291 safe. Diebold Inc.

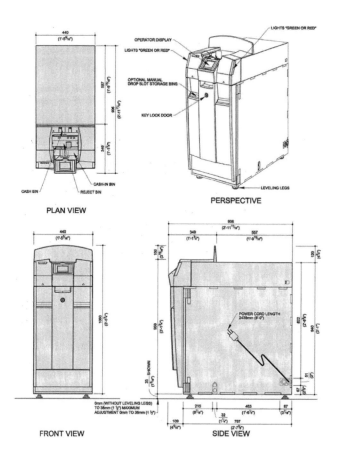

▶ Conventional drive-up teller room plan. The drive-up teller room is usually adjacent to the lobby tellers for cross-service. Foreman, Seeley, Fountain Architecture.

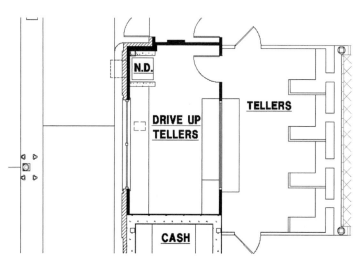

114

Teller Areas

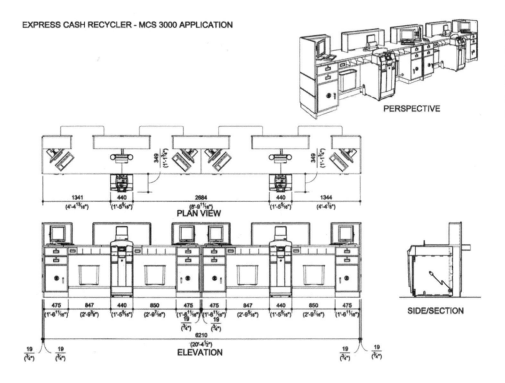

◀ Teller counters with cash recyclers. The machines are designed to fit precisely under standard counters and align with the adjacent under-counter system. Diebold Inc.

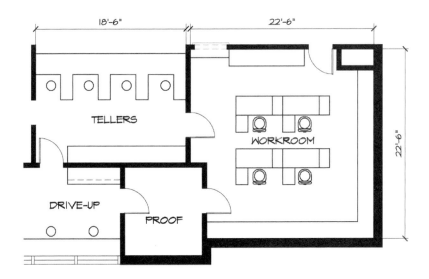

◀ Typical pre–Check 21 workroom and teller Room. ADC Architects.

TELLER ROOMS, WORKROOMS, AND ASSOCIATED EQUIPMENT

WORKROOMS

Depending on many factors, such as the method of check clearing employed and whether accounting or other activities are performed in-house, the workroom is usually adjacent to the tellers. The plan shown at right is typical in this way.

The equipment and space needs are significantly less after adoption of Check 21. The illustration at the bottom right shows the same workroom after Check 21 has been adopted. It indicates the new equipment needed and its placement, as well as the items that have been discarded. The original proof room was reused for new LAN equipment.

Casework, furniture, and furnishings are often selected or specified by designers; the specific equipment and its placement should be coordinated with the supplier. Some items, such as file cabinets, may be part of a designer-selected list. These are recommended to be fireproof, with a UL Class 350 1-hour rating anywhere they are used in a bank or credit union.

The power needs of specialized equipment must be noted and coordinated with engineers to ensure adequate and proper access, as well as for installation of outlets adequate to present and future operations. Many will be dedicated outlets for particular items. Some bankers prefer to have continuous power strips provided in workrooms in addition to dedicated outlets for equipment.

Some new branch facilities prefer to place the scanner and other items connected with Check 21 processing directly in the teller area. In the plan at right, the former proof room was selected for the new LAN server and teller computer. (The coin roller and shredder remained.) It is very important for architects to know the needs for all equipment items in order to provide not only for the required space but also for the correct power, data, and communication connections. While these illustrations indicate this particular bank's equipment and layout, each institution operates in an individual manner, which designers must understand to correctly plan these work spaces.

The key ingredient in the Check 21 process is the check scanner. These devices can scan large numbers of checks, both front and back, and thus allow electronic transfer to the clearing house or the Federal Reserve in a very short time, reducing or eliminating the "float" time previously associated with check-clearing. This greatly reduces workroom processing and assists in identifying fraudulent items sooner.

Workrooms

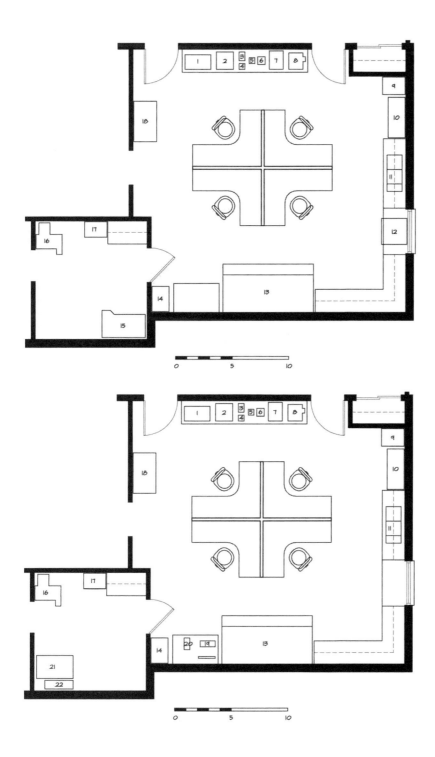

◀ Typical pre–Check 21 workroom plan and equipment. This room was designed for a single bank operation. It was connected to a small proof room at lower left, which led to the drive-up teller room.

Equipment:
1 Fax machine
2 Security camera and control system
3 Printer 900 (for cash advance)
4 Card-swipe device
5 Employee time clock
6 Label maker
7 Ricoh-IBM MICR ink printer
8 EFT router (ATM control)
9 Four-drawer legal file
10 Three-drawer flat file
11 Martin Yale auto-folder
12 Microfilmer (discarded after Check 21)
13 Power file (check storage)
14 Four-drawer legal file
15 Proof machine (replaced after Check 21)
16 Coin roller
17 Shredder
18 Office copier

◀ Workroom after Check 21 implementation. The items added for the new process are shown.

Equipment added:
19 Computer, keyboard, and monitor for Check 21 processing
20 Scanner and sorter for Check 21 processing
21 New LAN server
22 New computer for teller operations

TELLER ROOMS, WORKROOMS, AND ASSOCIATED EQUIPMENT

▶ Security camera monitor and control (item 2 in the plan on previous page). The security cameras, monitor, and control system is mandated by the Bank Protection Act, and although the monitor and control equipment may be installed anywhere in the institution, it is usually found in a bank workroom. Camera placement is important; the equipment supplier usually recommends locations, but architects and bankers should also know where they are needed.

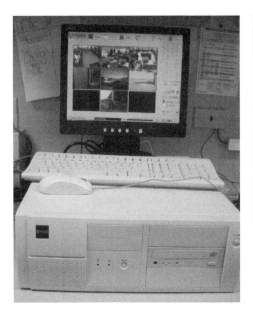

▶ Printer 900 and card swipe (items 3 and 4 in the plan on previous page). Card swipe equipment is now often placed at every teller station and is provided by that supplier.

▲ Check scanner and alignment device for Check 21 system (item 20 in the plan on previous page). This equipment scans the paper check and creates the electronic image that is then automatically sent to the clearinghouse. The alignment device (called a shaker) is used to accurately stack checks before they are fed into the scanner. After the scanning process, the paper checks are then kept on hand for a short time, after which they are shredded. Merchants now have acquired these devices, thus allowing for the ability at point-of-sale to electronically copy and transfer checks (a process called remote deposit capture). This effectively eliminates the normal float time in the funds transfer operation and allows the paper checks to be simply returned to the customer at the time of the transaction, already processed. The power requirements are auto-sensing from 100 to 240 VAC and from 47 to 63 Hz. Many banks simply lease these scanners, which are then maintained by the leasing company.

Workrooms

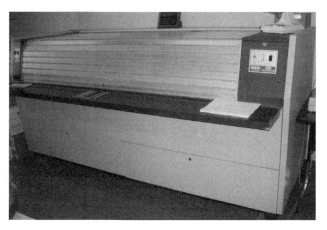

▲ Power file for check storage (item 13 in the plan on page 117). These large units are usually no longer needed after Check 21 truncation has been implemented. Banks, however, are required to hold paper checks for thirty days after processing, and some keep them longer. This file is also used to keep signature cards and was therefore retained even after the Check 21 system was adopted. The cards must be digitized, however, where there are multiple branch operations. Other appropriate short-term storage for processed checks must be provided if such power files are discarded.

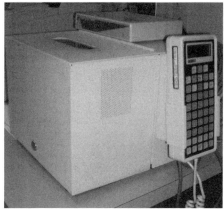

▲ ATM Relay Control (item 8 in the plan on page 117). This allows for island ATM control from within the bank building. Some future ATMs will be "smart" and will have active CCTV teller functions served by pneumatic tubes, and so essentially extend the teller operations to an island or walk-up ATM.

▲ Auto-folder, for statements (item 11 in the plan on page 117). While many branches have statements and other mailings sent out by outside contractors, these auto-folders are still used for an occasional mailing from the bank.

▲ MICR ink printer (item 7 in the plan on page 117). The magnetic ink character recognition feature of this printer allows for the appropriate code to be placed on cashier's checks and other documents. These may also be placed at the lobby teller area and at selected officers' desks.

TELLER ROOMS, WORKROOMS, AND ASSOCIATED EQUIPMENT

▶ *Computer monitor and keyboard dedicated to Check 21 (item 19 in the plan on page 117). This equipment is part of the system needed to implement the Check 21 process. The computer is located beneath the counter, and the keyboard and monitor are usually placed alongside the shaker and scanner. This setup can also be placed directly in the lobby teller room or wherever the check forwarding process is done.*

▶ *Proof machine. This new, compact machine is better and faster than older models and is used to provide the necessary code information on checks and other items occasionally needed even after the Check 21 system is implemented. This is usually placed in the workroom or teller room.*

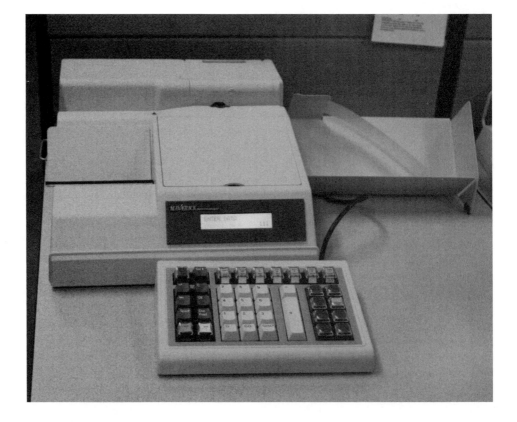

LAN EQUIPMENT ROOM

▲ Main server (at right) and computer (items 21 and 22 in the plan at bottom of page 117). These should be placed in a separate room if possible, and not in a location shared with utilities or fixtures connected to a water supply. The keyboard and monitor are necessary for service and maintenance operations. Most LAN rooms are now equipped with rack-mounted servers.

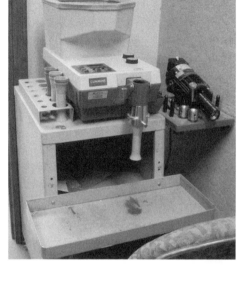

◀ Coin roller (item 16 in the plan on page 117).

◀ Shredder (item 17 in the plan on page 117). These are still needed after Check 21 implementation. Shredders are also used at some officers' desks and other interior locations.

TELLER ROOMS, WORKROOMS, AND ASSOCIATED EQUIPMENT

▸ Teller room currency counter.

▸ Teller room coin counter. These are needed in the lobby teller room and the drive-up teller room.

▾ Typical teller monitor and keyboard. Each teller station is equipped with a computer that is connected to the bank mainframe.

TELLER EQUIPMENT

Numerous items are needed in the teller rooms for lobby and drive-up operations. These are usually obtained from specialized sources separate from the main banking equipment provider. The pneumatic tube system is usually provided by the main equipment supplier.

OTHER EQUIPMENT

File Storage

In a typical branch operation, records are often kept in lateral or conventional file cabinets directly off the lobby, for access by bank officers and other personnel. In larger facilities there may be one or more rooms dedicated to file storage that make use of several types of cabinet arrangements. Some of these may be equipped with rail-mounted movable cabinets, as described below.

A comparative study by Tab Products Co. LLC, shows that in an identical room, the traditional four-drawer lateral file cabinet system provides for approximately 10.73 linear filing inches (LFI) per sq ft of space, while the seven-drawer units increase the LFI to 19.5 LFI/sq ft. The high-density open shelf system (unlikely to be suitable for a financial institution) further increases the file storage to 25.73 LFI/sq ft. The rail-mounted mobile system, however, reaches 53.6 LFI/sq ft; see figure at right.

The advantages of an optimal file storage system are said to include the following:

- Faster filing and retrieval times
- Increased operational efficiency
- Better space utilization
- Reduced file storage costs

Other Equipment

 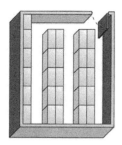

Traditional Filing Equipment
4-drawer lateral rollout cabinets with loc
Linear Filing Inches (LFI): 3,432
LFI/Sq.Ft: 10.73

◀ *File Storage Systems. This compares a traditional filing system and other methods as to storage capacities in a similarly sized room. A structural engineer is often needed to design or certify the building suitability for such loads. TAB Co.*

High Density Fixed Shelf Cabinets
7-high lateral end-tab locking cabinets
Linear Filing Inches (LFI): 6,240
LFI/Sq.Ft: 19.5

Space usage improved by 82%*

 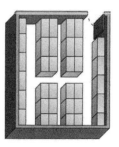

High Density Open Shelf Systems
7-high lateral end-tab shelving
Linear Filing Inches (LFI): 8,232
LFI/Sq.Ft: 25.73

Space usage improved by 140%*

Mobile System
Compacting end-tab shelving
Linear Filing Inches (LFI): 15,050
LFI/Sq.Ft: 53.6

Space usage improved by 339%*

TELLER ROOMS, WORKROOMS, AND ASSOCIATED EQUIPMENT

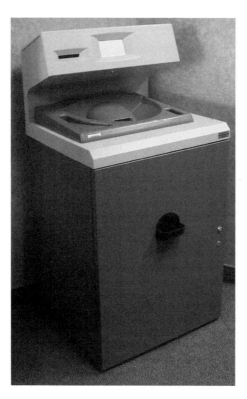

▶ *In-lobby coin receiver.*
Photo by HTG Architects.

A note of caution for this or any record storage system: a structural engineer should be consulted, whether the project is a new building or a renovation or addition. Owners and architects should also consider the fire rating of file room construction even if codes do not require it. Cabinets themselves should be fire rated to UL 350 1-hour ratings.

Coin Recievers

Coin receivers are a popular draw and help bring in new customers or members. A receipt is issued after the coins have been deposited, and a teller then refunds currency or accepts it as a deposit for the participating customer or member.

CHAPTER 10
SPECIALIZED EQUIPMENT

Much of the equipment shown in this chapter will be chosen by the institution's owners or financial equipment consultants. The details of its design and installation will usually be the responsibility of an equipment supplier or its representative. It is important, however, for architects and their consultants to understand the equipment functions and physical requirements, as matters such as access, connection requirements, and service needs must be addressed in design. Too often, architects and their consultants do not fully understand or correctly provide for these requirements. Building codes that call for a certain number of electrical outlets in a room, for example, do not account for the specific locations or needs of specialized equipment.

Provided here is a general guide to the equipment available. Power requirements are noted for each item, as these, and other utility requirements may vary significantly from one supplier to another. Adequate clearance around, or in the correct location, is very important to the service or resupply of an item such as an ATM or night-deposit receiving chest. Many items may not be needed for some projects, while others may require an extensive list of sophisticated equipment. The specific system or equipment needs must be decided on early, as they can impact the entire project.

These items included here represent a cross-section of those available and commonly used, along with some that are relatively new. Unless otherwise noted, all information shown in this chapter comes from Diebold Inc., Comco Systems, American Vault Products, the Hamilton Safe Company, and the NCR Company. These manufacturers and others are listed in appendix C.

DRIVE-UP UNITS

Used in a conventional drive-up (where tellers are in visual contact with customers), the customer drive-up units shown below have been in use for many years but have been steadily improved. These are Diebold VAT 21 units equipped with an overhead pneumatic tube delivery system. The standard tubes are 4½" diameter and are installed with 20" radius bends. The dual blower

▼ *Conventional drive-up customer units. These are fed by an overhead pneumatic tube system. The tellers have direct visual contact with the customers. Diebold Inc.*

SPECIALIZED EQUIPMENT

▸ *Remote drive-up teller system. This unit allows the drive-up to be located out of sight of the teller room, through the use of the audio, CCTV, and, in this case, an overhead pneumatic tube delivery system. It can serve cars arranged in almost any configuration or direction. The Comco 521 unit accommodates standard 4½" carriers supporting approximately 6 lb. ComCo Systems Inc.*

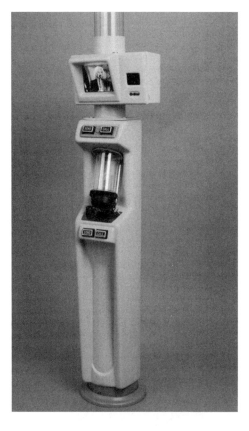

▸▸ *Private video teller system. This group of six ComCo LTS Series machines is served from a central location away from the units. The tellers may be located on a different floor or even in an adjacent building, allowing for possibly greatly increased security. These units may be placed to provide ADA accessibility as well. ComCo Systems Inc.*

motors are usually installed in the drive-up canopy and are able to support a carrier load of 6 lb in a standard operation.

These units have a standard communications system that allows the teller to communicate with different customers waiting in different lanes, while the customer terminal features send and call buttons. Some units are equipped with a raised base for access from vans and trucks while others feature dual controls. The units shown have a small 10" square footprint and may be installed on a narrow 24" island. It is important to maintain noise below objectionable levels; this system is said to operate at below 68 dB.

The teller workstation is subject to the following listings:

- UL 114 Office Appliance and Business Equipment
- Ul 291 Rain Test Specification

An optional CCTV feature allows these units to be operated by customer and teller situated out of direct visual contact.. A similar system is available with underground tubes.

REMOTE DRIVE-UP SYSTEMS

For an overhead tube delivery to function, a connection must be made through the canopy to the building. There are larger, commercial-size remote units available as well.

The unit illustrated at top right features dual controls that are accessible from both compact autos and larger SUVs and trucks. Care should be taken to avoid direct sun reaching the televised images at the customer units. The blower motors for these units may be installed in the canopy or inside the building. When they are installed in the canopy, an access panel is preferred. Most blower units are powered with 120V, 20 amp circuits The audio portion of the customer unit requires a low-voltage two-wire connection to the teller area placed in conduit below the drive or in the canopy. The unit control wiring may also be within the same conduit. This equipment should comply with the following listings or approvals:

- UL 114 Office Appliance and Business Equipment
- UL 291 Rain Test Specification
- C22 (CSA) No. 950

Personal Teller Machines

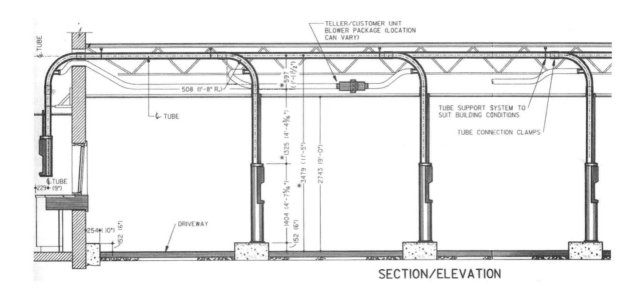

SECTION/ELEVATION

▲ *Typical overhead tube installation. A Diebold VAT 21 system. The lanes may extend to five or six in some installations.* Diebold Inc.

PERSONAL TELLER MACHINES

Personal teller machines should meet the following listings and approvals:

- UL-Class A Fire Rating (paint)
- UL-94 Flame Class rating (ABS; thermoplastic)

For underground systems, some manufacturers continue to suggest using a culvert system to allow for service access—a throwback to earlier designs, except that better, water-resistant steel culverts are now commonly used in the place of the older concrete. The pneumatic tubes are also the standard 4½" diameter with 20" or 24" radius bends. The specifications must conform to the UL 114 listing and UL 291 rain test requirements.

Most pneumatic systems for automobile drive-up lanes use carriers, as depicted on page 130. The larger carrier will accommodate loads of 12 lb. Experience has demonstrated that larger tubes and additional blower motors are needed for the increased load. Some bankers feel that because of the arm reaching involved, the larger loads are too heavy for customers and tellers alike, and therefore the commercial tellers are located

SPECIALIZED EQUIPMENT

▶ Remote teller system. A Diebold 13581 unit that may be installed as shown or in a multiple-unit group. Diebold Inc.

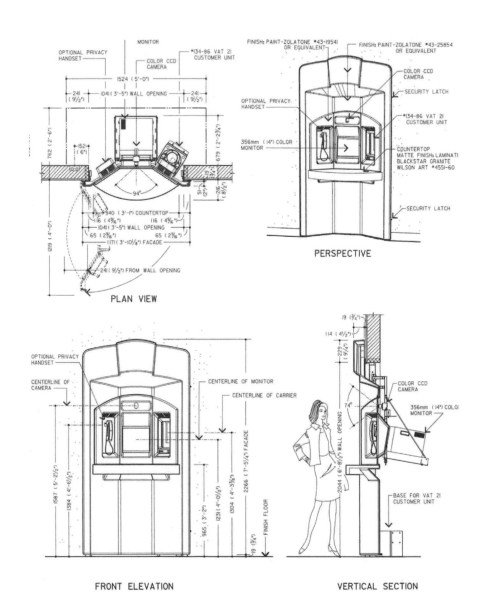

inside the building, where the lifting is mainly up and down with minimal reaching.

The commercial tubes are generally installed in an overhead system and usually located in a marked lane along with other standard customer units. The illustration at the top of page 131 depicts the larger teller unit (on the right side), along with standard units in the same counter arrangement inside the drive-up teller room.

Personal Teller Machines

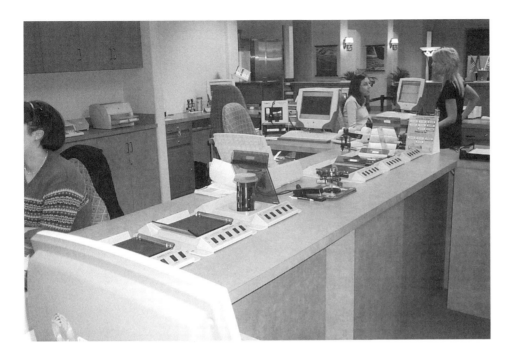

◀ *Remote teller room. A ComCo-equipped downloaded tube system in the remote teller room, with transactions conducted via CCTV and audio. ComCo Systems Inc.*

◀ *Remote teller room equipped with a ComCo overhead tube system. ComcCo has developed a new ecofriendly tube system that will qualify for LEED credits in any new or retrofit application. ComCo Systems Inc.*

SPECIALIZED EQUIPMENT

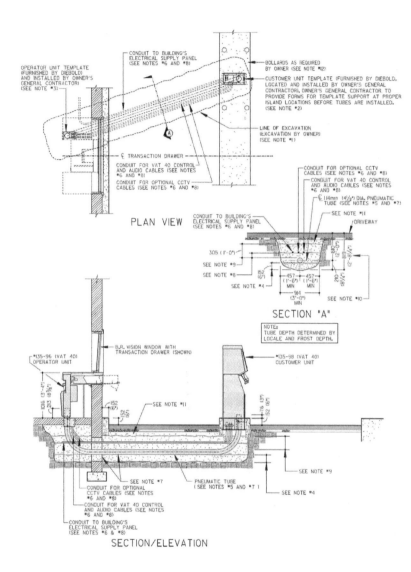

▲ Commercial carrier. This higher-payload carrier is for use in the 4 x 7" commercial tube system. ComCo Systems Inc.

▲ Standard carrier. This carrier is used in the majority of 4" and 4½" tube systems. ComCo Systems Inc.

▲ Underground pneumatic system, section/elevation. A configuration for a conventional direct-bury pneumatic tube system for the customer units (in this case Diebold VAT 23 units). The customer units are similar to those shown on page 125, except that the tube connection is from below and the blower package is installed in the customer terminal. These also may be equipped with CCTV video for a more remote installation. Diebold Inc.

Window and Drawer Units

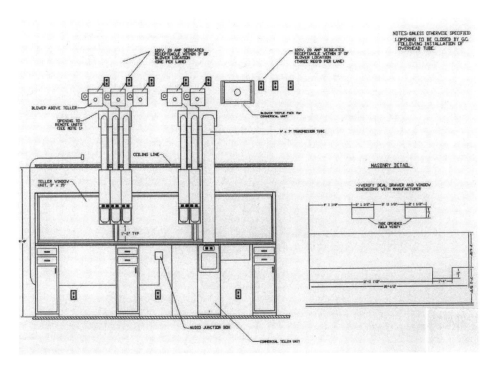

▲ Commercial teller unit (far right) alongside standard units. These tube systems allow a lane or other location to accommodate heavier and larger carriers and loads. ComCo Systems Inc.

▼ Commercial customer unit. These can handle heavier (to 12 lb) carriers. This unit is a ComCo model 900 and requires a 4 x 7" pneumatic tube. Similar commercial systems are now available using 8" diameter tubes. This unit is equipped with CCTV for communication between the customers and tellers. ComCo Systems Inc.

WINDOW AND DRAWER UNITS

The still-popular conventional window and drawer units are available in numerous sizes and types. Typically, the drawer is located at the first lane, while other lanes are served by pneumatic tube delivery. All are equipped with audio. It should be noted that the drawer unit usually requires a dedicated teller for its operation, whereas the other lanes may be served by any remaining tellers at the drive-up window.

Drive-up windows range from 4' or 5' wide single-width units for a single lane or walk-up, to 15' wide in three glass segments for multiple lanes. The deal drawer is usually located at the first window segment to the left, seen from the outside. The deal drawer units are 1' 6" to 2' 6" in width and are approximately 10" deep; they should meet a UL Level 1 rating.

Pictured on the following page is a Diebold Counterette deal drawer unit in a typical single-window arrangement, for a single drive-up lane or a walk-up location. Consideration must be given to the heating, ventilation, and air-conditioning system that surrounds a window/drawer unit because of the installation method and frequency of the opening and closing of the drawer. See appendix C for a list of manufacturers.

SPECIALIZED EQUIPMENT

▲ Multiple drive-up window and drawer installation. Diebold Inc.

◤ Single window and drawer. Diebold Inc.

▶ Typical double window elevations with deal drawer. Details are typical of available window and drawer units. Diebold Inc.

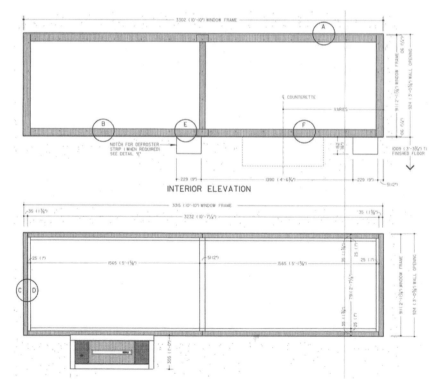

Window and Drawer Units

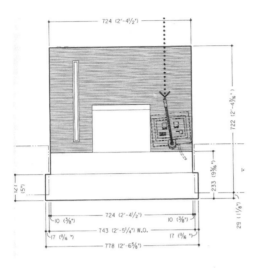

◀ *Drawer details. The drawer units are available with built-in heaters.* Diebold Inc.

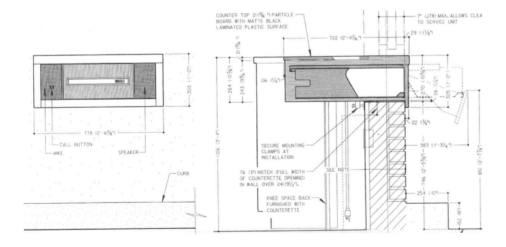

SPECIALIZED EQUIPMENT

▸ *Night depository.* Diebold Inc.

▸▸ *Night-drop safe.* Diebold Inc.

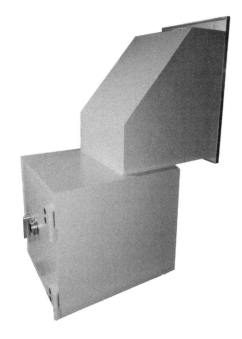

NIGHT DEPOSITORIES

Usually connected to a safe or vault, the after-hours depositories, as they are also called, are often located near the drive-up tellers. They are sometimes also placed at a main entrance for walk-up customers and less frequently in an island enclosure. Smaller envelope depository systems are also available; these are usually placed at a main entrance, for walk-up use. Some new branches use a larger receiving chest connected to the night depositories for secure storage, instead of a large walk-in safe deposit or cash vault. In these cases, armored car service is more frequent.

These depositories are usually manually operated and made of stainless steel, although they are also available in a composite steel filled with high-performance aggregate, as described later in this chapter. The standard models are made to accommodate bag or envelope deposits up to 7½ x 11". An envelope may be deposited without use of a key, but bag deposits are usually only made with a key. The bag opening is secured by a UL-listed pin-tumbler lock. The exterior face and deposit compartments are illuminated for night use, and the assembly is equipped with an alarm contact switch attached to the main alarm system. This contact is activated if tampering or removal by force is attempted. Standard features also include the following:

- Stainless steel exterior finish
- Forms storage compartment of 2¼" high, 12" wide, and 4½" deep
- Counterweighted access doors that assist with ADA accessibility standards
- Bag opening of 6" high, 12¾" wide and 9¼" deep

These units should meet or exceed UL 771 Anti Fish and Anti Trap features when

Safe Deposit Vaults

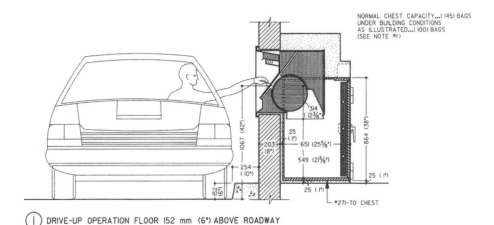

◀ Typical drive-up night deposit installation. The Securomatic Night Deposit and a Diebold 271-70 Receiving Chest. The receiving chests are also available in a composite construction of thin steel forms filled with high-performance aggregate similar to that used for vaults and doors. Diebold Inc.

installed with an acceptable chest and alarm system.

The standard installation height for drive-up units is 42" from pavement to handle. Walk-up units are placed at 48" from floor to handle; however, these units should also comply with ADA requirements in design and installation. Some units are available with an interface for adjacent ATM units for commercial customer use. These are unlocked electronically when a commercial deposit transaction is authorized and then relocked after a set period of time.

SAFE DEPOSIT VAULTS

Prefabricated Modular Vaults

In past years, banks and credit unions were constructed with site-poured concrete vaults that were very heavy and required massive amounts of steel reinforcement to be installed in two or more layers in walls, vault roofs, and floor slabs. These may have been 12–27" thick, depending on the rating needed. Prefabricated vaults of high-strength concrete or ceramic material are now available that can provide an equally secure space with much less wall and ceiling panel thickness and less weight, and requiring less construction time. They occupy a smaller footprint for the same inside dimensions. The Bank Protection Act requires each institution's board of directors to provide what is needed in the way of fire protection and security.

Most prefabricated vault panels are regular strength—that is, a high-density composite concrete mix that will provide at least 3,000 psi. Many provide much higher-strength panels of up to 12,000 psi, and there are also some very high-strength prefabricated vaults available, as described later. Prefabricated vaults allow for the following advantages over site-poured vaults:

- They are thinner than poured concrete vaults and therefore provide additional floor space inside the vault within the same footprint.
- Their lighter weight allows easier installation in upper stories.
- They are able to clear-span larger distances with a thinner structure.
- Their pre-engineering contributes to faster erection.

SPECIALIZED EQUIPMENT

▲ Prefabricated vaults. These new vault systems are secure, fire-resistant, fast to erect, and can often be placed in existing buildings where it would be unfeasible to site-pour a new concrete vault. American Vault.

- The vaults are more easily expanded or even relocated.
- They are designed for the most stringent seismic code compliance.
- Panels are UL listed for Class M, 1, 2, and 3 and meet ISO standards.
- They have precast conduit penetrations for alarm/electrical hook-ups.
- They have UL listed ports for HVAC hookup.

UNDERWRITERS LABORATORIES VAULT RATINGS

CLASS	RATING	THICKNESS (IN.)	APPROXIMATE WEIGHT (LB/SQ FT)
M	15 min.	3–4	42–56
1	30 min.	5	68
2	1 hour	7.5–9	102–123
3	2 hours	12	165

- They are eligible for investment tax credits and accelerated depreciation.

Underwriters Laboratories performs tests on the prefabricated vault panels to ensure they meet minimum requirements for burglary resistance. The table below indicates the class, rating, thicknesses, and weights (depending on the manufacturer) of regular-strength prefabricated vaults.

A particular vault design depends on several factors, such as the selection and sizes of the safe deposit boxes, the cash-volume needs of the facility, and whether a separate cash room or collateral room is needed. The bank's market analysis should determine these needs. It is much easier to construct an addition to a modular vault than to a site-poured one.

There are also available even lighter-weight modular vault panels constructed of ceramic-based material that uses steel fiber technology, reinforcing rods, and mild steel plate. These are available in UL Class 1 or 2 panels and have a compressive strength of approximately 30,000 psi, up to ten times greater than site-poured concrete. The Class 1 panels are 2.5" thick, weigh 45 lb per sq ft, and can be free-spanned to 16'. The Class 2 panels are 4" thick, weigh 60 lb per sq ft, and are capable of free spans up to 19' or more. These vaults are especially suitable when needed in the upper floors of a multi-story building and weight and access are critical.

Modular vaults are erected with panels butt-joined with welded seams along the back plate at ⅛" welds per 4" seam. The standard vault width is 9' 8", with lengths to 24' and a standard ceiling height of 8' 6". Shown at the top of page 139 are typical arrangements for a smaller vault of 10' 6" x

Safe Deposit Vaults

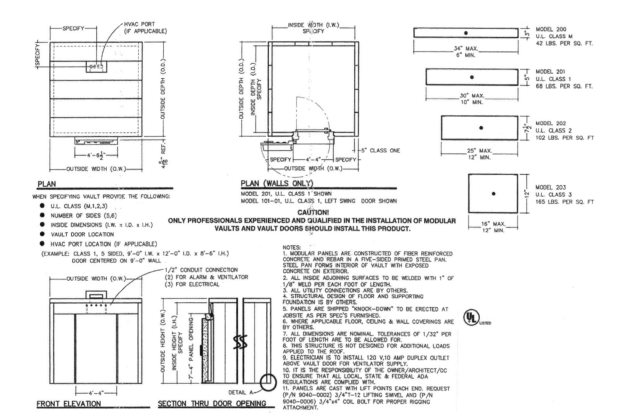

		Exterior Dimensions	Exterior Square Footage	Reinforced Concrete	Hamilton Safe Vault Panels
CLASS I	Reinforced Concrete (12" thick)	10'6"W x 14'0"L	147 sq.ft.		
	Hamilton Safe Vault Panels (5" thick)*	9'4"W x 12'10"L	119.8 sq. ft.		
			Space Savings: 27.2 sq. ft		
CLASS II	Reinforced Concrete (18" thick)	11'6"W x 15'0"L	172.5 sq. ft.		
	Hamilton Safe Vault Panels (8" thick)*	9'8"W x 13'2"L	127.3 sq. ft.		
			Space Savings: 45.2 sq. ft		
CLASS III	Reinforced Concrete (27" thick)	13'0"W x 16'6"L	214.5 sq. ft.		
	Hamilton Safe Vault Panels (12" thick)*	10'2"W x 13'8"L	139 sq. ft.		
			Space Savings: 75.5 sq. ft		

◀ *Space comparison, site-poured and modular vaults. This illustrates the space that may be saved by using prefabricated modular vaults. Hamilton Safe.*

▼ *Typical regular-strength prefabricated vault assembly. The section examples at the upper right show the thicknesses of various other prefabricated UL-rated vault panels that are available. A structural engineer should be consulted for the specific project conditions and related floor-slab requirements. American Vault.*

SPECIALIZED EQUIPMENT

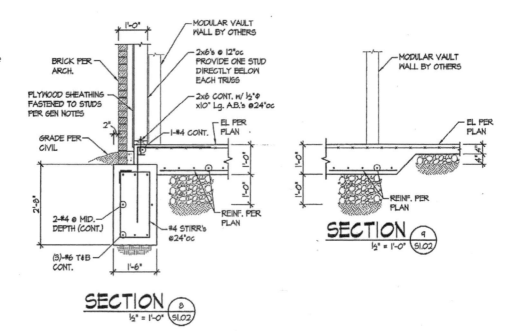

▶ Typical poured-slab section for modular vault. The drawing at the left depicts the outside wall condition, and the inside modular vault wall is at the right. WSKF Architects.

▶ Modular vault assembled at the construction site. The prefabricated components are shipped to the job site and erected in a relatively short time. The vault door is covered with a protective cover that is removed at completion of the construction. These high-strength concrete vaults are available in ratings from Class M rating (15 minutes) to Class 3 (2 hours). Diebold Inc.

Safe Deposit Vaults

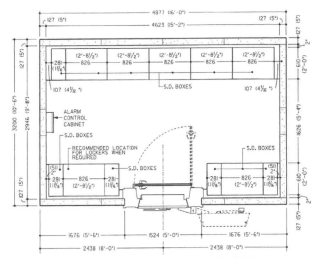

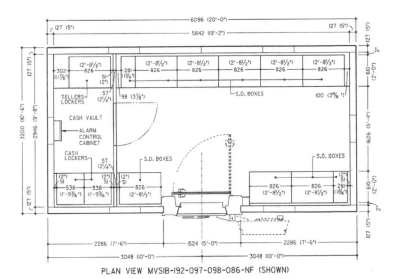

◀ Class 1 super-strength modular vault typical plan arrangements. These super-strength vaults offer higher ratings with thinner panels that weigh less. They are ideal for installations in upper floors of existing buildings and where space is limited. Diebold Inc.

16' and a larger one measuring 10' 6" x 20'. The recommended on-grade site-poured slab for these vaults should be 12" concrete and reinforced with a mat of steel #4 rods at 6" on center each way placed at the bottom of the slab, together with a mat of steel wire mesh placed at the top of the slab. Consult a structural engineer for specific circumstances.

The plans shown above depict the Diebold lightweight ceramic-based vault system using steel fiber technology, reinforcing

SPECIALIZED EQUIPMENT

▶ *Rotary wedge vault door. This door is available in Class 1 or 2 ratings. Diebold Inc.*

Vault Doors

Vault doors are available in the same rating classifications as the modular vaults, from UL Class M to Class 3 at 2 hours. The various manufacturers produce right-hand or left-hand swing doors with similar features. The most common features for Class 1 and Class 2 doors include the following:

- Composite construction with high-strength concrete and steel reinforcement
- Cladding in stainless steel or other durable material
- Adjoining vestibule construction of same material as the doors
- Clear openings of 37–52" wide by 79–80" high and thicknesses of from 10–16"
- Full-height stainless steel locking bars designed to prevent accidental lock-in
- Built-in illuminated ventilators
- UL-listed dual four-tumbler combination locks for controlled access
- Three-movement, 144-hour manual time locks
- Day gates of glass, acrylic, or with open bars, designed and equipped for ADA access

Options are also available for the following:

- Remotely activated electric day-gate locks
- Emergency phone built into the door frame
- Integrated light switches

Most of these doors are designed for installation with modular prefabricated vault systems that are supplied by the same manufacturer, but they can also be installed in site-poured concrete vaults. UL Class 3

rods, and mild steel plate. These are available in UL Class 1 or 2 panels, with an approximate compressive strength of 30,000 psi. Super-strength Class 1 panels are 2.5" thick and Class 2 panels are 4" thick, while regular-strength panels are 5" for Class 1 and 9" for Class 2. (If or when a regular-strength Class 3 panel is needed, the thickness is 12".) They are constructed with a double mat of #3 reinforcing rods spaced at 3" centers each way. The interior of the panels is lined with 11-gauge plate steel. The plans indicate suggested locations of safe deposit boxes and the relative positions of vault doors. The panels should meet or exceed UL 608 standards.

Safe Deposit Vaults

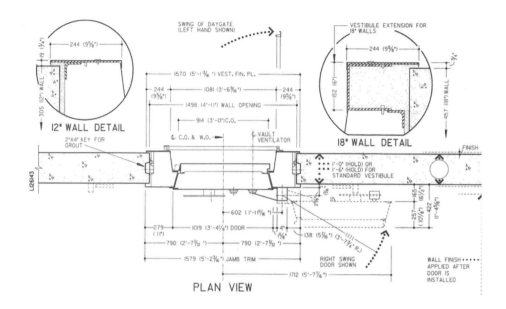

◀ *Typical plan detail of a Class 2 vault door installation.* Diebold Inc.

doors are also available and have similar features to those listed above. Most doors are also available without the need for a pit, allowing for a floor-level threshold. This also provides an antiskid surface for smooth access.

Doors with a rotary wedge and continuous hinge system are also available that provide a UL Class 2 or 3 rating. These are 16" thick and equipped with the some of the same standard features described above, but rather than a series of individual locking bolts or a locking bar, they are equipped with a single rotary wedge. This wedge spans the full height of the door and is sandwiched in its center. These doors also have the following features:

- A 120-hour time lock to prevent unauthorized opening.
- Electronic door contact sensors that determine when the door has been closed.
- Randomly located thermal and mechanical relocking devices.
- A built-in sensor indicates when the rotary wedge is in place.
- When the door is open, an antilock-in device is automatically activated.

Most safe deposit vault doors are UL Class 1 or 2, although Class 3 doors are available, measuring 10–16" thick. A full-height locking bar is used and ventilators are built in. A three-movement, 144-hour manual time lock is standard. Most doors are also equipped with ADA-compliant day gates and hardware and may be installed in either prefabricated or poured-in-place vaults.

The photograph on the following page shows the biometric access device installed adjacent to the vault. Many institutions are now using these devices, which read handprints. The customer or member then needs only his/her deposit box key for unescorted access to the vault. The biometric reader measures nominal 9" wide, 12" high, and 9"

SPECIALIZED EQUIPMENT

▶ *Biometric vault access. These biometric systems allow customers or members to access a safe deposit vault without assistance from bank personnel.* HTG Architects.

deep. It is normally mounted adjacent to the vault door at a height to allow ADA access as well.

The computer and software system is usually located in a secure space along with other LAN equipment. The power requirement is 12–24 VDC or 12–24 VAC, 50–60 Hz, 7 watts.[1]

The features of this system are as follows:

- Increased security at less expense
- Eliminates signature cards
- Integrates into existing systems
- Customers access the vault with a security number, then with a handprint on the biometric reader.
- The system unlocks the vault day gate with a customer's security code and biometric data verification. The day gate then automatically closes and relocks. (Customers can unlock the day gate from the inside when they are ready to leave.)
- A software application and computer are dedicated to operate the entire system,

1 Information from Hamilton Safe Company, 2007.

which records the security number, the customer's name, the time and date of the log-in, and the sequence of entry.

Safe Deposit Boxes and Lockers

Although most bankers, if they have decided to incorporate safe deposit vaults in their projects, have their equipment suppliers handle the arrangements for their installation, it is helpful for architects and designers to understand something of their design detail, construction, and installation. Small and large openings are available in single 11 1/16" or triple 32 1/2" widths. Four standard height/width section sizes are available at 6 5/8" high x 11 1/16" wide, 6 5/8" high x 32 1/2" wide, 11 1/16" wide x 22 1/4" high, and 32 1/2" wide x 22 1/4" high. All are 24" deep. Another standard size opening of 7 x 10" is sometimes used. Safe deposit boxes are usually constructed from welded zinc-coated steel, with plated front frames of zinc alloy. The hinges are brass and the sections have built-in locking clips at the rear to maintain alignment. There are guide pins at the front to prevent shifting, and screws in vertical side members to attach adjoining sections. Doors are 1/2" thick on edge with stainless steel fronts. Locks are listed for the following:

- UL 175-70 specifications
- Seven customer tumblers and seven guard tumblers
- Each side independently changeable, with double changeable locks
- Ability to change keys on-site

There are now available computer-controlled locking systems that allow quicker and better supervision of the boxes, and that work in concert with customer keys as well as the biometric readers for vault access.

Security Lockers

When the secure storage of bulk currency or large volume of coins or negotiables is required, security lockers are available. These are usually constructed of ¼" solid steel plate with ½" steel plate doors. They may be surfaced with polished steel or stainless steel cladding. The doors are also available with an aluminum alloy finish. Interiors are normally painted. They are also available in the composite material constructed of thin steel forms filled with high-performance aggregate.

Flat boltwork is used to secure top and bottom in addition to deadbolts that are used on the hinge side of the opening. They have adjustable shelving that can support 400 lb each. Roller suspension drawers are also available in one-, two-, or three-drawer units, and the lockers have either left- or right-hand door swings. They are equipped with standard UL-listed safe deposit box locks.

Teller Lockers

These lockers are used for less bulky items and to store teller cash trays. They are constructed of ⅛" solid steel plate, with doors of ½" steel plate. Cladding is either polished or stainless steel, and interior surfaces are painted. These are available in 19" or 24" depths for use in vaults or chests.

Safes and Security Chests

Available in a variety of sizes and capabilities, most safes are constructed of high-strength steel that meets UL 15-minute performance and TL-15 or TL-30 door attack performance ratings. (Similar UL-rated safes and chests are also available in composite construction.) Doors are secured by 1" diameter plated and case-hardened steel bolts. These are equipped with both "live" bolts on the strike side of the chest and

◀ Section, typical safe deposit box. Hamilton Safe.

◀ Security or cash lockers. Diebold Inc.

SPECIALIZED EQUIPMENT

Teller lockers. Diebold Inc.

Typical safe. This Cash Guard safe by Diebold is available in many sizes, UL-rated TL-15 or TL-30. This installation is connected through-wall to a night depository. Diebold Inc.

fixed "dead" bolts on the hinged side for security. A variety of alarm components are available. These safes are offered with the following standard security features:

- Energy-absorbing doors that obstruct prying attempts
- Built-in interior lockers with brass hinges
- Standard UL-listed Group 1 electronic combination locks or Group 2M key-locking combination locks
- Stainless steel three-point bolt work
- Relocking devices
- Spy-proof combination dials
- Alarm-ready heat sensor and door contacts
- A variety of alarm components available after installation
- Ratings of UL TL-15, TL-30, insurance services office (ISO), mercantile "ER," and bank "BR"

There are also options that provide for the following features:

- Individually lockable storage compartments for bulk cash or cash trays
- Alarm packages that vary from a simple door contact switch to a comprehensive facility alarm system installed in the safe
- Mechanical combination locks and two-movement time locks
- Time delay, dual combination, two-combination, manager/clerk, duress with silent alarm, bolt sensor switch, and multiple users
- Digital combination locks

TL-15 models are available in unit sizes from nominal 31" high, 19" wide, and 23" deep to 72" high, 40" wide, and 31" deep. TL-30 models are available in unit sizes from nominal 31" high, 19" wide, and 25" deep to 72" high, 40" wide, and 33" deep.

Composite Safes and Lockers

To help offset the cost of steel and at the same time provide for increased security, composite safes and chests have been devel-

Automated Teller Machines

oped with thin steel forms filled with the same high-performance aggregate and concrete mix as is used in modular prefabricated vaults. These are UL-rated and offer the following advantages:

- UL-listed for TL-15 and TL-30 ratings
- Exterior finish in light gauge steel
- Available in safes, teller-receiver chests, night depository chests, teller chests, and portable vaults

AUTOMATED TELLER MACHINES

Since the first ATMs were developed in 1967, they have been constantly refined and improved with new options and functions. There are numerous models of ATMs

◀ Composite safe. Composite safes are made of steel formed with a very high-performance aggregate used in prefabricated modular vaults. Hamilton Safe.

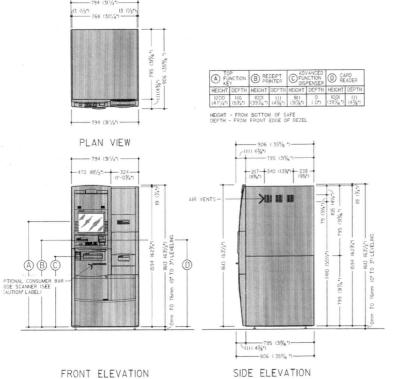

◀ Freestanding lobby ATM. The unit depicted is a Diebold Opteva 720 Advanced-Function ATM. It may be located in a group and is available with front- or rear-loading capability. It also is equipped with a ½" UL-rated steel safe. Diebold Inc.

SPECIALIZED EQUIPMENT

▶ *Through-wall drive-up ATM. A Diebold Opteva 740 Advanced-Function Through-wall ATM with a ½" UL 291 Label I security chest. Diebold Inc.*

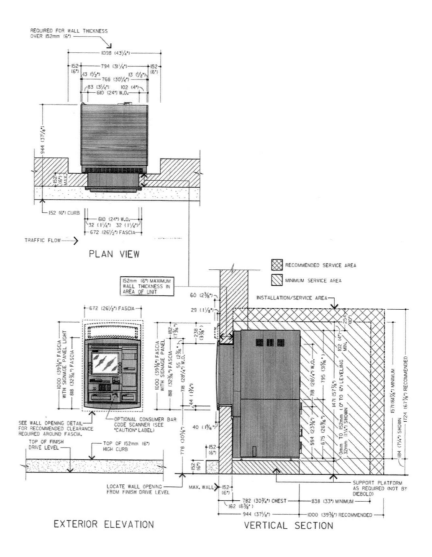

available, from simple cash dispensers to full-function machines. Here we will consider four general categories:

1. Walk-up lobby ATMs (freestanding or through-wall)
2. Through-wall drive-up ATMs
3. Island drive-up ATMs
4. Through-wall walk-up ATMs (for exterior customer use)

Freestanding Lobby ATM

A walk-up freestanding lobby ATM usually has the following features:

- May be freestanding or installed through wall
- Features a 12" or 15" color LCD display for advertising and cross-selling
- Has touch-screen options and an encrypting PIN pad

- Has headphone jack
- Is equipped with a universal camera mount
- Dispenses and receives envelopes
- Accepts envelope-free checks for direct-deposit verification and credit
- Has bulk note acceptor for up to 100-note bundles for deposit and account credit
- Has manual-insert card reader with motorized and Smart Card options
- Has printer options with high-resolution graphics
- Is available with UL 291 Level 1 safe, or CEN I, CEN III, or CEN IV chests

Through-Wall Drive-Up ATM

A through-wall drive-up ATM usually has features similar to a lobby ATM but may also have the following:

- Lighted signage panels or options for brand enhancement
- UL 291 Level I security chest

Freestanding Drive-Up ATM

One of the most-used ATMs for a bank or credit union is the island-installed machine. These are commonly placed at the outside island of a conventional drive-up facility or on a separate freestanding island separated from the drive-up or even the bank. The most common features are as follows:

Customer Interface
- A 12" or 15" LCD, FDK (function display key), or touch-screen color display with sunlight readability, and an optional privacy filter
- A keyboard with EPP (PCI compliant) stainless steel or polycarbonate and optional alphanumeric keyboard
- A card reader: Smart Dip, IMCRW with Smart option HiCo
- Integrated media entry and exit indicators (MEEI)
- Audio: optional high-quality public audio
- Advert panel: standard or with optional backlight
- Barcode reader: 2D barcode supports both 1D and 2D documents

Dispenser
- 2 or 4 cassettes: bunch presenter, retract and purge capability
- Dual dispense 2x4 (8 cassettes)

Deposit
- Cash deposit and recycling options; accepts and validates 100–200 notes per transaction
- Supports multicurrency deposit, remote download of templates
- Intelligent check deposit: scalable check deposit with up to 30 checks in a single bunch
- Envelope depository/dispenser

Printers
- Receipt printer: 80 mm 203 dpi graphics thermal printer
- Journal printer: 80 mm 203 dpi graphics thermal printer
- Statement printer: 80 column thermal printer with document capture and 2ST

Security
- USB protection and parts validation
- Uninterruptible power supply (UPS)
- Safes: CEN L or UL 291 Level 1

SPECIALIZED EQUIPMENT

▶ Drive-up island ATM requirements. Although this NCR 90e ATM may be placed on a 36" island, many manufacturers require a greater width. Bollards protect the ATM unit but must not interfere with replenishment or service. NCR.

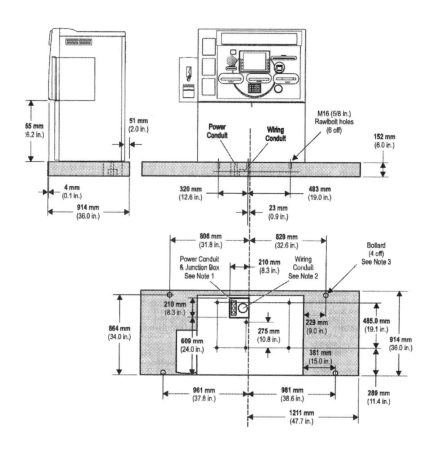

Operating Platform
- 440 2.0GHz, 512MB–2GB
- 2 Duo/13 GHz 2GB
- 80GB or 160GB hard drive
- DVD and floppy disk drives

Software
- Windows XP Pro

Premanufactured Freestanding ATM Enclosures and Canopies

There are numerous manufacturers of these enclosures and freestanding canopies. They will custom design an enclosure or canopy for any ATM unit and site location. Some will also accommodate a night depository. Lighting, electrical, and mechanical requirements are important to coordinate with any installation. See appendix C for manufacturers.

ALARM AND BUILDING SECURITY SYSTEMS

Numerous options and systems are available; they are usually designed and specified by a security expert provided by the supplier. It is very important, however, that architects, engineers, and interior designers become famil-

Alarm and Building Security Systems

iar with this equipment, what it is designed to do, how it is installed, and its power and space requirements.

In a typical bank alarm installation, the system will consist of the following:

- An alarm control panel with a keypad and a wireless receiver and battery backup
- Money clips
- Hold-up buttons (at each teller and officer desk)
- Motion detectors (at entrances, lobby and other areas)
- A vault audio system
- Alarms at all safes
- ATM alarm
- Door monitors (contacts)
- Glass breakage monitors
- Single-station smoke detectors
- Height-strip camera at main entrance doors
- The system should meet UL Grade AA line security and UL 1076 and 1610 requirements for alarm monitoring and control applications.

These are usually equipped with a regular monitoring program, with a monitored digital backup. A closed-circuit television system is included, with the following features:

- Black and white or color cameras strategically placed for optimal monitoring of the building interior and exterior
- Outdoor housings for cameras outside the building
- Image monitor
- Separate dedicated camera power supply
- Time-lapse VCRs
- Black and white or color multiplexer Security cameras are linked by a digital

◀ Drive-up island ATM. This is the latest NCR Drive-up ATM with state-of-art features. NCR.

◀ Typical exterior camera installation. These cameras are connected to the security control and monitor system placed in the workroom of this bank.

SPECIALIZED EQUIPMENT

video management system to a hybrid NVR server, an IP camera server, or a commercial off-the-shelf server. They are capable of remote management via LAN, WAN, and ISPN. They also have the following features:

- ATM text insertion
- Time, date, text, or alarm search
- Real-time operation
- Multiple zones of motion detection

Other items that are increasingly used in bank security are Dinion cameras, which produce very high-resolution images, and height-strip cameras, which are discreetly installed on or near a door frame and produce sharp eye-level images of anyone who passes.

OTHER EQUIPMENT

Traffic Control and Specialty Lighting and Signage

A number of different specialty lighting fixtures are available for the financial industry. The ones listed here are not usually a part of the building lighting system but are normally a part of the specialty equipment supplied to a bank or credit union. These include the following:

- Drive-thru message signs; includes "blank-out" LED direct-view, neon backlit, and incandescent backlit examples.
- Directional and informational signs, including non-illuminated panel and overhead clearance and lane signs as well as freestanding directional signs.
- ATM message signs, including ATM/teller lane signs.
- LED and incandescent traffic controller lights; vertical and horizontal configurations. These are the most common of those used in branch drive-up canopies to control lanes.
- Direct-view LED signs.
- Variable message and segment signage.

FORMS DISPENSER

Not often used but available for interior or exterior use, this dispenser is usually mounted on a stand and set at an adjustable height for access by cars or trucks. Normally equipped with a stainless steel housing and a Plexiglas front windscreen for a clear view of the contents, it is loaded from the rear.

CHAPTER 11
CASE STUDIES

This chapter shows different types of financial institutions, from small neighborhood branch facilities to larger full-service branches with drive-ups, to urban core area projects that rely completely on walk-in customers and large headquarters banks that offer the complete range of financial services. For the most part, the branch institutions are dedicated to customer service, but there are also facilities that concentrate on operational efficiency and employee job comfort.

Some of the projects featured here are renovations—one of a former great banking hall newly restored to employ twenty-first-century banking methods, and another a former fast food restaurant transformed into an unlikely but successful bank. There are credit unions that exhibit branding brilliance, banks and credit unions that feature the concierge pod for customer service, and a credit union that serves walk-in customers with remote teller machines.

Some of the projects have been developed on very small sites, and others are sited on their ample land with an eye toward expansion. Drive-up facilities are shown that allow for extensive stacking space for waiting vehicles; others are limited to only one or two lanes. Drive-up equipment is presented with both overhead and underground pneumatic systems. Some projects are one story, while others are two or more floors. Most are equipped with the latest specialized bank equipment. Some feature large walk-in safe deposit vaults, while others rely on safes or chests and use regular armored car services to deliver currency and other valuables.

Most of these institutions have been designed to use Check 21 clearing and do not require the large workrooms formerly needed. Most have been designed with drive-up lanes, except those in dense urban centers, which have larger teller-line operations. Some feature lobbies surrounded by permanent offices, and others have open desks with fewer dedicated offices. The projects are scattered throughout the United States and exhibit various architectural styles and design themes, some historic and others regional. Many have a particular brand image. Other projects are prominent for their sustainability planning; one has earned LEED Platinum certification.

Bank and credit union prototypes are also shown, along with site-specific information about a particular location. The descriptions of the projects come from designers, owners, and, in some cases, media sources. In most of these case studies, the site and floor plans are presented, together with exterior and interior photographs.

The size in square feet of the various projects is indicated, along with the completion dates; however, in most cases the owners did not wish to divulge the construction costs of their projects. More complete contact information for the architects is presented in appendix E.

CASE STUDIES

NORLARCO CREDIT UNION
Fort Collins, Colorado; EHS Design

The CEO of Norlarco Credit Union knew that his institution was solid but needed a new image and brand concept, both to differentiate it from increasing competition and to increase market share. He also wanted to expand into new markets with an image that would "wow" the community and competition.

EHS Design, the architects, and Weber Marketing Group, the branding consultant, studied the members' characteristics and preferences, analyzed the market conditions and competitors, and recognized an opportunity. The Fort Collins community was interested in the environment and exercise.

Paul Seibert, CMC, a principal with EHS Design and also an expert in brand strategy, says, "We connected the members' lifestyle with Norlarco's business focus, creating a physical fitness–financial fitness retail branch concept.... No other financial institution in the city or state had made this connection." Norlarco's management readily accepted this concept, and EHS Design has applied it to its freestanding branches and minibranches located on university campuses.[1]

The benefits to Norlarco's strategy include a unique and positive new image that significantly differentiates its branches from

[1] Paul Seibert, message to author, October 12, 2007.

▼ Site plan, Norlarco Credit Union, Fort Collins, Colorado. The site layout positions the branch for high market visibility, safe pedestrian access, and face-up drive-up banking. Parking is available on-site and at adjacent lots. EHS Design.

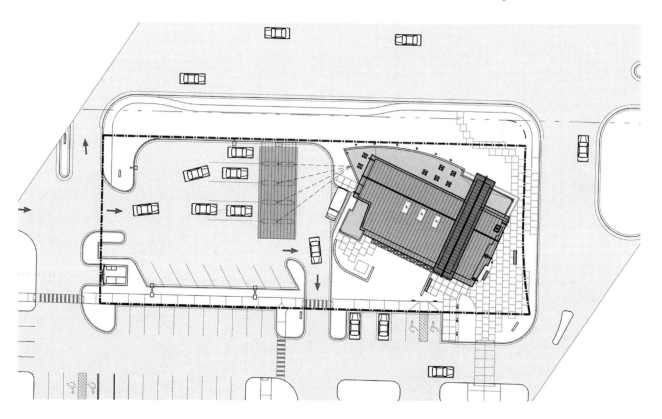

the competition. They are focused on members' interests and needs, while encouraging nonmembers to join. This new branch business model also provides a more effective way to deliver services by using employees in multiple roles and allowing members to use remote delivery services.

The new retail branch concept is described as "highly professional, expressive, fun, engaging, and directly related to target members' interests through the use of sports equipment as work-surface supports, PC stands, merchandising kiosks, and accessories. This connection to its members is more than just visual; it is three-dimensional and tactile."[2]

The resulting project is a very successful example of design and brand strategy. The basic design, with a greeter and waiting area at the main entry and then a path to the lobby tellers, is very effective. The sports items incorporated into the design, such as bicycles for the check stand support and skis for display kiosks, are very fitting. The conventional tellers are arranged in a curved plan that faces a queue line with open desks for officers and customer representatives.

2 Naomi Berg, EHS Design, conversation with the author, February 11, 2008.

▼ Floor plan, Norlarco Credit Union, Fort Collins, Colorado. The main entrance, at lower right, leads to the greeter and education area by the fireplace. A through-wall ATM is in the entrance vestibule. The imaginative floor plan provides additional branding opportunities along the path to the teller line, such as the online tech center station. EHS Design.

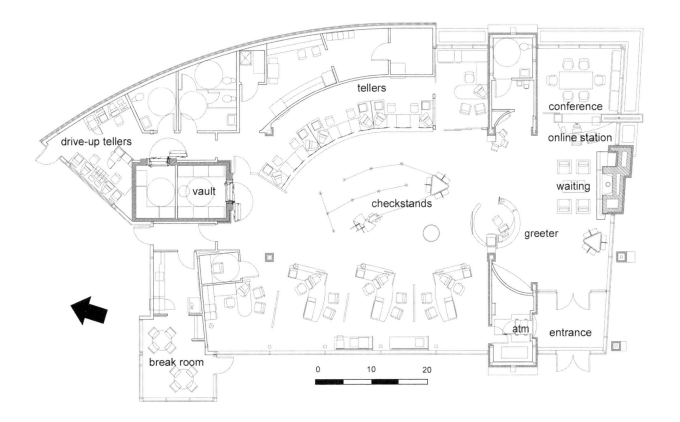

CASE STUDIES

FARMERS BANK OF NORTH MISSOURI
Saint Joseph, Missouri; WSKF Architects

This bank, headquartered in a small northwestern Missouri town, needed to expand to Saint Joseph, a much larger city to the south, and its owners wanted a new building that would convey the image of modern convenience and service. Several operational requirements were part of the program for the new project. Interior tellers needed to be convenient and accessible from vestibule entrances on two sides of the main lobby and also be placed adjacent to the drive-up tellers. A conventional drive-up should accommodate four lanes, but a separate drive access needed to be made for a through-wall ATM (see p. 54).

The main site access is from the south, so the building is oriented thus. Customer parking is also from that point of access, and because of the resulting circulation, employee parking and drive-up access are on the north side facilitated by another access drive extending from the main thoroughfare to the east. While most bankers prefer to have

▶ Site plan, Farmers Bank of North Missouri, Saint Joseph, Missouri. A major thoroughfare to the east of the site provides direct access to the north building entrance and to the drive-up. The street to the south provides access to the main customer entrance. The site allows for future expansion to the north side of the building. Illustration by Kaw Valley Engineering.

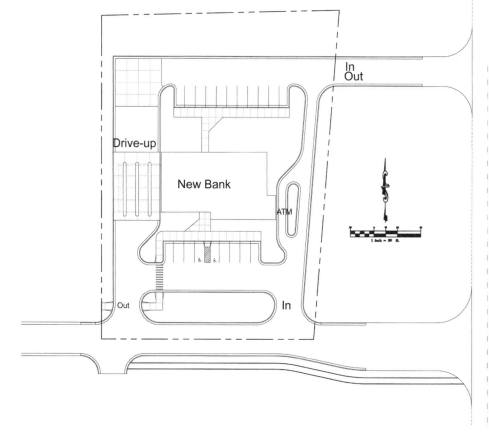

FREESTAR Bank

◀ Floor plan, Farmers Bank of North Missouri, Saint Joseph, Missouri. Entrances on both sides of the lobby lead directly to the teller line. A through-wall ATM located at the far right may be serviced and replenished from inside the building, resulting in much less of a security risk. The building was designed to provide for expansion to the north. WSKF Architects.

one main entrance, this owner wished to have access to the building from both north and south. Another consideration was that space for expansion be left on the north side of the building.

The program provides for both vestibule entrances and a spacious lobby, with offices for the president, a loan officer, and an insurance officer, as well as cubicles for administrative and service representatives. It was designed for ample natural light through the clerestory windows, made possible by the elevated drive canopy; the sloped roof extending from the drive-up and across the lobby makes the feature easily achieved, with light entering from the north, east, and south. The through-wall ATM, replenished from the interior, saves in security and operational expense.

A safe deposit vault and a coupon booth are provided adjacent to the four-teller line, which is in front of the four-lane drive-up teller area. A conventional overhead system of pneumatic tubes serves the drive-up lanes. One of the lobby teller stations is lowered to desk height to accommodate seated or handicapped customers. A workroom placed by the teller area contains the night depository and receiving safe.

The 5,014 sq ft building was completed in early 2002.

FREESTAR BANK
Downs, Illinois; Bailey Edward Design, Ellen B. Dickson, AIA

The president of FREESTAR Bank had a vision to create a cross-marketing facility that would increase his banking operation. By providing "destination" products and services through retail establishments such as a café and a dry cleaner, the bank would gain exposure to a wider range of potential clients. This facility provides the customer with a one-stop shopping experience, as well as allowing the bank to soft-sell additional banking services such as loans, financial planning, and online investments to its broader customer base.

The bank is strategically located near a growing bedroom community and on a

CASE STUDIES

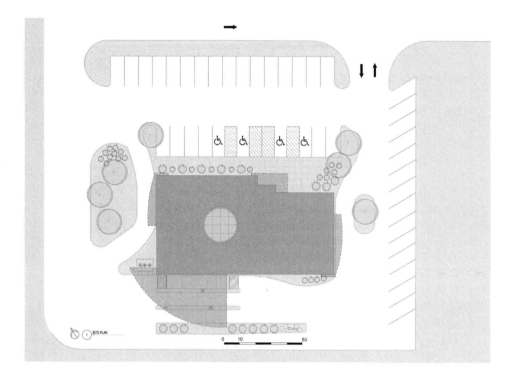

▶ Site plan, FREESTAR Bank, Downs, Illinois. The site access allows for three points of drive-up service—from the west, south, and east. Separate lanes are provided for an ATM at left and dry-cleaner pickup window at right, in addition to the drive-up lanes. Bailey Edward Design.

main route from an interstate highway to a major corporate headquarters. Target demographics include younger, two-income families that appreciate the convenience of being able to access money at the cash station, drop off their dry cleaning, and grab a cup of coffee and a muffin all in one trip. It is possible for customers to conduct all business transactions without leaving their cars. The dry-cleaning pickup window is on the east side of the building, and an additional lane accommodates a through-wall ATM on the west side.

The building was designed with a contemporary look both inside and out. The main entry leads straight into the "community" area between the retailers and the bank. A comfortable customer lounge area is designed as a place to have a coffee or a casual meeting, or use a laptop. This lounge also provides a perfect location for new marketing materials as well as television viewing that can double with bank promotional videos.

A large 20' skylight in the center of the lobby provides significant natural light and is reminiscent of classic bank designs. Conventional teller counters are arranged around part of the circular lobby, and offices are located at the opposite side. A workroom is adjacent to the tellers, but access is through the break room. The open glass for offices allows bankers constant oversight of foot traffic. Another useful feature is that the manager's office provides good observation of the lobby and at the same time a view of the drive-up. Color contrasts in the décor and furniture add to the contemporary appeal of the building.

The project exhibits a very imaginative

Hyde Park Bank

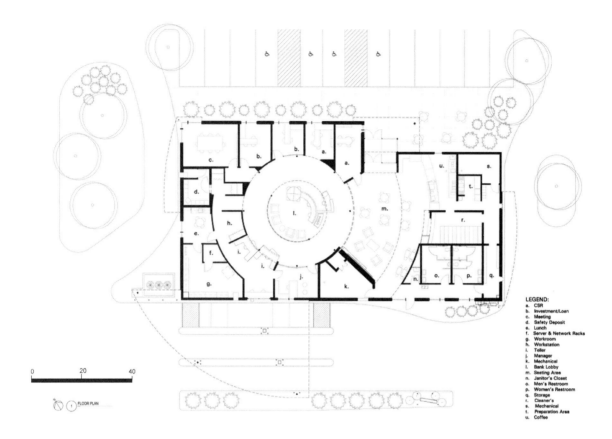

▲ Floor plan, FREESTAR Bank, Downs, Illinois. A large circular skylight directly above the lobby center acts as a central organizing element for the bank. The coffee shop, dry cleaner, and public toilets are at the right. Bailey Edward Design.

floor plan and a clean modern exterior with an unusual curved drive-up canopy that also echoes the circular plan features within the building. The coffee shop/deli and dry cleaner are said to be very popular with customers and are successful attractions for the public, as had been envisioned by the owner and architect.

Construction of the 6,788 sq ft bank was completed in December 2005.

HYDE PARK BANK
Chicago, Illinois;
Florian Architects

At a time when so many of the former great banking halls have been abandoned or converted into some unidentifiable segment of commercial real estate, this project transformed the former bank "through a dramatic play of modernist and classic vocabularies" (Kamin 2005, pp. 136–138). The 10,000 sq ft project was the winner of a 2005 AIA Honor Award and has been described as being "as much a transformation as a renovation."

In bringing modern banking features to this classic hall, the architects placed receptionist stations near each of the monumental open stairs. Various officer stations were placed behind each in an open arrangement, and the teller line is adjacent in the center-south side of the hall. An Internet banking area, flanked by the building elevators and a fire-stair, is opposite the tellers on the north

CASE STUDIES

▶ Main lobby floor plan, Hyde Park Bank, Chicago, Illinois. The skillful use of the grand hall's space is shown by the placement of the new banking functions that complement the building's classical past. The large teller line is needed in this urban location. Florian Architects.

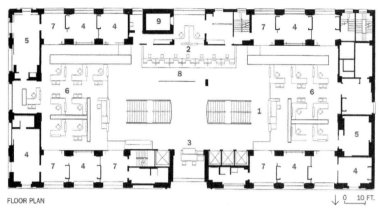

1. Reception
2. Teller line
3. Internet banking
4. Executive offices
5. Conference rooms
6. Banking officer stations
7. Waiting lounges
8. Queuing line and kiosk
9. Vault

▶ Hyde Park Bank, Chicago, Illinois. The original building was designed by architect K. M. Vitzthum in 1928. The building exterior was kept intact.

◀ Interior, showing personal banking station. A personal banking representative can assist customers with various needs and products. The marble and trim of the station complement the existing floors and walls. Barbara Karant/Karant+Associates Inc.

side, and there are five customer waiting lounges scattered around the periphery of the hall.

Executive offices, conference rooms, work areas, and workstation files are placed in the balance of the surrounding margins of the hall, freeing it of visual clutter. Indirect lighting that is reflected off of the regilded ceiling adds to the desired effect. Travertine and maple surfaces blend very well with the building walls, and the metal mesh screen walls separate the offices from the lobby of the great hall in a delicate but functional manner. The light is diffused at workstations by the use of translucent glass, and direct sun is kept from the interior with shading devices.

The architect decided to complement rather than obscure the bank's classical past and described his effort to "create an uplifting interior" but not in a formal sense. He did not want the bank's customers to feel required to "come in (wearing) a three-piece suit" (Kamin 2005, p. 137).

As described by Blair Kamin in an *Architectural Record* article about this project, "A bank doesn't have to be dumbed down architecturally to be approachable and functional. There is a middle ground between history and freshness, grandeur and intimacy, ceremony and informality. That is a lesson worth heeding for all historic bank halls in an age that seems to value them less and less" (Kamin 2005, p. 138).

The interior was completed in 2005 and a significant amount of exterior renovation was completed in March of 2008, which involved masonry restoration, a new entrance canopy, new revolving doors, exterior paving and landscape work. The bank remained open while all of this work was completed.

CASE STUDIES

▼ Site plan, Madison National Bank signature branch, Merrick, New York. Parking and circulation are arranged around the irregular site, with the two drive-up lanes on the building's east side. JRS Architect, P.C.

MADISON NATIONAL BANK
Signature Branch, Merrick, New York; JRS Architect, P.C.

The design philosophy of this project was to incorporate aspects of the local neighborhood into the branch, and thereby increase the comfort level of customers for the new start-up bank. The brand design was inspired by the late-nineteenth-century Romanesque architecture of Henry H. Richardson. His multicolored brickwork, dramatic arches, and rounded roof turrets may be seen in this distinctive building. The entrance vestibule occupies a round turretlike feature that leads to the main lobby and a waiting area that surrounds the fireplace.

As customers enter this branch, they find themselves in an area that includes a working fireplace, flat-screen televisions, and other amenities meant to evoke a living room feeling. The 4,200 sq ft building also uses wood trusses that have a hand-carved appearance, with distinctive curved lower chord members.

Unlike most new branch facilities in the United States, this bank has a traditional teller counter with six stand-up tellers and a night teller station that can be locked off for after-hours service; however, since it is in an urban

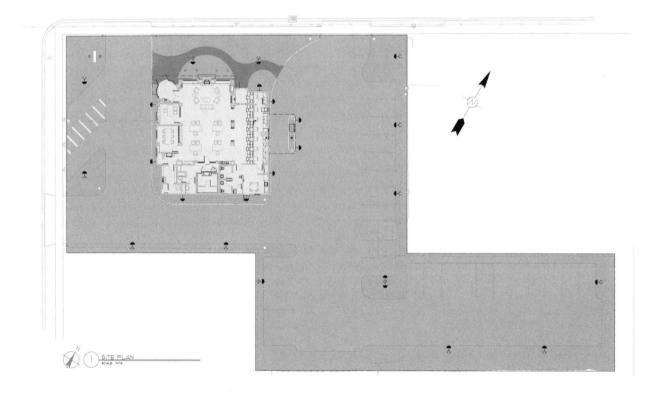

location, it only has two drive-up lanes. The second lane is equipped with an ATM as well as a pneumatic tube customer unit.

Grouped around the main lobby are a private office, a conference room, and a copy room. At the back of the lobby are a prefabricated vault with two coupon booths, the public restrooms, and a break room. Within the lobby are four open desks for banking officers and staff. Files are built into one side of the lobby.

Although this bank operates with a traditional line of stand-up tellers, it seems attractive and adequate to customers and staff alike, so future branches are planned to continue with this design theme.

The building was constructed in 2007.

PILOT BANK
Tampa, Florida; NewGround

Originally named Temple Terrace Bank for its home location, a suburb of Tampa, this bank client desired a new image. The architects and in-house brand experts created a new brand that was to be customer-focused and progressive and would also differentiate itself in Tampa's saturated financial market. The result was Pilot Bank, and the consulting firm also assisted the owners in finding suitable locations, with the highest growth potential, to consider for the new branch.

With the use of focus groups, mystery shoppers, and product and purchasing analysis together with market research, the designers found the optimum location for the new branch and developed the new brand name, logo, and subsequent brand experience that would demonstrate the new customer-focused approach.

The aeronautical imagery became a metaphor for soaring higher and achieving dreams. This project then became the impetus for converting the bank's six other facilities to the same theme and brand identity.

The building is designed with a main bank entrance and a secondary lobby entrance with stairs and an elevator for access to the upper floors. The bank lobby leads to the tellers with a path that features an investment center, a business center, a lifestyle center, and a kids' center. The tellers are placed in a split counter arrangement that also includes computer banking teller assistance. Seat stools are also used at the teller stations, providing additional customer comfort, and a prominent flat-screen television monitor is located behind the tellers. The adjacent drive-up tellers use a televised system for service to the drive lanes.

The bank has four meeting rooms for customer assistance instead of the usual officer's

▲ Floor plan, Madison National Bank signature branch, Merrick, New York. The main entrance at upper left leads to the lobby waiting area and fireplace. A traditional six-station teller line is to the right. The plan shows a well-thought-out arrangement for all customer and staff needs and demonstrates that a traditional line is still feasible. The walk-in vestibule at the upper right allows for after-hours service while the main bank is closed. JRS Architect, P.C.

CASE STUDIES

▶ Site plan, Pilot Bank, Tampa, Florida. This is an effective use of a site to provide stacking and parking under an upper-floor area. Access to the elevator and stairs can be locked off for upper tenant use. NewGround.

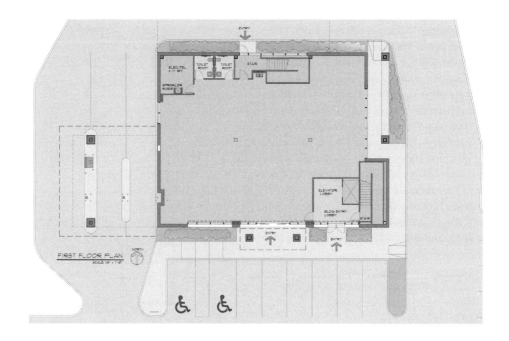

▶ Floor plan, Pilot Bank, Tampa, Florida. The floor plan shows an innovative use of alternative products and services placed directly along the path to the tellers. The investment, business, and lifestyle centers are in can't-miss proximity. The kids' center is also a popular feature. This bank uses cash recyclers for lobby and drive tellers, and although the drive is attached to the building, it uses remote customer units for drive-up teller services. NewGround.

desk and side chair arrangement. There are also offices for business lending and a manager's office with access to an adjacent off-site workstation area. A room for IT/video equipment is located across from an employee lounge. The bank has a safe deposit box vault with counters as well as a coupon booth. Toilets are off a rear corridor that has access to an electrical and phone equipment room at the building's northwest corner.

The second floor extends over the drive and parking below, and is planned for leased space to separate tenants or for future expansion of the bank. The modern design features stucco and glass with a metal standing-seam roof. Exterior diagonal struts at the walls present an ideal location for downspouts that normally clutter a building facade.

OLD NATIONAL BANCORP HEADQUARTERS
Evansville, Indiana; HOK (Design Architects) and VPS Architecture (Principal Architects)

The new Old National Bancorp building in Evansville, Indiana, is an 8-story, 251,000 sq ft office tower joined to an adjacent 3-story pavilion and a glass atrium on a site larger than a city block. The entire complex is called Old National Place. It houses one of Old National's banking centers and serves as the bank's headquarters; it includes a multilevel garage and landscaped plaza for public events. The structure offers a river view from virtually any location within the building, and 90 percent of the offices have direct access to sunlight.

The new headquarters represents a new design concept for the now 174-year-old financial institution. One of the most notable differences is the extensive use of glass all around the building envelope. The design transparency gives the facility an open, airy atmosphere that is new to this traditional financial organization. The expanses of glass around the entire building were incorporated for several reasons, with the proximity to the Ohio River being an important one, as well as the energy savings this design offered.

Old National connects the bank's employees to each other and to the community. Previously these employees were spread out

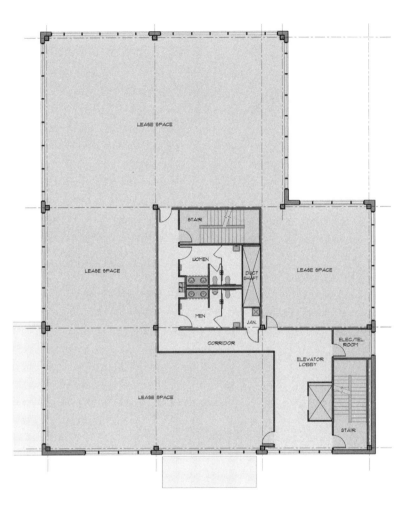

▲ Second-floor plan, Pilot Bank, Tampa Florida. The second floor provides lease space for one or more tenants and presents views for all sides of the building. Restrooms, janitor's closet, and the second stair are located in the center core. NewGround.

CASE STUDIES

▶ *Site and floor plan, Old National Bancorp Headquarters, Evansville, Indiana. The Ohio River is immediately beyond the street at the top of the plan and contributes a picturesque setting for the new bank. The four-lane remote drive-up facility is shown at the right within the attached parking garage. HOK Design.*

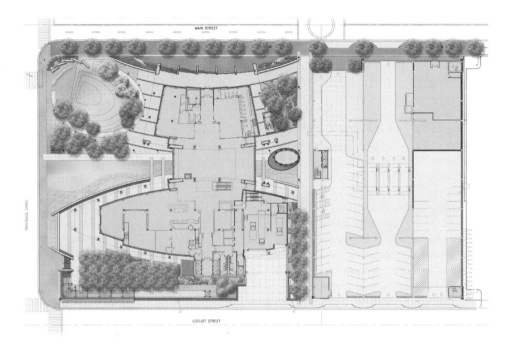

▶ *Old National Place and the Ohio River, Old National Bancorp Headquarters, Evansville, Indiana. A view of the wide Ohio River is available from virtually every office and floor. Photo by Sam Fentress.*

over several floors in their existing building and in other downtown locations. In the new building, it is possible to bring together many functions that were previously 3 or 4 stories apart and in separate buildings. Many private offices were eliminated, providing an open design that gives banking departments added space and the flexibility to function more efficiently. Enclosed spaces such as the remaining private offices, the boardroom, and theater were moved to the building core, thereby allowing daylight to spill in from the floor-to-ceiling windows. The project features a daylighting system and has automatically dimmed fixtures based on ambient light levels.

The building's elliptical shape and curtain-wall system are designed to maximize the sunlight, while a daytime lighting system uses mini-optical light-shelves to reflect sunlight inward, and the automatic dimming system adjusts interior lights according to need. It is estimated that these systems will provide substantial energy cost savings annually.

The project received an Award of Merit Commercial from Midwest Construction. The Saint Louis office of HOK worked on the project with VPS Architecture, local architects in Evansville.

RIVER BANK
Osceola, Wisconsin;
BKV Group Architects

The River Bank's Osceola, Wisconsin, headquarters facility is a 23,000 sq ft, 2-story multiplex financial services center for the

◀ *River Bank, Osceola, Wisconsin. Lobby interior facing the main entrance. The 2-story entrance provides ample natural light to the interior and the open stair. The waiting area is shown at left, and the greeter station is at the right.* Photo by Steve Bergerson.

CASE STUDIES

▶ Second-floor plan, River Bank, Osceola, Wisconsin. The second floor contains a gallery of offices and open workstations that look down on the lobby floor. An abundance of natural light is made possible by windows surrounding the lobby and by the clerestory ribbon windows at the south. BKV Group Architects.

▶ First-floor plan, River Bank, Osceola, Wisconsin. The customer path leading from the entrance to the tellers presents several opportunities for marketing new products and services as well as Internet and investment stations. ATMs are available for walk-up and drive-up customers. BKV Group Architects.

Osceola and St. Croix River Valley communities. The internal spatial concept consists of a 2-story atrium with south-facing clerestory windows that provide daylighting for the bank's interior volume.

This project effectively uses the method of brand identification along the customer path. From the entrance, through to the tellers, customers are met by a consecutive series of opportunities that promote interactive financial services. First, the customer representative greets them, and there is a very comfortable waiting area with a fireplace and flat-screen television for customers who need to wait there. The next opportunity is an online banking station, where customers can check on their own accounts or surf the Internet. A third feature before the customer arrives at the teller counter is an investment center. A number of open desks with private offices behind them provide specific banking services along the lobby path.

A traditional teller line for four stand-up tellers is adjacent to the drive-up teller room, and the drive-up features five lanes with an ATM at the last lane. A safe deposit vault and coupon booths are also near the teller area. The elevator and a second stair are at the opposite end of the main lobby. A file room provides for a movable filing system near the main stair and is accessible from both floors.

A monumental main stair is adjacent to the building entrance and leads to the second floor. The second floor wraps around the lower lobby and provides office space for loan offices, insurance, securities brokerage, and retail banking, all overlooking the first floor. Brightly colored banners that advertise various products, services, and other brand-related themes are connected to the 2-story columns in the main lobby.

The exterior of the building is designed to provide a visual connection to the 2-story scale and character of the nearby downtown by using brick at the first floor and the pavilionlike articulation of the hipped roof, 2-story columns, and windows. These clerestory windows effectively use the sun to illuminate the entire open lobby. The intent was to maintain a reflection of both the residential community and the downtown together, in a complementary building design. The pylon sign in front is a feature less frequently used for other new bank buildings because of increasingly restrictive sign ordinances.

The 2-story entrance connects the downtown streetscape with the atrium lobby. The project is very successful in its planning and functional endeavors.

MOUNTAIN STATE BANK
Cumming, Georgia; Foreman Seeley Fountain Architecture

This bank, located at the foothills of the Appalachian Mountains north of Atlanta, is noteworthy for its Arts and Crafts–style design. The traditional bank and drive-up design follows the style very well, and it is carried from the exterior treatment of varied-color stone, smooth stucco, and painted wood trim through to the interior fixtures and darkly stained interior trim. The coffered wood ceiling also provides a dramatic contrast to the interior lighting, and the floor tile design brings in the exterior stone coloring. The dark-colored standing-seam roof also complements the design theme.

This project also shows how a temporary (mobile) bank building can be used during construction in order to get a head start on opening for business. The plan is the classic layout of a central lobby surrounded by open desks and private offices behind them, all with a view to the teller line. The four lobby tellers face out to the offices for the manager and five loan officers as well as a closing/conference room. The drive-up tellers are directly behind the lobby tellers for cross-service in the usual fashion.

The four open-desk customer service representatives are located adjacent to the main entrance, in front of loan offices, and in front of the main vault. The main vault is to the left of the tellers and features a second compartment for a cash vault and second vault door, accessible by the tellers and directly behind the night deposit. At the other side of the teller area are a workroom, break room, and separate record vault.

The manager's office has a separate conference table and private restroom (see p. 88). A waiting area is to the left of the

CASE STUDIES

▼ Floor plan, Mountain State Bank, Cumming, Georgia. The traditional teller line is immediately visible from the main entrance and surrounding offices as well. The main safe deposit vault is adjacent to a cash vault that is accessible by the drive-up tellers. The manager's office has a small conference table for less formal discussions, and the plan features a separate record vault for file storage. The vestibule entrance that helps keep comfort higher and energy costs lower is a good idea even in the southern part of the United States. Foreman Seeley Fountain Architects.

lobby. Public toilets are to the left of the vault, and there is a separate room for a sprinkler service behind them. A room for the server and LAN equipment is adjacent to the conference room and the lobby.

The four-lane drive-up has room for future expansion, including a bypass lane (this

from the area formerly occupied by the temporary facility). Although the Arts and Crafts–style dark wood trim, coffered ceilings, floor tile, and colored stone do not necessarily reflect a deep-south stereotype, they all relate well to the surrounding countryside and are refreshing in their selections.

ROCK SPRINGS NATIONAL BANK
Rock Springs, Wyoming; NewGround

This prosperous western Wyoming bank was quite simply out of space and needed a new main office that would allow for future growth and establish a solid foundation in the revitalized downtown area of Rock Springs, which now houses the community's professional market area.

The architects created a new main office that accommodated the bank's current operational requirements, as well as its projected growth needs. Careful consideration was also given to the impact that the anticipated growth would have on back-office departments that were responsible for maintaining customer service functions. The new 31,185 sq ft, 2-story main office features an entrance plaza anchored by a striking 50 ft clock tower.

The grand entry point leads to an elegant lobby and a greeter's station that serves to direct customers to their appropriate destination. Adjacent to that is a waiting area surrounded by a stone fireplace with a large flat-screen television and rich leather chairs. The tellers are arranged in a curving counter that has a separate drive teller area behind. Across from the tellers is a resource center. Adjacent to the tellers is a large safe deposit vault and an attached cash vault with direct access from the teller areas. A safe deposit clerk provides assistance for vault access as well.

Rock Springs National Bank

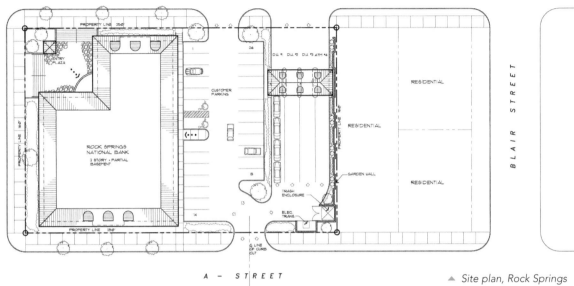

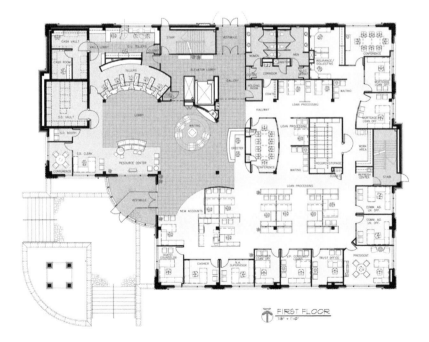

▲ Site plan, Rock Springs National Bank, Rock Springs, Wyoming. The four-lane face-up drive-up on the east side of the site is separated by the parking that extends across the east side of the bank; the customer units operate via CCTV and buried pneumatic tubes. An ATM is at the far right lane. NewGround.

◀ First-floor plan, Rock Springs National Bank, Rock Springs, Wyoming. The main entrance is at the southwest corner of the bank; however, a second public entrance at the north side of the building can be locked off to provide access directly to the upper floor. Note the large safe deposit vault attached to a second cash vault and cash room. NewGround.

CASE STUDIES

▲ Second-floor plan, Rock Springs National Bank, Rock Springs, Wyoming. The second floor accommodates a 70-seat meeting room, separate offices for internal audit and chief financial officer, human resources, and the bank's bookkeeping department, as well as the computer department. A large computer room and separate server room are included. NewGround.

A separate rear entrance allows stair and elevator access to floors above and below, and can be locked off from the main bank. A training room, boardroom, and additional offices are located on the second floor.

Separate departments are provided for insurance and collections, mortgage lending, and a large loan-processing department on the first floor. Offices are also provided for new accounts, consumer lending, agricultural lending, a trust office, and an impressive president's office. Waiting areas are placed at various locations throughout the first floor.

The building's exterior is a pleasing combination of stone, brick, cut stone lintels and sills, and round-arch second-floor window heads that blend with a standing-seam roof featuring rounded ventilators.

FRANDSEN BANK & TRUST
Forest Lake, Minnesota;
HTG Architects

This project represents a relatively new direction in financial institution planning and service delivery. It demonstrates an early use of "concierge pod" stations instead of a traditional teller line (see p. 70). The benefits of serving more customers with fewer staff have been previously mentioned in this text, and this is one of the projects selected to illustrate those features.

The open floor plan of the 6,600 sq ft building encourages the flow of customers between the greeter station, waiting space, concierge area, coffee bar, Internet station, and self-service information kiosk. This latter feature promotes bank product information and brand image through a system using a touch-screen computer with a sound-directed headphone feature. The concierge stations are equipped with cash recycling systems—secure vault-like machines that are shared between two associates, allowing the intake and dispersing of cash (see p. 172). Studies by the technology's manufacturers have shown these machines to be more accurate than humans, and they can significantly reduce the bank's full-time employee count.

Inherent in this design is a separate drive-up teller room behind the lobby tellers. Adjacent to the drive-up tellers are a workroom, private offices, and the safe deposit vault. Opposite the lobby are additional banking offices, a president's office, a real estate banking office, and a conference room. Clerestory windows provide daylighting for the lobby.

The willingness of the leadership and staff of Frandsen Financial—Frandsen Bank & Trust's parent company—to experiment with a new banking delivery system (through this new technology and the concierge concept) represents the company's desire to think beyond the box. Frandsen Financial believes this new bank, situated in the growing Forest Lake community, will provide for additional opportunities to reach new customers by standing apart from a traditional banking facility.

This building serves as a marketing tool for the company, providing a first point of contact and a unique impression on existing

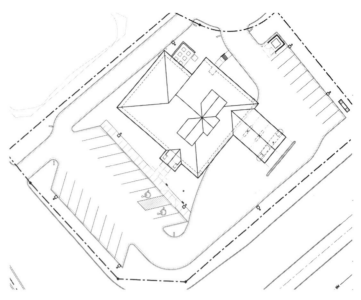

▲ Site plan, Frandsen Bank & Trust, Forest Lake, Minnesota. The standard counterclockwise flow of traffic extends past the angle parking around to the conventional drive-up. The hip-roofed building has an extended high gable roof with clerestory glass for natural light distribution to the entire lobby. HTG Architects.

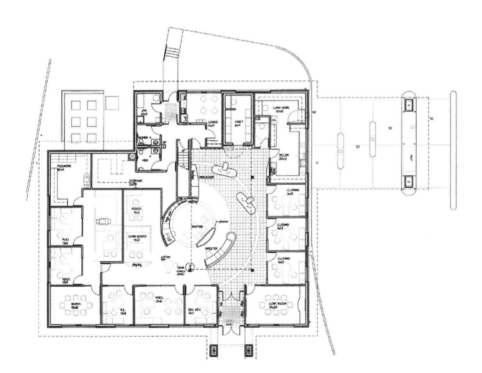

◀ Floor plan, Frandsen Bank & Trust, Forest Lake, Minnesota. The entrance vestibule leads directly past the greeter, who can assist and direct customers to appropriate destinations. The concierge pods are just beyond the greeter and circular waiting area. The concierge staff is trained to offer customers much more than traditional teller services. HTG Architects.

CASE STUDIES

▶ *Greeter desk, Frandsen Bank & Trust, Forest Lake, Minnesota. A combination of light- and dark-colored wood is carried throughout the bank. The greeter desk is placed to assist and direct customers. Interior plants and landscaping add to the effect. HTG Architects.*

▶ *Customer service representative side of concierge pod, Frandsen Bank & Trust, Forest Lake, Minnesota. The cash recycler shown in the foreground permits faster and more accurate service to customers by trained staff. HTG Architects.*

customers. The simple yet sleek design extends inside, with a convergence of curves, wood finishes, tile, and modern amenities and technologies.

HOME STATE BANK
Willmar, Minnesota;
KKE Architects

In this 2-story, 14,126 sq ft bank can be seen the architecturally popular trend of offsetting elements at different angles to create more interesting forms and spaces for site and floor plans. Located on a key site in Willmar, where U.S. Highway 12 bends in a slightly more easterly direction, the 2-story glass lobby and pylon sign of the Home State Bank are designed to function as an icon for the western part of the city, and as a window into the community.

Home State has been a key financial institution in the Kandiyohi County area since the 1920s, and sought to build a new headquarters that reflected its progressive banking philosophy and long-time commitment to the community. The site, a 1.85-acre tract located within a larger development, was used to maximize visibility, provide some dedicated parking, and allow for simple, easy access to the drive-up. The north-facing stone end-wall acts as a signboard for incoming traffic from the east.

The main entrance vestibule leads to the main lobby and a fire stair. The main lobby then contains a conventional teller line, and adjacent to that an elevator. The sawtoothed plan provides for a variation of offices surrounding the extended lobby, and a curved center core intersects the angled office lines on the first floor of the 2-story structure. This center core holds file space and a workroom as well as public toilets and a second stair.

A safe deposit vault and a coupon booth are located to the other side of the lobby tellers. The traditional plan elements have the drive-up tellers behind the lobby tellers for the four-lane drive-up. Both an ATM and a customer unit are placed at the last lane. Other features of the first floor are a separate closing room and a kids' room.

The second floor provides space for the president's office and boardroom to one side of the 2-story lobby. A break room and kitchen are designed with a folding partition to allow the outer corridor space to be included for larger events. Other facilities are additional offices, a processing and workroom, records storage, and a server room.

The contemporary building is constructed with stone, and copper-detailed and assembled in a traditional manner. The interior geometry, with its juxtaposed angle office plan, provides for traditional functional relationships with a nontraditional look. All offices have a view to the customer entrance to enable bankers to see and welcome customers. The 2-story glass-enclosed lobby provides a dramatic welcoming space for the community.

A wide-screen television monitor projects new products and services from a niche in the curved stone wall along the lobby. The colors and furnishings are matched to the unusual design theme, and the use of a large eagle sculpture accents the waiting area, along with an antique safe.

The building was occupied in December of 2005.

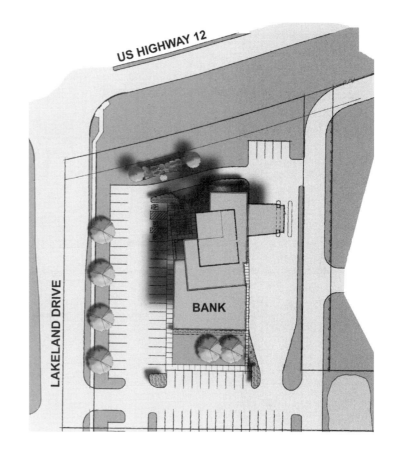

▲ Site plan, Home State Bank, Willmar, Minnesota. The corner location along the highway and thoroughfare provides an opportunity for showcasing the bank to a large group of potential customers. The drive-up exit to the side street behind helps reduce the traffic within the site. KKE Architects.

CASE STUDIES

▶ *Second-floor plan, Home State Bank, Willmar, Minnesota. The president's office and boardroom are to the left of the break room and assistant areas. A folding wall opens this space for special events. Additional offices, a server room, a storage room, and records are adjacent to a large processing room and work area to round out the second floor. KKE Architects.*

▶ *First-floor plan, Home State Bank, Willmar, Minnesota. The unusual plan places interior spaces at different juxtaposed angles than the usual rectangular room design. The open lobby extends up through the second floor to the roof above. KKE Architects.*

COLONIAL BANK, ANTHEM BRANCH
Henderson, Nevada;
Dr. Robert A. Fielden, NCARB, FAIA, Architect

Colonial Bank has become one of Nevada's major business and investment institutions, providing real estate and construction loans to developers and small corporations. The owners wished to create the illusion of a large building, but also to make it sensitive to the environmental impact it would create. The architects approached the challenge by using simple techniques to create a "mirage" in the desert. The resulting design sought to achieve a building that incorporates basic sustainable qualities as well as current technologies while maintaining the visibility and marketability that were desired by its owners.

Located within an existing shopping development, the project site was selected after a number of other sites were considered. Two feet of additional fill were brought into the site in order to better manage the water runoff and to create additional height for better visibility. Because of sign restrictions, the architects used walls to support the drive-up canopies, and this also helped give an added dimension to the facade of the building.

The design was significantly influenced by the environmental factors of wind, sun, and water. The main entrance is shaded by a large overhang that prevents the direct sun from hitting the southwest building face or the main south facade. Vertical louvers and horizontal planes allow the wall of the lobby to be open while shading the facade. The entry faces south and is set back from the

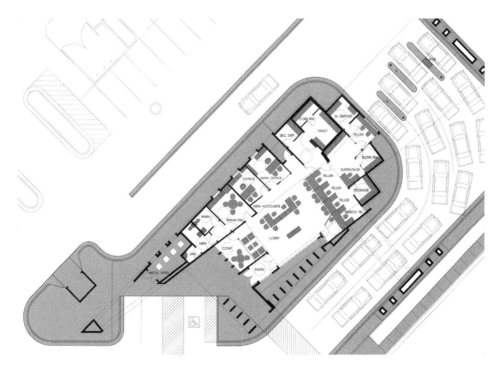

◀ Floor plan, Colonial Bank, Anthem Branch, Henderson, Nevada. The compact plan provides for a vestibule entrance, and lobby leading to the teller area, with a customer service desk and offices on the opposite side of the building. The drive-up tellers are at the far end, and a safe deposit vault is between. Great care was taken to screen items such as air-conditioning condensing units and even the waiting cars as they queue in the drive-up lanes. RAFI Architects.

CASE STUDIES

▸ Exterior view of Old Colonial Bank, Henderson, Nevada. View toward the main entrance. The relatively narrow site is well planned for the full-service bank. RAFI Architects.

▸▸ Floor plan, Wachovia Bank at Eagles Landing Financial Center, Stockbridge, Georgia. The carefully thought-out plan shows the progression of customers as they proceed to the teller line, to the community center, or to financial counseling, the vault, or an office. The six tellers are able to serve a large walk-in customer base, while the drive-up is equipped with three lanes. The branch uses safes placed adjacent to the teller manager and a safe deposit vault as well. Gensler Architects.

western facade in order to keep the southwestern winds from entering the building.

The vestibule also prevented the wind from entering the building and helped maintain a consistent inside temperature, thereby providing additional energy savings. Another design decision contributing to sustainability is the use of native plants that require relatively little watering. Whereas many projects of this type end up with unsightly mechanical equipment in plain view, this project located equipment such as condensing units in a partially hidden yard.

One product that is featured very successfully in the building is a skylight called a Solatube. It is designed to bring in natural light without the radiant heat that usually accompanies such devices, thereby significantly helping reduce energy costs. Although the project was not submitted for LEED certification, it has been found to exceed the basic qualifications for such a rating.

The 3,171 sq ft bank building was completed in March 2003.

WACHOVIA BANK AT EAGLES LANDING FINANCIAL CENTER
**Stockbridge, Georgia;
Gensler Architects**

The merger between Wachovia and First Union (and now with Wells Fargo) created an opportunity to develop a new prototype bank and brand image. The architects were given the task of designing three different freestanding bank branch concepts plus a kit of parts for new and existing locations, including those in an urban infill. This first freestanding prototype serves as a brand showpiece.

The new brand strategy responded to an emerging customer focused, product-driven business development. New products and services included everything from savings accounts to insurance policies. In collaboration with the bank's in-house design team, the architects fashioned an evolving solution that met the client's goals. Flexibility became a required feature, and even though the program requirements continued to change,

Wachovia Bank at Eagles Landing Financial Center

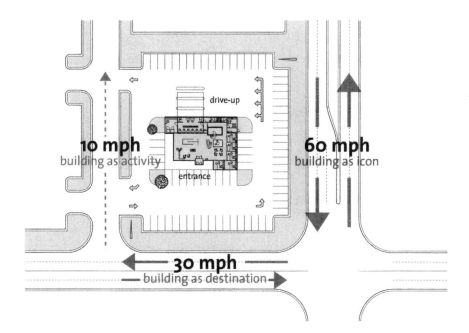

◀ Site plan, Wachovia Bank at Eagles Landing Financial Center, Stockbridge, Georgia. The prototype site plan places the building at an intersection of a major thoroughfare and a secondary street, with access from a side street. It provides for parking around the building and counterclockwise traffic flow to the three-lane conventional drive-up. Gensler Architects.

eventually resulting in the three prototype scales, the basic design remained consistent.

This project example shows the suggested typical site use with a four-lane drive-up, the suggested floor plan, and the resulting building design. Several areas of the lobby are dedicated to customer assistance and marketing/brand emphasis opportunities: a seated waiting area, a community center, a writing desk, a focus room, and the teller counter and back wall areas.

The interior features a traditional six-station stand-up teller counter and a back area for two drive-up tellers. A teller manager's office is also provided. The safe deposit vault is directly available from the lobby, and behind it are public restrooms and the employee lounge.

The building lobby is enclosed with glass, and glass bands surround part of the office area as well as the upper wall area above the tellers and front canopy. Color and texture have been carefully chosen to reflect the brand image, and they will be used

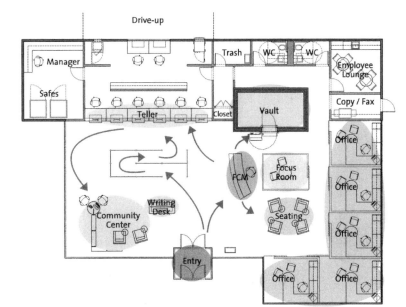

in all of Wachovia's other facilities. The building features a distinctive curved roof that references the new brand logo.

The project was opened in the fall of 2003.

177

CASE STUDIES

▶ Site plan, St. Cloud Federal Credit Union, Sartell, Minnesota. The single access point to the site provides for traffic to move in a conventional counterclockwise direction toward the five-lane drive-up. The parking is adjacent to main drive as it extends around the building. HTG Architects.

▶▶ First-floor plan, St. Cloud Federal Credit Union, Sartell, Minnesota. One of the significant features is use of the concierge pods. The distinctive circular lobby includes a greeter station, a work area, and a waiting area as well as the pods. Stairs and an elevator are accessible in a vestibule entrance. HTG Architects.

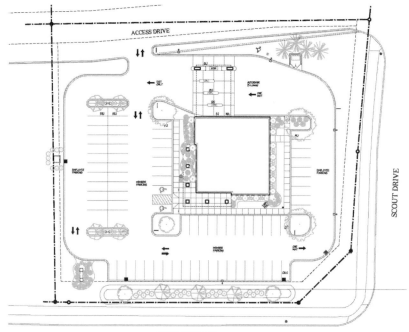

ST. CLOUD FEDERAL CREDIT UNION
Sartell, Minnesota; HTG Architects

St. Cloud Federal Credit Union is in a new 2-story building that makes use of the concierge station concept. The new facility features a lobby with two separate concierge stations that have four member positions instead of a conventional teller line. From these stations, member service representatives provide many financial services, including typical teller transactions. The main entrance vestibule has stair and elevator access to the upper and lower floors and leads directly to the main lobby and a greeter station. The waiting area is situated at the center of the main lobby, where customers are encouraged to relax, have a cup of coffee, or use the online connection to the Internet and monitor their own accounts.

Surrounding the lobby on the first floor are three member offices, three lending offices, a manager's office, a flex office, and a fire-rated file room. The file room features track-mounted movable cabinets for high-density storage. Behind the concierge area of the lobby are the drive-up tellers, cash workroom, and the head teller's office. A second stair and a unisex toilet are placed at the opposite side of the lobby, together with a secondary exit door.

The second floor has additional offices, a large boardroom, the accounting department, and a call center. There are also public restrooms and a break room. The main server equipment is located in a separate

St. Cloud Federal Credit Union

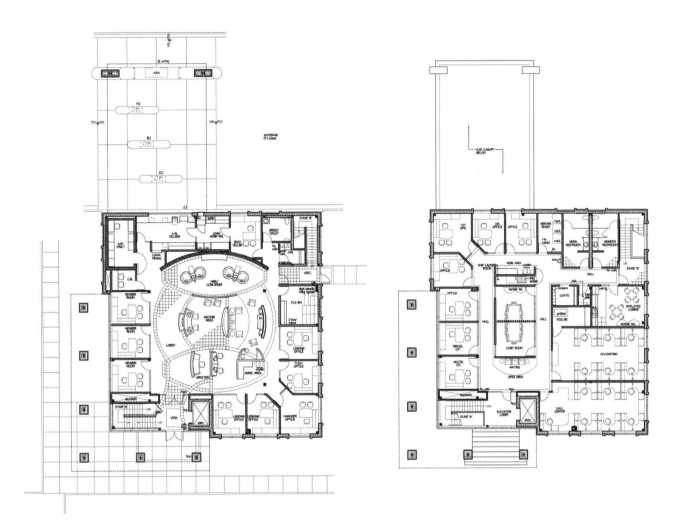

▲ Second-floor plan, St. Cloud Federal Credit Union, Sartell, Minnesota. Various offices, a large conference room, the accounting department, and a call center are located on the second floor, along with a fire-rated server room, the employee lounge, and public toilets. HTG Architects.

fire-rated room as well. A partial basement provides space for storage, mechanical equipment, and the elevator equipment room.

Among the new technology features in this bank is the use of biometric vault access. A hand scan and password allow members to enter the vault one at a time without being accompanied by an employee (see p. 142). Inside this vault, the boxes are single-keyed and members may view the contents in the privacy of the vault itself or in an adjacent coupon booth.

The open floor plan, accompanied by private areas such as the closing rooms, gives members options for fast, simple transactions and more private meetings with in-depth discussions. The closing rooms, when used in concert with the concierge stations, create a place for the credit union staff to provide members with information on a variety of products and to complete more

CASE STUDIES

▶ *Exterior with main entrance, St. Cloud Federal Credit Union, Sartell, Minnesota. The well-defined entrance is a focal point for member access to the 2-story headquarters building. HTG Architects.*

complicated transactions. These rooms are sometimes used as "universal" rooms with identical filing systems, so that if one were occupied, another may be used with ease. This concept allows the employees to move about onto the retail floor where they are able to interact with the credit union members face-to-face without the barrier of a teller line or an office wall.

NORTH FORK BANK, LONG BEACH BRANCH
Long Beach, New York;
JRS Architects

There are numerous examples of fast-food and other restaurants that have been converted to banks although the process is usually very difficult and costly. The cost is often comparable to, or even more than, new construction. Site issues can also be difficult, and where there is a drive-up, it is sometimes convenient to place it in the same location as the restaurant's former "to-go" window. This bank uses that design strategy and was able to add a second lane for an island ATM.

This successful conversion resulted in a repurposed building with very little resemblance to its fast-food predecessor. The use of new materials, finishes, colors, and some image-changing wall construction helped to avoid any reminders to the building's original function. The main entrance is very close to the first drive-up lane, but it is separated by the walk and curb. The entrance also contains another through-wall ATM for

North Fork Bank, Long Beach Branch

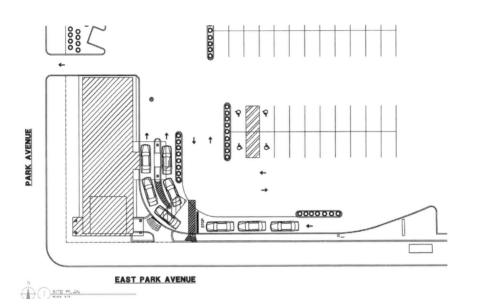

◀ Site plan, North Fork Bank, Long Beach Branch, Long Beach, New York. In order to use the existing building and site, the parking remained as previously planned, and the bank's drive-up is situated between the drive and adjacent sidewalk, providing for the two lanes. JRS Architects.

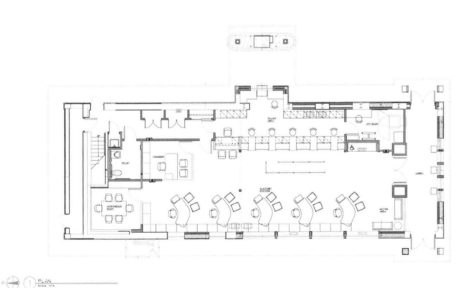

◀ New bank floor plan, North Fork Bank, Long Beach Branch, Long Beach, New York. The increasingly popular Internet station located behind the greeter desk is handy to the other lobby features. The relatively narrow resulting lobby space has been divided between the open officer desk area and the teller line with six stations. A manager's office and a conference room are located at the back, along with the restroom and stair to a mezzanine. It worked out for the new drive-up teller to occupy the existing alcove from a previous fast-food serving window. JRS Architects.

walk-up customers, which is available after hours.

This new retail branch sought to capture the ambience of nearby Long Beach with a red-tiled roof, white stucco, and structural accents of large wood beams and copper guttering. This also is an example of a successful branch design that has only one pri-

181

CASE STUDIES

vate office (for the manager) and a small conference room, but it provides five open-desk locations for other banking officers and assistants.

There are six lobby teller locations (one to accommodate seated customers), and one position behind the teller line to serve the drive-up. Teller counters, floors, and a coffee bar are of decorative stone accented by wood trim. A restroom and janitor's closet are at the back of the building, together with a small mezzanine area above for mechanical equipment.

ALOHA PACIFIC CREDIT UNION Honolulu, Hawaii; EHS Design and Weber Marketing Group, together with Honolulu-based Ushijima Architects and Glen Mason Architects

This project is in a renovated building in Honolulu that serves as the flagship design and branding image for this fast-growing credit union. The 5-story building is co-owned by the Aloha Pacific Credit Union and another investor. Aloha Pacific (formerly named the City and County Employees

▶ *First-floor plan, Aloha Pacific Credit Union, Honolulu, Hawaii. The main entrance is to the left and starts the engineered member experience. The group of six remote teller machines serves the lobby customers, while an additional tube is placed near the customer service representative. Walk-up ATMs are provided at the main entrance and at the main street side of the building.* Ushijima Architects.

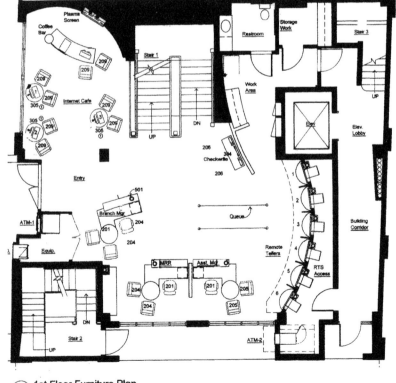

◀ Aloha Pacific Credit Union Honolulu, Hawaii. Remote teller machines. Although it required about a year for customers to readily accept the RTM system, they are now quite comfortable with it. The positions provide privacy, a soft material to stand on, and clear operating instructions.

Credit Union) renovated the building and occupies the first and second floors as well as the basement, for a total area of 4,500 sq ft of the 9,000 sq ft building.

In downtown Honolulu, as in other major metropolitan centers, an automobile drive-up is not usually provided because of land scarcity and costs, but this credit union makes very effective use of remote personal teller machines, with greeters and personal service representatives to help direct the members to the appropriate destination. These customer service representatives are also able to provide member assistance in using the remote teller machines that are prominently displayed in the main lobby area.

The use of the remote teller machines in this project was a significant change in how the institution was to operate. Whether its members would accept the seemingly impersonal communications with televised tellers was not known. Wallace Watanabe, its president, indicated that it took about a year for members to become comfortable with the system. The members eventually became accustomed to it, however, and now are at ease in its use. The resulting savings in teller time per transaction has been a great success, and other Aloha Pacific branches are now using the same machines.

Better security also results from having all teller operations on the lower floor in a secure room, away from any robbery threat. Cash

183

CASE STUDIES

▲ Remote teller workroom, Aloha Pacific Credit Union, Honolulu, Hawaii. The workroom provides a secure environment to serve the branch and future "smart" ATM machines. Three tellers are able to serve the RTMs located above. Note the cash recycling machines between the tellers, which greatly facilitate the speed and accuracy of transactions.

recycling machines are also used in concert with the remote teller equipment. Mortgage lending, commercial lending, and the branch president's offices are located on the second floor.

A new entrance was designed for the building, and a through-wall ATM is positioned nearby. A coffee bar is across from the service desk, and the credit union makes very effective use of branding features such as flat screens and advertising displays on all floors. Other features include an elevator, second stair, additional offices, a break room, mechanical equipment rooms, and public restrooms on the ground floor. Each floor is 1,500 sq ft.

The remodeling of the credit union, together with the new exterior design, was completed in 2007. The building exterior renovation was designed by Mason Architects. The Aloha Pacific Credit Union architectural design was by Ushijima Architects, and the interior design features were by EHS Design.

WATERMARK CREDIT UNION HEADQUARTERS FACILITY
Seattle, Washington;
IA Interior Architects

Watermark Credit Union has been in Seattle for more than forty years and took over a historic 1929 building to house its headquarters. "The primary goal was to create an office that flexed to its ever-changing needs. Amenities and a youthful design attitude—so that all employees know they are appreciated and come to work with a renewed sense of purpose—were also priorities."[3]

Since this is the headquarters facility, all of the credit union's administrative functions happen here, such as human relations, finance, training, marketing, legal, IT, and the data center. The building also houses a call center, member service, and lending functions. This facility, unlike others featured in this chapter, is dedicated more to employee needs than to members, whose needs are accommodated by the credit union's numerous branch offices.

The design team "studied employee functions and workflow in order to position groups with shared work activities in close proximity. Shared amenities such as break areas, a conference center, and training rooms were centralized in the building for easy access."[4]

The break area is near the main entrance, and the large conference and training space is located on the middle floor for easy access by all. Individual work space is designed to be flexible in order to adapt to changing

---

3 Mark Gribbins, senior associate and design lead, IA Interior Architects, to author, December 2008.
4 Mark Gribbins, to author, January 8, 2009.

Watermark Credit Union Headquarters Facility

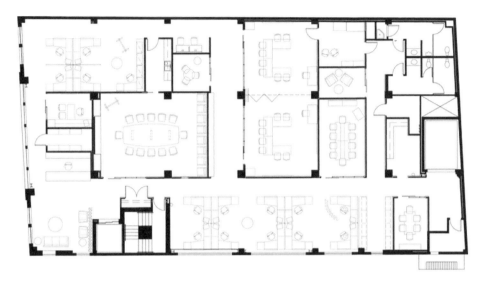

◀ Second-floor plan, Watermark Credit Union, Seattle, Washington. Numerous plan configurations are evident, from small meeting rooms for 3 or 4 people, to large conference rooms that accommodate 20 or more. Different workstation options are also provided, depending on the required function. A call center is located on the fifth floor. IA Interior Architects.

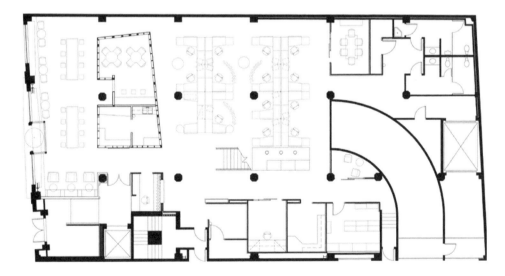

◀ First-floor plan, Watermark Credit Union, Seattle, Washington. The project is designed more for employee needs and workplace efficiency than for members. Because it is a headquarters facility, members do not need to come to it for services. IA Interior Architects.

work styles and functions. The credit union had to have a space that would allow adaptation to ongoing experimentation with new business concepts.

The basic "internal" design theme was to promote a message of human interaction, professional growth, and an effective business environment. The "external" message, which is also the design theme of the credit union's branch facilities, is directed at member needs and promoting its products and services.

CASE STUDIES

▲ *Interior from stair, Watermark Credit Union, Seattle, Washington. The slim horizontal stair cables help project the overall modern and open architectural treatment.* Photo by Nick Merrick/Hedrich Blessing.

The resulting design provides for team and meeting spaces located on each floor immediately adjacent to staff; gathering areas, such as a "living room," a "coffee house," and a "clubhouse" setting; and formal spaces such as the boardroom. The "Epic Center," which is a key area for employee interaction, is a freestanding pavilion within a 2-story space that serves as a coffee bar and an Internet café. It is wrapped with recycled embossed resin panels with a water ripple pattern. The concentric rings are Watermark's signature. Watermark takes great pride in the northwest-native ferns, reclaimed wood flooring, and recycled content of the resin panels used in the building.

The 40,000 sq ft space was completed in June 2008.

FIVEPOINT CREDIT UNION
Bridge City, Texas; NewGround

Originally called Texaco Community Federal Credit Union, this organization was the leading credit union in southeast Texas but needed to increase its financial and member position in early 2003. Established in 1935 by employees of the Texaco Oil refinery, this credit union was steeped in company history, commanded great loyalty for this heritage. Its leadership, however, was seeking to increase its competitive advantage in this highly aggressive marketplace and beyond.

NewGround identified the financial needs of the busy local consumers and established the innovative concept of "fill-up station convenience" as the catchphrase credo of the new credit union image. That led to the brand slogan "America's Financial Convenience Store," connecting the credit union to the target audience rooted in Texaco Oil.

The new name, FivePoint, was the next brainchild of NewGround, derived from the Texaco Oil Company's well-known star logo. This prototype design was the physical manifestation of the FivePoint brand, with a circular layout that allows members easy access to all services offered. FivePoint was soon launched publicly with a brand campaign that positioned this credit union as an even stronger financial leader in southeast Texas.

Fivepoint Credit Union

The floor plan provides for a brightly colored member service center via a circular counter arranged within the star that is outlined on the lobby floor. Surrounding this counter are a waiting area, a well-lit display board that describes the products and services offered, a loan center, an online center, a "Kids' Korner," and a teller services area that makes use of concierge stations and cash recycling machines. A painted mural that wraps around part of the upper lobby's circular wall depicts activities important in members' lives.

A workroom is located behind the teller services area, and houses the space for the remote pneumatic tube–fed drive-up located behind the credit union. A walk-up night depository is also placed at the workroom exterior wall. Two private offices and a manager's office are located off of a main corridor that also leads to a file room and small vault. A break room and restroom are also provided.

The 2,495 sq ft space was completed in April 2005.

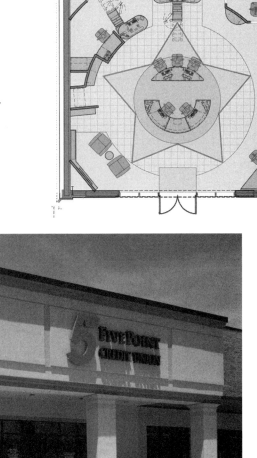

▲ Prototype floor plan, FivePoint Credit Union, Bridge City, Texas. The star brand icon provides a fitting model for the floor plan uses that surround it. NewGround.

◀ Exterior view, FivePoint Credit Union, Bridge City, Texas. The main entrance facade displays the distinctive FivePoint brand as well. The night depository may be seen at the left, and a drive-up is barely visible at the far left rear of the credit union. NewGround.

CASE STUDIES

BANNER BANK
Boise, Idaho; HDR Architects, with The Architects Office, (Price, Sanders, Cooper and Rhees) and Cornerstone Design, Interior Design

This project is very significant in that it was one of only twenty LEED Platinum projects at the time of its completion. The 11-story multitenant building is anchored with the bank occupying the first floor of approximately 10,500 sq ft of the 195,000 sq ft structure. The bank is laid out on a conventional plan accessed from a large central lobby that extends well into the building. This core has fire stairs, elevators, and toilets grouped around it. The bank extends around the core with additional offices and provides a drive-up at the first-floor level. The bank, as well as the entire building, is designed with the sustainable features that have contributed to its distinction.

The principal factors that resulted in the LEED Platinum certification of the building are as follows:

- It uses 50 percent less energy than a similar sized conventionally constructed building. The lighting system and its controls make use of fluorescent T-8 fixtures with continuous dimmable ballasts. Perimeter fixtures are controlled by photosensors to dim light and thereby meet

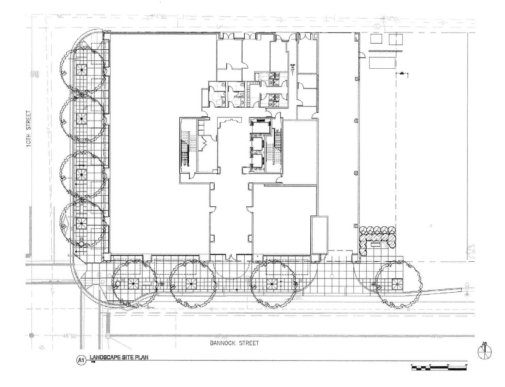

▶ Site plan, Banner Bank, Boise, Idaho. The downtown site location is within an area offering ten community services, which was a benefit in the effort to achieve the LEED Platinum rating. The building plan, with no interior columns other than the inner core, allows greater flexibility in each floor's space planning. HDR Architects.

target luminance values. All lights in enclosed offices, break rooms, and workrooms are activated by motion sensors using both ultrasound and infrared technologies. Conference rooms and some reception areas are fitted with "override switches" in addition to motion sensors, for greater illumination control.
- It uses 65 percent less water than a similar conventional building. (The design captures rainwater and uses 100 percent of its gray water to flush urinals and toilets.)
- The building is constructed with 42 percent recycled materials based on costs, and the total cost was no greater than a conventionally constructed project of similar size.
- It incorporates hundreds of sustainable design features, which added no increase in cost or time of construction.
- It was built on a former brownfield site, offering new life to a downtown neighborhood.
- It makes use of castellated steel beams that are lighter but deeper than standard steel beams, and are made with holes in their webs so that mechanical and electrical equipment can pass through them.

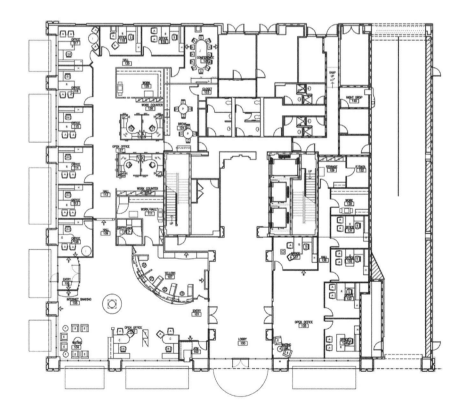

◀ *Floor plan, Banner Bank, Boise, Idaho. The bank extends around the perimeter of the building. The main bank entrance leads to the lobby and a teller line arranged in a curved plan across from open desks and a waiting area. Private offices, cubicles, workrooms, a break room, and a conference room are located beyond the lobby. A walk-up ATM is adjacent to the main building entrance. The single drive-up lane is served by a televised customer unit and pneumatic tube operation.* The Architects Office.

CASE STUDIES

The castellated beams allowed designers to dispense with internal columns on floors, adding greater flexibility to tenant spaces and contributing to the building's overall sustainability by facilitating tenant fit-outs. These also resulted in far fewer smoke detectors being required because of the web openings.

- It features numerous design elements that add flexibility and convenience for the diverse tenants who will occupy the building during its anticipated 100-year life span.

The Banner Bank project was the subject of a documentary film by Ben Shedd, entitled *Green is the Color of Money* and available at www.deepgreen.tv.

CHAPTER 12
THE FUTURE OF BANK ARCHITECTURE

These pages have described many of the various types of bank buildings and methods of delivering financial services in the United States today. Where will these methods lead us, and how will the industry be affected by the changes that we are now seeing and the further changes we anticipate? Today, a wide range of delivery systems is being used in financial institutions, but many banks are still operating with traditional teller lines and conventional drive-up facilities.

Most new branch banks in the suburbs provide for drive-up banking, while most in dense urban areas, where adequate land acquisition is not economically feasible, do not. Some still use the older method of check clearing, retaining and forwarding the paper check until it is cleared and then sent back to its maker, but more institutions are converting to the electronic advantages of Check 21. In the near future, it is unlikely that banks will continue to operate apart from the Check 21 system.

More automation is being implemented in branch operations, and the use of flat screens for customer information and marketing opportunities is now widespread. "We'll go from more efforts at personalization and perhaps, better coordination of the Internet and ATM channels, and then move to cash recycling and deposit automation," states Greg Lowell, a Reston, Virginia–based senior manager for Accenture (Bielski 2007, p. 33).

The next progression is teller-assisted functionality, which has evolved to the idea of "concierge stations" (see chapter 7). Many new branches are now using these, which allow more customers or members to be served by fewer employees, resulting in greater profit. The stations also provide for more subtle marketing opportunities. "Imagine brochures [are] being replaced by interactive kiosks that can, in effect, get the customer far more involved in financial planning—these devices can get the customer engaged far more easily than a brochure" (Bielski 2007, p. 33).

It is likely that banks will become increasingly more retail-oriented and thus will assume an environment that is more conducive to retail-oriented sales and service.

Changes in the drive-up design with face-up configurations, closed-circuit television (CCTV) customer and teller equipment, and more distant placement of car lanes allows for much greater flexibility in the location and site adaptation of the drive-up itself.

ATMs, which have become so prevalent in this country (and the world), have actually declined in average transaction volumes and, on a direct basis, are losing money (Bielski 2007, p. 33). Kiosks, meanwhile, have seen increasingly greater use in numerous locations, from airports to supermarkets and large retailers. While banks have been slow to adopt them, more new facilities are successfully using remote teller machines in lobbies and other locations. Some institutions have adapted so completely to this approach that all of their branches are so equipped. (See chapter 11, case study of the Aloha Pacific Credit Union in Honolulu, Hawaii.) As younger customers or members

THE FUTURE OF BANK ARCHITECTURE

▶ New Hyde Park Bank Technical Center, Chicago, Illinois; Florian Architects. This futuristic new facility will be added to the Chicago area Hyde Park banking organization.

enter the workforce, they bring enhanced abilities in use of higher-tech systems and equipment. Their ease in using the Internet, wireless systems, and other technological advances will alter banking practices in the United States.

An increasing concern in the banking industry has been the prospect of large retailers or discounters entering into banking. Debit cards, low-cost check cashing, and money transfers are already among the services offered by these large organizations. Groups such as Prosper.com are increasing their market share through Internet lending to borrowers who might not otherwise qualify for a loan. A part of their clientele, however, may come from people who wish to "avoid the government red-tape that comes with banking transactions" (McVicker 2007, p. 18).

Prosper.com has in fact made more than $65 million in loans since its launch in February 2006. The effect is that banks must try to compete with a much less regulated industry, and as of this writing there are far reaching-regulatory changes being considered in Washington, D.C., as a result of the subprime mortgage debacle and worldwide economic decline of recent years. More regulation will not necessarily be a benefit to the industry; nor will it be without a cost to consumers.

The Future of Bank Architecture

How these conditions settle will have a direct impact on the design and construction of financial institutions. Many lending institutions are now providing Internet stations for their clients, with ready assistance in lobbies and elsewhere, and now there are banks that are accessed solely by call center or with the Internet, even though some of those had not been expected to last. New banks such as the rapidly growing Internet-oriented ING Direct are fast becoming the replacement for the older, less flexible banks of the past. Their message of "savings" instead of just "lending" has obviously resonated well with their increasing customer base.

The use of the scanners that came with Check 21 has created the remote check capture capability now being used by banking commercial customers, which will soon also be available to consumers. The resulting immediacy in funds transfer and elimination of traditional "float time," as well as the ability to detect fraudulent activity sooner, will dramatically change the face of banking in the United States, and eventually the world. These changes will then be seen in the design and planning of banks and credit unions as well.

Another instrument beginning to affect banking is the use of a personal cell phone or personal digital assistant (PDA) to conduct personal banking. With a cell phone it is now possible to view and monitor account activities, check balances, receive alerts, and transfer funds between accounts. An early participant in this trend was the United Bank of Michigan in Grand Rapids. This bank determined to stay ahead of the competition and implemented the Fiserv ITI mobile banking solution in October 2007. It reports that while customer demand prior to implementation was limited, the demand has steadily increased and virtually every new customer now chooses the service.[1]

In a recent article in *Ten*, the publication of the Federal Reserve Bank of Kansas City, Bill Medley maintains that "shifting consumer attitudes leads to growing acceptance." He describes wide acceptance of online banking by younger consumers and adds:

> While e-banking products such as online bill payment, debit cards, and direct deposit have continued to gain widespread acceptance, consumers and banks are already focusing on emerging technologies such as mobile payments. Not surprisingly, surveys show that it's the youngest group of consumers—those born after 1980—that is most receptive to using cell phones or PDAs to pay for things and carry out bank transactions.[2]

Another, much larger bank to enter this market is Wachovia (recently merged with Wells Fargo), in the launching of its "On the Go Banking" Initiative. Since it rolled out the new program in September 2007, Wachovia has had an average of 9,000 sessions per day by users of Windows Mobile and RIM devices. In peak periods the demand is much greater, and during December, holiday shoppers logged on to Wachovia's banking site for as many as 12,000 sessions daily.[3] It is interesting to

---

1 "ITI Rolls out Integrated Mobile Banking for Handheld Devices," Trading Markets, March 18, 2008, http://www.tradingmarkets.com/.site/news/Stock%20News/1217463.

2 Bill Medley, "e-banking evolves," *TEN, Federal Reserve Bank of Kansas City*, spring 2009.

3 Jacqueline Emigh, "Wachovia Reaches Out To Handhelds," Windows in Financial Services, http://windowssfs.com/TheMag/tabid/54/ArticleType/ArticleView/ArticleID/1868/PageID.

note that while Wachovia is rapidly integrating this Windows mobile banking feature, it has also constructed many new prototypical branches throughout the United States in recent years.

Other institutions have decided to limit their customer base to only those with high net-worth holdings. One prominent banker predicts that the banks of the future will be limited to Internet-based operations that serve the mainstream public, and high-end institutions that limit their customers to exclusively those who have a high net worth.

While the current global financial crisis is indeed formidable and more U.S. banks have failed in recent years, this country has experienced similar difficulties in the past. The lessons learned from the Reconstruction Finance Corporation's handling of banks in the Great Depression in the 1930s, the Resolution Trust Corporation's handling of the savings-and-loan crisis in the 1980s, and the Federal Deposit Insurance Corporation's handling of the 1984 failure of Continental Illinois bank all point to the ability of this country to emerge stronger and wiser.

The prediction that the United States will become a "cashless and paperless" society has not yet been borne out, and some banking experts believe it will be many years, if ever, before it will. Likely, financial services will continue to be offered from new and renovated buildings, designed to exhibit memorable brand identities, that are continually being upgraded with new technologies and customer-friendly features, even as many personal banking needs are increasingly being met through use of cell phones, PDAs, and the Internet.

APPENDIX A
FEDERAL BANK REGULATORS

Information in this appendix is from www.federalreserve.gov/address.htm (accessed April 13, 2008).

Board of Governors of the Federal Reserve System
20th Street and Constitution Avenue, NW
Washington, DC 20551
(202) 452-3000
www.federalreserve.gov

FEDERAL RESERVE BANKS

Boston
600 Atlantic Avenue
Boston, MA 02205
(617) 973-3000
www.bosfrb.org

Chicago
230 South LaSalle Street
Chicago, IL 60604
(312) 322-5322
www.chicagofed.org

New York
33 Liberty Street
New York, NY 10045
(212) 720-5000
www.newyorkfed.org

St. Louis
One Federal Reserve Bank Plaza
Broadway and Locust Streets
St. Louis, MO 63102
(314) 444-8444
www.stlouisfed.org

Philadelphia
Ten Independence Mall
Philadelphia, PA 19106
(215) 574-6000
www.philadelphiafed.org

Minneapolis
90 Hennepin Avenue
Minneapolis, MN 55401
(612) 204-5000
www.minneapolisfed.org

Cleveland
1455 East Sixth Street
Cleveland, OH 44114
(216) 579-2000
www.clevelandfed.org

Kansas City
925 Grand Boulevard
Kansas City, MO 64198
(816) 881-2000
www.kansascityfed.org

Richmond
701 East Byrd Street
Richmond, VA 23219
(804) 697-8000
www.richmondfed.org

Dallas
2200 North Pearl Street
Dallas, TX 75201
(214) 922-6000
www.dallasfed.org

FEDERAL BANK REGULATORS

Atlanta
1000 Peachtree Street NE
Atlanta, GA 30309
(404) 498-8500
www.frbatlanta.org

San Francisco
101 Market Street
San Francisco, CA 94105
(415) 974-2000
www.frbsf.org

FEDERAL RESERVE BRANCH LOCATIONS

New York
Buffalo
Key Center, 40 Fountain Plaza
Suite 650
Buffalo, NY 14202
P.O. Box 961, Buffalo, NY 14240-0961
(716) 849-5000

Cleveland
Cincinnati
150 East Fourth Street
Cincinnati, OH 45202
P.O. Box 999, Cincinnati, OH 45201-0999
(513) 721-4787

Pittsburgh
717 Grant Street
Pittsburgh, PA 15219
P.O. Box 299, Pittsburgh, PA 15230
(412) 261-7800

Richmond
Baltimore
502 South Sharp Street
Baltimore, MD 21201
P.O. Box 1378, Baltimore, MD 21201
(410) 576-3300

Charlotte
530 Trade Street
Charlotte, NC 28202
P.O. Box 30248, Charlotte, NC 28230
(704) 358-2100

Atlanta
Birmingham
524 Liberty Parkway
Birmingham, AL 35242
(205) 968-6700

Jacksonville
800 Water Street
Jacksonville, FL 32204
P.O. Box 929, Jacksonville, FL 32231-0044
(904) 632-1000

Miami
9100 Northwest 36th Street
Miami, FL 33178
P.O. Box 520847, Miami, FL 33152-0847
(305) 591-2065

Minneapolis
Helena
100 Neill Avenue
Helena, MT 59601
(406) 447-3800

Kansas City
Denver
1020 16th Street
Denver, CO 80202
Terminal Annex – P.O. Box 5228, Denver, CO 80217-5228
(303) 572-2300

Oklahoma City
226 Dean A. McGee Avenue
Oklahoma City, OK 73102
P.O. Box 25129, Oklahoma City, OK 73125
(405) 270-8400

FEDERAL BANK REGULATORS

Omaha
2201 Farnam Street
Omaha, NE 68102
P.O. Box 3958, Omaha, NE 68103
(402) 221-5500

Dallas
El Paso
301 East Main Street
El Paso, TX 79901
P.O. Box 100, El Paso, TX 79999
(915) 544-4730

Houston
1801 Allen Parkway
Houston, TX 77019
P.O. Box 2578, Houston, TX 77252-2578
(713) 659-4433

San Antonio
126 East Nueva Street
San Antonio, TX 78204
P.O. Box 1471, San Antonio, TX 78295-1471
(210) 224-2141

San Francisco
Los Angeles
950 South Grand Avenue
Los Angeles, CA 90015
Terminal Annex – P.O. Box 2077, Los Angeles, CA 90051
(213) 683-2300

Nashville
301 Rosa L. Parks Boulevard
Nashville, Tennessee 37203-4407
P.O. Box 4407, Nashville, TN 37203-4407
(615) 251-7100

New Orleans
525 St. Charles Avenue
New Orleans, LA 70130
P.O. Box 61630, New Orleans, LA 70161-1630
(504) 593-3200

Chicago
Detroit
1600 East Warren Avenue
Detroit, MI 48207-1063
P.O. Box 1059, Detroit, MI 48231
(313) 961-6880

St. Louis
Little Rock
Stephens Building
111 Center Street, Suite 1000
Little Rock, AR 72201
P.O. Box 1261, Little Rock, AK 72203-1261
(501) 324-8300

Louisville
National City Tower
101 South Fifth Street
Louisville, KY 40202
P.O. Box 32710, Louisville, KY 40232-2710
(502) 568-9200

Memphis
200 North Main Street
Memphis, TN 38103
P.O. Box 407, Memphis, TN 38101-0407
(901) 523-7171

Portland
1500 SW First Avenue
Portland, OR 97201
P.O. Box 3436, Portland, OR 97208
(503) 276-3000

FEDERAL BANK REGULATORS

Salt Lake City
120 South State Street
Salt Lake City, UT 84111
P.O. Box 30780, Salt Lake City, UT 84125
(801) 322-7900

Seattle
2700 Naches Avenue SW
Renton, WA 98057
P.O. Box 3567, Seattle, WA 98124
(425) 203-0800

FEDERAL DEPOSIT INSURANCE CORPORATION (FDIC)

National Office
550 17th Street NW
Washington, DC 20429
(877) 875-3342
www.fdic.gov

Regional Offices

Atlanta
10 Tenth Street #800
Atlanta, GA 30309-3906
(800) 765-3342

Boston
15 Braintree Hill Office Park #100
Braintree, MA 02184-8701
(866) 728-9953

Chicago
500 W. Monroe Street #3300
Chicago, IL 60661-3697
(800) 944-5343

Dallas
1601 Bryan Street
Dallas, TX 75201
(800) 568-9161

Kansas City
2345 Grand Boulevard #1200
Kansas City, MO 64108-2638
(800) 209-7459

Memphis
5100 Poplar Avenue #1900
Memphis, TN 38137-1900

New York
20 Exchange Place, 4th Floor
New York, NY 10005
(800) 334-9593

San Francisco
25 Jessie Street at Ecker Square #2300
San Francisco, CA 94105-2780
(800) 756-3558

OFFICE OF THE COMPTROLLER OF THE CURRENCY (OCC)

Washington, DC Office
Independence Square
250 E Street SW
Washington, DC 20219-0001
(202) 874-5000
www.occ.gov

Central District Office, Chicago
One Financial Place #2700
440 S. Lasalle Street
Chicago, IL 60605
(312) 360-5800

Northeast District Office, New York
340 Madison Avenue, 5th Floor
New York, NY 10173-0002
(212) 790-4000

Southern District Office, Dallas
500 N. Akard Street #1600
Dallas, TX 75201
(214) 720-0656

Western District Office, Denver
1225 17th Street #300
Denver, CO 80202
(720) 475-7600

APPENDIX B
STATE BANKING ASSOCIATION WEBSITES

Alabama
www.alabamabankers.org

Arizona
www.azbankers.org

Arkansas
www.arkbankers.org

California
www.calbankers.com

Colorado
www.coloradobankers.org

Connecticut
www.ctbank.com

Delaware
www.debankers.com

Florida
www.floridabankers.com

Georgia
www.gabankers.com

Illinois
www.ilbanker.com

Indiana
www.indianabankers.org

Iowa
www.iowabankers.com

Kansas
www.ksbankers.com

Kentucky
www.kybanks.com

Louisiana
www.lba.org

Maine
www.mainebankers.com

Maryland
www.mdbankers.com

Massachusetts
www.massbankers.org

Michigan
www.mibankers.com

Minnesota
www.minnbankers.com

Mississippi
www.msbankers.com

Missouri
www.mobankers.com

Montana
www.montanabankers.com

Nebraska
www.nebankers.org

Nevada
www.nvbankers.org

New Hampshire
www.nhbankers.com

New Jersey
www.njbankers.com

New Mexico
www.nmbankers.com

New York
www.nyba.com

North Carolina
www.ncba.com

STATE BANKING ASSOCIATION WEBSITES

North Dakota
www.ndba.com

Ohio
www.ohiobankersleague.com

Oklahoma
www.oba.com

Oregon
www.oregonbankers.com

Penn.
www.pabanker.com

Puerto Rico
www.abpr.com

South Carolina
www.scbankers.org

South Dakota
www.sdba.com

Tennessee
www.tnbankers.org

Texas
www.texasbankers.com

Utah
www.uba.org

Vermont
www.vtbanker.com

Virginia
www.vabankers.org

Washington
www.wabankers.com

West Virginia
www.wvbankers.org

Wisconsin
www.wisbank.com

Wyoming
www.wyomingbankers.com

U.S. Virgin Islands
www.vibankers.com

For these states, call:

Alaska
(907) 777-3011

Hawaii
(808) 524-5161

Idaho
(208) 342-8282

Rhode Island
(401) 276-2637

APPENDIX C
BANK EQUIPMENT MANUFACTURERS

ACTRON INC. 1351 Jarvis Elk Grove, IL 60007 Ph. (847) 364-4810 T Fax (847) 439-5556	Drive-up lane signs & lights
ADT SECURITY Ph. (800) 492-2238	Vaults and doors Remote teller systems
AIRTUBE SYSTEMS 5322 Rafe Banks Drive, Ste. B Flowery Branch, GA 30342 Ph. (800) 231-4156 Fax (770) 965-8456 www.aerocom.de	Remote teller systems
AMERICAN VAULT CO. 7500 Mars Drive Waco, TX 76712 Ph. (254) 776-0100 www.americanvault.us	Prefab vaults and doors Safes and deposit boxes Windows and deal drawers Remote transaction systems Night deposits and chests
ARCA TECH SYSTEMS 1403 S. Third St. Ext. Melbane, NC 27302 Ph. (919) 442-5200 www.arcatechsystems.com	Cash dispensers Cash recyclers
AUDIO AUTHORITY 2048 Mercer Rd. Lexington, KY 40511 Ph. (859) 233-4599 or (800) 322-8346 TF Fax (859) 233-4510 www.audioauthority.com	Audio/video teller intercom

BANK EQUIPMENT MANUFACTURERS

BAVIS & ASSOCIATES
201 Grandin Road
P.O. Box 337
Maineville, OH 45039
Ph. (513) 677-0500
Fax (513) 677-0552
www.bavis.com

Deal drawers and vision windows

BOSCH SECURITY SYSTEMS
130 Perinton Parkway
Fairport, NY 14450
Ph. (800) 289-0096
Fax (585) 223-9180
www.boschsecurity.us

Security controls and systems
Surveillance cameras

BRIDGEMAN SECURITY
510 West Washington Boulevard
Montebello, CA 90640
Ph. (323) 724-5880 or (800) 334-6060
Fax (323) 727-0236
bridgeman@socalsafe.com

Safe deposit boxcs
Teller lockers

COLLIER SAFE CO.
P.O. Box 955
Odessa, FL 33556
Ph. (813) 920-2090
Fax (813) 920-5091
www.colliersafe.com

Modular vaults
Vault doors
Night depositories
Windows
Remote teller systems
Safe deposit boxes

COMCO SYSTEMS INC.
306 W. Overly Drive
Lake Dallas, TX 75065
Ph. (800) 533-3794
Fax (940) 498-9937
www.comcosystems.com

Complete bank equipment
Automatic remote teller systems
Private video teller systems
Vaults and doors
Night deposits
Windows and drawers
Safes and boxes

CUSTOM VAULT CO.
4 Research Drive
Bethel, CT 06801
Ph. (203) 403-4205
Fax (203) 403-4206
www.customvault.com

Prefab vaults and doors

BANK EQUIPMENT MANUFACTURERS

CUMMINS-ALLISON 852 Feehaville Drive Mt. Prospect, IL 60056	Coin sorter
DIEBOLD INC. 818 Mulbury Road SE P.O. Box 8230 Canton, OH 44707-3256 Ph. (800) 999-3600 T www.diebold.com	Complete bank equipment Remote teller systems Vault systems Night deposits Windows and deal drawers Security systems Safes and boxes ATMs
EMPIRE SAFE CO. 6 E. 39th Street New York, NY 10016 Ph. (212) 684-2255 or (800) 543-5412 www.empiresafe.com	Safe deposit boxes Teller lockers Under-counter equipment Prefab vaults and vault doors Drive-up windows
EXACQ TECHNOLOGIES 7202 E. 87th Street #115 Indianapolis, IN 46256 Ph. (317) 845-5710 T www.exacq.com	Surveillance systems Software and servers
FENCO INC. 4422 Route 130 South P.O. Box 1238 Burlington, NJ 08016-1238 Ph. (800) 486-8484 Fax (609) 387-0803 www.fencobankequipment.com	Modular counters Under-counter pedestals Vault and safe interiors
FIREKING SECURITY GROUP 101 Security Parkway New Albany, IN 47150 Ph. (800) 457-2424 www.fireking.com	Safes CCTV systems
FUJITSU Ph. (888) 385-4878 www.fujitsu.com	ATMs Cash recyclers

BANK EQUIPMENT MANUFACTURERS

GREYFIELD
4510 Port Union Road
Hamilton, OH 45011
Ph. (513) 860-1785
Fax (513) 860-4933
gestes@fuse.net

Audio/video teller intercom

HAMILTON SAFE CO.
3143 Production Drive
Fairfield, OH 45014
Ph. (513) 874-3733 or (800) 876-6066
Fax (513) 874-3967
www.hamiltonsafe.com

Complete bank equipment
Vaults and vault doors
Drive-up systems and tubes
Safe deposit boxes
Lockers and chests
Night deposits
Security systems
Entrance control systems

HERITAGE INDUSTRIES
905 Centennial Road
Wayne, NE 68787
Ph. (402) 375-4770
www.heritageind.com

ATM enclosures

HIS INTERSECURE SYSTEMS LTD.
1092 Lower Delta Road
#04-06/07 Tiong Bahru Ind. Estate
Singapore 169203
Ph. (65) 6272 7353
Fax (65) 6273 3073
www.hiss.com.sg

Prefab vaults and doors

KASO OY
Box 27 (Lyhtytie)
Fin-00751 Helsinki, Finland
Ph. (358) 9 346 81
Fax (358) 9 3860 021
www.kaso.fi

Prefab vaults and doors
Safe deposit boxes

C. R. LAURENCE CO.
hardware
www.crlaurence.com

Bullet-resistant windows and

MGM SECURITY GROUP
Montreal, Canada
Ph. (514) 328-2504 or (866) 327-4688
www.mgmsecuritygroup.com

Safes
Composite safes

BANK EQUIPMENT MANUFACTURERS

NATIONAL BURGLER AND FIRE ALARM ASSN.   Represents alarm system industry
2300 Valley View Lane #230
Irving TX, 75062
Ph. (888) 447-1689
www.alarm.org

NCR CO.   ATMs
1700 S. Patterson Boulevard   Self-service terminals
Dayton, OH 45479   Cash recyclers
Ph. (937) 445-1936 or (800) 225-5627
www.ncr.com

NOVACOMM INC   Access-control vestibules
231 Ruby Avenue, Ste. E
Kissimmee, FL 34741
Ph. (407) 932-4266
Fax (407) 932-4276
www.novaacu.com

SAFEGUARD SECURITY SERVICES LTD.   Bullet-resistant windows and doors
5926 Corridor Parkway   Transaction drawers
Schertz, TX 78154   Package receivers
Ph. (210) 661-8306 or (800) 880-8306   Bullet-resistant fiberglass
Fax (210) 661-8303 F
www.armortex.com and www.frag-stop.com

SCHNEIDERS VETTER GLASS   Security vision windows
2224 S. 162nd Street
New Berlin, WI 53151
Ph. (262) 754-0866
info@svglass.com

SCHWAB CORP.   Vault doors
P.O. Box 5088   File room doors
Lafayette, IN 47903
Ph. (765) 447-9470
Fax 765 447-8278
www.schwabcorp.com

SECURITY CAMERAS DIRECT Security cameras
#1 Security Cameras Direct Way
Luling TX 78648
Ph. (830) 401-7000 or (800) 316-6027
Fax (830) 875-9010
www.scdlink.com

SIGNAL TECHNOLOGIES Signage & lane lights
4985 Pittsburg Avenue
Erie, PA 16509-6206
Ph. (877) 547-9900
Fax (814) 835-2300
www.signal-tech.com

SPECO TECHNOLOGIES Cameras & security systems
200 New Highway
Amityville, NY 11701
Ph. (800) 645-5516
Fax (631) 957-9142
www.specotech.com

TAB PRODUCTS CO. LLC Movable files and high-density storage
605 Fourth Street
Mayville, WI 53050
Ph. (920) 387-3131,
(920) 387-1995, or
(800) 827-3288
Fax (920) 387-1808
www.tab.com

TCP PRECISION IND. CO. LTD Vault doors and safes
No. 3-3, Lane 4 Safe deposit boxes
Cheng Tien Rd.
Tu Cheng City, Taipei Hsien, Taiwan
Ph. (886) 2-22672233
Fax (886) 2-22672980
www.tcp.com.tw

TRANAX TECHNOLOGIES ATMs
30984 Santana
Hayward, CA 94544
Ph. (510) 324-2224 or (888) 340-2484
Fax 510 324-2240
www.tranax.com

VAULT STRUCTURES INC. Drive-up systems and tubes
3640 Work Drive Vaults
Fort Myers, FL 33916 Safes and lockers
Ph. (239) 332-3270 or (800) 226-3990 Night deposits
Fax (239) 332-5593 Safe deposit boxes
www.vaultstructures.com Lockers
 Windows and drawers

WILLIAMSON SAFE CO. Safes and lockers
5631 State Route 73
Hillsboro, OH 45133
Ph. (937) 393-9919
Fax (937) 393-9586
www.wsco.net

WILSON SAFE CO. Under-counter equipment
3031 Island Avenue Safes
Philadelphia, PA 19142 Cash deposit safes
Ph. (800) 345-8053
www.wilsonsafe.com

APPENDIX D
FINANCIAL WEBSITES

ACS X9 Committee (Financial Standards)	www.x9.org
American Banking Association	www.aba.com
American Community Bankers	www.acbankers.org
American Society for Industrial Security	www.asisonline.org
American Stock Exchange	www.amex.com
Bank Administration Institute	www.bai.org
Bank Marketing Association	www.bmanet.org
Banker's Round Table	www.bankersround.org
BITS (Financial Services Round Table)	www.bitsinfo.org
Bond Market Association	www.bondmarkets.com
Committee on Global Finance System	www.bis.org/cgfs
Conference of State Bank Supervisors	www.csbs.org
Consumer Bankers Association	www.cbanet.org
Credit Union National Association	www.cuna.org
Electronic Check Organization	www.electronic-check.org/
Export-Import Bank	www.exim.gov
Electronic Funds Transfer Organization	www.efta.org
Electronic Clearing Services	www.electronicclearingservices.com
Federal Bank Information Infrastructure Committee	www.fbiic.gov
Federal Deposit Insurance Corporation	www.fdic.gov
Federal Financial Institution Exam Council	www.ffiec.gov
Federal Home Loan Bank	www.fhlbanks.com
Federal Reserve Bank, Washington, D.C.	www.federalreserve.gov
Federal Reserve of Kansas City, Missouri	www.kc.frb.org
Financial Management Service	www.fms.treas.gov
Financial Services Information Sharing and Analysis Center	www.fsisac.com
Financial Services Technology Consortium	www.fstc.org
Futures Industrial Association	www.futuresindustry.org
Graduate School of Banking, Colorado	www.gsbcolorado.org

FINANCIAL WEBSITES

Graduate School of Banking at Louisana State Uuniversity	www.gsblsu.org
Graduate School of Banking at Wisconsin University	www.gsb.org
Independent Community Bankers of America (ICBA)	www.icba.org or: http://ecc.nacha.org
International Trade Administration	www.trade.gov
Investment Bankers Association	www.investmentbankersassociation.org
Investment Company Institute	www.ici.org
Mortgage Bankers Association	www.mortgagebankers.org
NASDAQ	www.nasdaq.com
National Association of Federal Credit Unions	www.nafcu.org
National Automated Clearinghouse Association	www.nacha.org
National Burglar and Fire Alarm Association	www.alarm.org
National Credit Union Administration	www.ncua.gov
National Investment Bankers Association	www.nibanet.org
New York Clearing House	www.nych.org
New York Stock Exchange	www.nyse.com
Office of the Comptroller of the Currency	www.occ.treas.gov
Office of Thrift Supervision	www.ots.gov
Risk Management Association	www.rmahq.org
Securities Industry and Financial Markets Association	www.sifma.org
Small Business Administration	www.sba.gov
U.K. Financial Sector Continuity	www.fsc.gov.uk
U.S. Government	www.usa.gov
U.S. Treasury	www.ustreas.gov

APPENDIX E
FEATURED PROJECT ARCHITECTS AND DESIGNERS

BAILEY EDWARD DESIGN (BE DESIGN)
900 N. Franklin # 604
Chicago, Il 60610
Ph. (312) 440-2300
www.bedesign.com

BKV GROUP
222 N. 2nd Street
Minneapolis, MN 55401
Ph. (612) 339-3752
www.bkvgroup.com

CORNERSTONE DESIGN
1005 E. Park Boulevard
Boise, ID 83712
Ph. (208) 384-1422
www.cornerstoneinteriordesign.com

EHS DESIGN
One Union Square
600 University Street #1818
Seattle, WA 98101
Ph. (206) 223-4999
www.ehs-design.com

FIELDEN ARCHITECTS PH. (RAFI)
155 S. Water Street #220
Henderson, NV 89015
Ph. (702) 435-6401
www.rafi-nevada.com

FLORIAN ARCHITECTS
432 N. Clark Street #200
Chicago, IL 60610
Ph. (312) 670-2220
www.florianarchitects.com

FOREMAN SEELEY FOUNTAIN ARCHITECTS
5855 Jimmy Carter Boulevard #218
Norcross, GA 30071
Ph. (770) 729-8433
www.fsfarchitects.com

GENSLER ARCHITECTS
2020 K Street NW #200
Washington, DC 20006
Ph. (202) 721-5200
Fax (202) 872-8587
www.gensler.com

HDR ARCHITECTS
8404 Indian Hills Drive
Omaha, NE 68114-4098
Ph. (402) 399-1000 or (800) 366-4411
Fax (402) 399-1238
www.hdrinc.com

HOK ARCHITECTS
211 N. Broadway #700
Saint Louis, MO 63102
Ph. (314) 421-2000
www.stlouis@hok.com

HTG ARCHITECTS
9300 Hennepin Road
Minneapolis, MN 55347
(Also offices in Phoenix, AZ, and Tampa, FL)
Ph. (952) 278-8880
www.htg-architects.com

FEATURED PROJECT ARCHITECTS AND DESIGNERS

IA INTERIOR ARCHITECTS
257 Park Avenue South #800
New York, NY 10010
Ph. (212) 672-0262
Fax (212) 867-8852
www.interiorarchitects.com

KKE ARCHITECTS
300 1st Avenue North
Minneapolis, MN 55401
Ph. (612) 339-4200
www.kke.com

MASON ARCHITECTS
119 Merchant Street #501
Honolulu, HI
Ph. (808) 536-0556
www.masonarch.com

MCHARRY ARCHITECTS
2780 SW Douglas Road
Miami, FL 33133
Ph. (305) 445-3765
www.mcharry.com

MYEFSKI COOK ARCHITECTS
716 Vernon Avenue
Glencoe, IL 60022
Ph. (847) 835-7081
www.myefskicook.com

NEWGROUND
15450 South Outer Forty Drive #300
Chesterfield, MO 63017
Ph. (636) 898-8100
www.newground.com

JOHN R. SORRENTI, ARCHITECTS PH. (JRS)
181 E. Jericho Turnpike
Mineola, NY 11501
Ph. (516) 294-1666
www.jrsarchitect.com

THE ARCHITECTS OFFICE
499 Main Street
Boise ID 83702
Ph. (208) 343-2931
Fax (208) 343-1306
www.taoidaho.com

USHIJIMA ARCHITECTS
1110 University Avenue #302
Honolulu HI 96822
Ph. (808) 946-9544

VPS ARCHITECTURE
528 Main Street #400
Evansville, IN 47708
Ph. (812) 423-7729
www.vpsarch.com

WSKF ARCHITECTS
110 Armour Road
North Kansas City, MO 64116
Ph. (816) 300-4101
www.wskfarch.com

BIBLIOGRAPHY AND REFERENCES

Asacker, Tom. 2005. *A Clear Eye for Branding*. Ithaca, N.Y.: Paramount Market Publishing.
Belfoure, Charles. 2005. *Monuments to Money*. Jefferson, N.C.: McFarland.
Bielski, Lauren. 2007. "Branch Design." *ABA Banking Journal* (August): 25–28.
Burchard, John, and Albert Bush-Brown. 1950. "Drive Ins." *Architecture Record* (August): 131–139.
———.1961. *The Architecture of America*. Boston: Little, Brown.
Carlton, Jim. 2007. "Citigroup Tries Banking on the Natural Kind of Green." *The Wall Street Journal* online. http://online.wsj.com/article_print/SB118895273112917574.html (accessed September 5).
Fisher, Dan M. 2006. *Capturing Your Customer, The New Technology of Remote Deposit*. Fargo, N.D.: The Copper River Group Publishing Co.
Federal Reserve. 2008. "The Life of a Check." http://www.federalreserveeducation.org/fre_director/print.cfm? (accessed February 2).
Freed, Eric. 2007. "Ask the Expert: Top 10 Green Building Questions." Sustainable Design Forum, 2006–2008. http://www.sustainabledesignforum.com/articles.asp?id=20 (accessed April 22).
Heathcote, Edwin. 2000. *Bank Builders*. Chichester, UK: Wiley-Academy.
Hilgert, Jackie. 2005. "Bank Midwest Redefines the Customer Experience." *The Financial Review* 10.01: 20–21.
Hines, Thomas.1979. *Burnham of Chicago*. Chicago: University of Chicago Press.
Hopper, Leonard, and Martha Droge. 2005. *Security and Site Design*. Hoboken, N.J.: John Wiley & Sons.
Kamin, Blair. 2005. "Hyde Park Bank." *Architecture Record* 3:136–138.
Klebaner, Benjamin. 1990. *American Commercial Banking*. Boston: Twayne Publishing.
Kohn, Meir. 2004. *Financial Institutions and Markets*. New York: Oxford University Press.
Kuhlman, Arkadi, and Bruce Philp. 2009. *The Orange Code: How ING Direct Succeeded by Being a Rebel with a Cause*. Hoboken, N.J.: John Wiley & Sons.
Lathrop, Alan, et al. 1984. *Prairie School Architecture in Minnesota, Iowa, Wisconsin*. Minneapolis, Minn.: Minnesota Museum of Art, Catalog of Exhibition.
Mayer, Thomas. 1987. *Money Banking and the Economy*. New York: Norton & Co.
McVicker, Earl. 2007. "From Walmart to Prosper: Where Do Banks Fit In?" *ABA Banking Journal* 7: 18.
Moore, Carl H. 1987. *Money: Its Origin, Development and Modern Use*. Jefferson, N.C.: McFarland.
"A Native American Proverb." 2008. From Sustainable Design Forum 2006–2008. http://www.sustainabledesignforum.com/files/articles/sunsetdrivecasestudy.pdf (accessed April 22).

Peña, William. 1977. *Problem Seeking*. Boston: CBI Publishing.
Pepe, Michele. 2007. "Banking on Success." *Building Long Island* (May–June): 41–42.
Post, Karen. 2005. *Brain Tattoos*. New York: Amacom Books.
———. 2007. *Square Foot Costs, Bank Costs*. Kingston, Mass.: R. S. Means Publishers.
Severini, Lois. 1985. *The Architecture of Finance: Early Wall Street.* Ann Arbor, Mich.: UMI Research Press.
Smith, John B. 1987. *Planning Fundamentals for Financial Institutions*. Hamilton, Ohio: Mosler Co. Facilities Planning Group.
Stein, Joel, and Caroline Levine. 1990. *Money Matters: A Critical Look at Bank Architecture.* Houston: McGraw-Hill and the Parnassus Foundation.
Streeter, Bill. 2007. "2 Banks Take the LEED." *ABA Banking Journal* (August): 29.
Sullivan, Bob. 2007. "Agency Warns Banks of Al-Qaida Risk." Dept. of Homeland Security, the ABA, and the OCC. MSNBC: http://www.msnbc.com/id/3072757 (accessed August 26).
Tahmincioglu, Eve. 2008. "First Step: Second Life." *BusinessWeek Smallbiz* (August/September).
Van Rensselaer, Mariana G. 1969. *Henry Hobson Richardson and His Works*. Dover Publications.
Weingarden, Lauren. 1987. *Louis H. Sullivan: The Banks*. Cambridge, Mass.: MIT Press.
Williams, Jonathan. 1997. *Money: A History*. New York: St. Martin's Press.

PRODUCT CATALOG REFERENCES

American Vault. 2007. *Product Catalog*. Waco, Tex.: American Vault Co..
ComCo Systems. 2007. *ComCo Systems: The Future is Now.* Dallas, Tex.: ComCo Equipment Co..
Diebold. *Drive-up Banking Applications, Concepts and Strategies Guide*. Columbus, Ohio: Diebold Inc.
Diebold Product Application Services (PAS). PAS is part of the Customer Business Solutions group within Diebold Inc. PAS provides professional services to Diebold customers in a variety of ways, including assisting architects and contractors throughout the design and construction phases of a bank or credit union project. Using product data sheets, drawings, and renderings of Diebold products, PAS is a resource for proper application and installation of Diebold Products into a customer's new or existing facility. PAS associates are neither architects nor professional engineers but experts in financial equipment applications and are involved in the development of hundreds of branch projects each year. These projects include traditional and nontraditional financial branches, self-service, in-store, and retail locations. © Diebold Incorporated, 1994–2009. All rights reserved.
Hamilton Safe. Product literature. Fairfield, Ohio: Hamilton Safe. 2004–2009.

BIBLIOGRAPHY AND REFERENCES

WEBSITE REFERENCES

Bank Holding Companies. http://en.wikipedia.org/Bank_holding_company (accessed October 28, 2007).

Bank of the Internet. http://www.bankofinternet.com (accessed October 28, 2007).

Check Clearing. http://www.advfn.com/money-words_term_6468_check_clearing.html (January 23, 2008).

ComCo Systems Inc. http://www.comcosystems.com (accessed December 12, 2007).

Commercial Banks. http://www.investorwords.com/featureadjumboros.html (accessed October 2, 2007).

"Comptroller of the Currency Responsibilities." http://www.occ.gov (accessed October 21, 2007).

EHS Design. http://www.ehs-design (accessed October 20, 2007).

The Federal Reserve Bank. http://federalreserve.gov (accessed September 17, 2007).

Federal Reserve. "Payments System." http://www.federalreserve.gov/paymentsystems/truncation (accessed February 3, 2008).

First Bank of the United States. http://www.en.wikipedia.org/wiki/First_Bank_of_the_United_States (accessed September 15, 2007).

HTG Architects. http://www.htg-architects.com (accessed October 27, 2007).

Merchants National Bank. http://en.wikipedia.org/wiki/Image:MerchantsNatlBankWinonaMN.JPG (accessed September 24, 2007).

Microsoft Surface Computer. http://www.microsoft.com/surface (accessed October 9, 2007).

National Association of Federal Credit Union Administrations. http://www.nafcu.org (accessed October 2, 2007).

National Credit Union Administration. http://www.ncua.gov/AboutNCAU/Index.htm (accessed October 29, 2007).

National Farmers Bank. http://en.wikipedia.org/wiki/Image:OwatonnaBank.JPG (accessed September 21, 2007).

Office of the Comptroller of the Currency. http://www.occ.gov (accessed September 15, 2007).

Office of Thrift Supervision. http://www.infoplease.com/ce6/bus/A0843804.html (accessed October 9, 2007).

The Private Bank. http://www.theprivatebank.com (accessed October 29, 2007).

Second Life. http://secondlife.com (accessed April 19, 2008).

The 12 Federal Reserve Districts. http://www.federalreserve.gov/otherfrb.htm (accessed October 23, 2007).

INDEX

Accenture, 191
access. *See also* Americans with Disabilities Act (ADA); entrances
    building design, 91–94
    site planning, 39
accounting facilities, building design, 90
acoustics
    HVAC systems, 103
    mechanical room, 101
    plumbing, 103
advertising, branding, 17. *See also* branding
Agawam Bank (Springfield, Massachusetts), 3
age level, cash dispensing and cash recycling, 65–66
airport locations, building design, 81
air quality, indoor, HVAC systems, 98
alarm and building security systems, specialized equipment, 148–50
Aloha Pacific Credit Union (Honolulu, Hawaii) case study, 72, 182–84
amenities, lobby and waiting areas, 87
Americans with Disabilities Act (ADA)
    building design, 39, 91–94
    community meeting spaces, 86
    entrances, lobby and waiting areas, 87
    plumbing fixtures, 103
    teller stations, 63
American Vault Products, 125
The Architects Office (Price, Sanders, Cooper and Rhees), 188–90

architectural styles
    banking history, 3–4, 6
    branding function, 17
    prototypical design, 80
Asacker, Tom, 17
Ascend Credit Union (Murfreesboro, Tennessee) case study, 21–23, 68
ASI Federal Credit Union (West Wego, Louisiana), 70, 72
Atelier Pacific Architecture, Inc., 18
audio systems. *See also* closed-circuit television (CCTV)
    drive-up banks
        floor plan, 66–67
        site planning, 51
    remote teller system, floor plan, 69
automated teller machine (ATM), 8. *See also* electronic banking; online banking
    branding, 24–25
    canopy design, 55
    floor plan, 62
    future prospects, 191
    lighting, 105
    resupply, 125
    site planning, 39, 45, 46–47, 53–55
    specialized equipment, 145–48

Bailey Edward Design, 155–57
bank holding companies, functions of, 14
bank holiday of 1933, 6
banking, historical perspective, 1–8, 12–13
banking institutions, 12–15
    bank holding companies, 14

    branding function, 17–18
    commercial banks, 13
    credit unions, 14–15
    investment banks, 13–14
    nationally-chartered banks, 13
    savings and loan association (S&L), 14
    savings banks, 14
    state-chartered banks, 12–13
Bank of England, 1
Bank of North America, 2
Bank of the Internet (San Diego, California), 83
Bank Protection Act of 1968 and amendments of 1991 (BPA), 8, 11–12, 135
Banner Bank (Boise, Idaho) case study, 95, 96, 103, 188–90
bathrooms. *See* toilets
BKV Architects, 61, 87, 165–67
Blodgett, Samuel, 2
boardroom
    building design, operational space, 88–90
    plumbing fixtures, 103
boutique bank/shop design, 78
branch bank, conference/board rooms and closing rooms, 88–90
branding, 17–25. *See also* marketing
    Ascend Credit Union (Murfreesboro, Tennessee) case study, 20–23
    ATMs, 54
    automated teller machine (ATM), 53
    branding function, 17–18
    future prospects, 24–25

215

INDEX

branding, *continued*
   ING Direct (New York, New York) case study, 23
   lobby and waiting areas, 87
   North Fork Bank (New York, New York) case study, 23–24
   North Shore Credit Union (Vancouver, British Columbia) case study, 18–20
break rooms, 90, 91, 103
budgeting, programming, 32
building codes
   automated teller machine (ATM), 127
   community meeting spaces, building design, 86
   design, 91–94
   HVAC systems, 97–103
   site planning, 39
   specialized equipment, 125
building design, 61–96. *See also* drive-up banks; floor plan
   boutique bank/shop, 78
   cabling systems, 108
   call centers, 81–82
   ceiling space, 101
   codes, 91–94
   commissioning, 109
   community meeting spaces, 86
   construction costs, 94–95
   deregulated services, 84
   floor number considerations, 84–86
   floor plan, 61–72
   future prospects, 191–94
   HVAC systems, 97, 100
   mall, airports, and in-store locations, 81
   mechanical room, 101–2
   online banking tellers, 82–83
   operational space, 87–91
      accounting facilities, 90

      conference/board rooms and closing rooms, 88–90
      lobby and waiting areas, 87
      offices, 88
      vaults, 90
      workrooms, 90
   prototypical design, 80
   remodeling, 72–78
   select-market banks, 83–84
   specialized equipment, 108–9, 125
   sustainability, 95–96
   utilities, 94
building openings, energy efficiency, HVAC systems, 100
building permits
   drive-up banks, site planning, 45–46
   signage, site planning, 59–60
building space, programming, 28, 32
business hours. *See also* personnel; productivity
   automated teller machine (ATM), 54
   drive-up banks, 38
   remote teller system, 70

cabling systems, 108
call centers, building design, 81–82
canopies
   drive-up banks, 48, 50, 51
   site planning, 55–59
cash dispensing and cash recycling
   equipment for, teller areas, 113–15
   floor plan, 64–66
   remodeling, 78
ceiling space, HVAC systems, 101
cell phones, 193
Check 21 (Check Clearing for the 21st Century (Check 21) Act of 2003), 8
   floor plan considerations, 62

   future prospects, 191–93
   programming checklist, 29
   workrooms, 116–20
Check Clearing for the 21st Century (Check 21) Act of 2003. *See* Check 21 (Check Clearing for the 21st Century (Check 21) Act of 2003)
check clearing operations, floor plan, 61–62
check stands, floor plan, 64
China, 1
circulation
   drive-up banks, 33, 35, 37
   site planning, 39
Civil War (U.S.), 3, 13
clearances
   canopy design, 55–59
   specialized equipment, 125
closed-circuit television (CCTV). *See also* audio systems
   alarm and building security systems, 148–50
   future prospects, 191
   remodeling, 72, 77–78
   site planning, 44–45, 50, 51
   specialized equipment, 126
closing rooms, building design, operational space, 88–90
coinage, 1
coin receivers, 123
colonial America, 1–2
Colonial Bank, Anthem Branch (Henderson, Nevada) case study, 175–76
Comco Manufacturing Co., 72
Comco Systems, 125
commercial banks, functions of, 13, 14
commercial lanes, drive-up banks, site planning, 52–53
commissioning, 109

INDEX

communications. *See also* electrical systems; electronic banking; telephone systems
    electrical systems, 107
    specialized equipment, 108–9
community meeting spaces, building design, 86
concierge station
    floor plan, 62, 68–69
    future prospects, 191
conditioning zones, HVAC systems, 98
conference rooms, building design, operational space, 88–90
construction costs, building design, 94–95. *See also* costs
construction permits, site planning, 41
construction process
    commissioning, 109
    HVAC systems, 100
consultants, programming, 30
Continental Illinois Bank, 194
controls
    HVAC systems, 102
    lighting, 107
cooperation, programming, 32
Cornerstone Design, 188–90
costs
    construction costs, building design, 94–95
    cost estimates, programming, 32
    drive-up banks, 38
    HVAC systems, 98–101
credit cards, 8
credit unions, functions of, 14
culverts, pneumatic tubes, drive-up banks, 33, 35, 37, 127. *See also* trench installations
customer service representatives
    concierge station, floor plan, 68–69
    floor plan, 62

data equipment, building design, 108–9
debit cards, 8, 192
deregulated services
    banking industry, 14
    building design, 84
Dickson, Ellen B., 155–57
Diebold Inc., 41, 46, 55, 59, 72, 125
direct-bury installations, drive-up banks, site planning, 51–52
disabled customers. *See* access; Americans with Disabilities Act (ADA)
dispensing. *See* cash dispensing and cash recycling
doors
    energy efficiency, HVAC systems, 100
    vault doors, safe deposit vaults, 140–42
drainage. *See also* pneumatic tubes; trench installations
    building design, 94
    canopy design, 45, 59
drinking fountains, building codes, 92
drive-up banks, 33–38. *See also* building design; floor plan
    contemporary, 37–38
    future prospects, 191–93
    historical perspective, 33–37
    lighting, 105
    remodeling, 72–78
    site planning, 39
        commercial lanes, 52–53
        conventional, 44–47
        direct-bury and trench installations, 51–52
        face-up lanes, 47–50
        tandem island customer units, 50
    specialized equipment
        conventional, 125–26

        remote, 126
        window and drawer units, 131–33
    teller
        floor plan, 66–67
        programming checklist, 29
        temporary facilities, 42
dual banking system, regulatory agencies, 12
ductwork, HVAC systems, 97

EHS Design, 61, 69, 152–53, 182–84
electrical systems, 104–8. *See also* utilities
    building design, 94
    cabling, 108
    communications, 107
    direct-bury installations, drive-up banks, 51
    lighting, 104–7
    power supply, 107
    security equipment, 109
    specialized equipment, 108–9, 125
electronic banking, 8. *See also* automated teller machine (ATM); online banking
    branding, 24–25
    building design, 82–83
    future prospects, 191–94
Elmslie, George G., 4
emergency power supply, 107
energy efficiency
    building design, 95–96
    HVAC systems, 100
    lighting, 107
English Queen Anne style, 3
entrances. *See also* access
    lobby and waiting areas, 87
    site planning, 39
environmental concerns, drive-up banks, 38

217

INDEX

equipment. *See also* specialized equipment
   coin receivers, 123
   file storage, 122–23
   mechanical room, 101–2
   specialized, programming checklist, 30
   teller requirements, 122
   teller rooms, programming checklist, 28–29
   teller stations, under-counter, 111–15
   workrooms
      Check 21 LAN systems, 116–20
      programming checklist, 29
Europe, medieval, 1
EvoBank (IITG Architects concept), 69
Exchange National Bank (Chicago, Illinois), 33
executive offices, building design, 88
exterior lighting, 105

face-to-face transactions
   cash dispensing and cash recycling, 65–66
   remote teller system, 69–70
face-up lanes, drive-up banks, site planning, 47–50
Farmers Bank of North Missouri (Saint Joseph, Missouri) case study, 154–55
feasibility, site planning, 39
Federal Credit Union Act of 1934, 6–7
Federal Deposit Insurance Corporation (FDIC), 6
   commercial banks, 13
   functions of, 12
   listings for, 198
   savings and loan associations (S&Ls), 14
   state-chartered banks, 13

Federal Reserve Act of 1913, 3
Federal Reserve System
   banking institutions, 13
   functions of, 10–11
   listing of, 195–98
Federal Savings and Loan Insurance Corporation (FSLIC), 14
Fielden, Robert A., 175–76
file storage
   equipment, 122–23
   lobby and waiting areas, 87
financial panics, 3
financial system, 9–15. *See also* banking institutions; regulatory agencies
financial websites, listing of, 208–9
fire protection
   automated teller machine (ATM), 127
   file storage, 122–23
fire sprinkler systems, plumbing, 103–4
First Bank of the United States, 2
First National Bank (Nashville, Tennessee), 33
Fiserv ITI mobile banking, 193
Fivepoint Credit Union (Bridge City, Texas) case study, 186–87
floor number considerations, building design, 84–86
floor plan, 61–72
   cash dispensing and cash recycling, 64–66
   check clearing operations, 61–62
   check stands, 64
   concierge station, 68–69
   drive-up banks, 33
   drive-up teller counters, 66–67
   programming, 61
   remote teller system, 69–72

   teller pod stations, 67–68
   teller stations, 63–64
Florian Architects, 157–59
Foreman Seeley Fountain Architecture, 167–68
forms dispenser, specialized equipment, 150
Frandsen Bank & Trust (Forest Lake, Minnesota) case study, 69, 170–72
free banking movement, 13
free charter laws, 2
freestanding automated teller machine (ATM), 54
   drive-up ATM, 147–48
   lobby ATM, 146–47
Freestar Bank (Downs, Illinois) case study, 155–57
French Second Empire style, 3
furnishings, lobby and waiting areas, 87

Gensler Architects, 23, 78, 176–77
geothermal systems, HVAC systems, 100–101
glare. *See also* lighting; sight lines
   canopy design, 55
   site planning, 39, 45
   task lighting, 104
Glass-Steagall Act of 1933, 12
Glenn Mason Architects, 182–84
goldsmiths, banking history, 1
Gramm-Leach-Bliley Act of 1999, 8
Great Depression, 4, 6–7, 194
Great Northern Bank (Osceola, Wisconsin), 87
Great Northern Bank (Saint Michael, Minnesota), 84–86
Greek style, 3
green buildings, design, 95–96. *See also* LEED ratings
greeter stations. *See* concierge station

INDEX

ground-source HVAC systems, 100–101
GWP Brand Engineering, 79

Hamilton, Alexander, 2
Hamilton Safe Company, 125
HDR Architects, 103, 188–90
headquarters
    conference/board rooms and closing rooms, 88–90
    emergency power supply, 107
    offices, 88
    Old National Bancorp Headquarters (Evansville, Indiana) case study, 163–65
    Watermark Credit Union Headquarters Facility (Seattle, Washington) case study, 81, 184–86
heating, ventilation, and air conditioning systems (HVAC). *See* HVAC systems
HOK, 163–65
Home State Bank (Willmar, Minnesota) case study, 172–74
Howe, George, 6
HTG Architects, 69, 170–72, 178–80
Hughes, Charles Evans, III, 7
HVAC systems, 97–103
    acoustics, 103
    building codes, 97
    building design, 97
    ceiling space, 101
    conditioning zones, 98
    construction process, 100
    costs, 98–100
    energy efficiency, 100
    geothermal systems, 100–101
    indoor air quality, 98
    lobby, 102
    mechanical room, 101–2

overview, 97
    radiant effect, 102–3
    sustainability, building design, 95–96
    technology rooms, 103
    temperature controls, 102
    temperature levels, 97–98
    vaults, 103
Hyde Park Bank (Chicago, Illinois) case study, 157–59

IA Interior Architects, 81, 184–86
indoor air quality, HVAC systems, 98
ING Direct (New York, New York) case study, 23, 78, 82
institutional type, programming checklist, 27–28
in-store locations, building design, 81
insulation, energy efficiency, HVAC systems, 100
International Building Code (IBC), 91
Internet social networks, electronic banking, 82–83
investment banks, functions of, 13–14
Italianate style, 3

Jackson, Andrew, 2
JRS Architects, 23–24, 160–61, 180–82

kiosk. *See* teller pod stations
KKE Architects, 84–86, 172–74
Kuhlmann, Arkadi, 23, 79

lamp color index, 106
landscaping, site planning, 39, 41. *See also* site planning
LAN systems
    equipment room for, 121
    HVAC systems, 103
    workrooms, Check 21, 116–20

lawn sprinkler systems, plumbing, 103–4
LEED ratings
    building design, 95–96
    pneumatic tubes, 72
Lescaze, William, 6
lighting. *See also* glare
    electrical systems, 104–7
    energy efficiency, HVAC systems, 100
    site planning, 39
    specialized equipment, 150
light levels, recommended, 106
lobby
    building design, operational space, 87
    HVAC systems, 98, 102
Lowell, Greg, 191

Madison National Bank, Signature Branch (Merrick, New York) case study, 160–61
mall locations, building design, 81
manager offices, building design, operational space, 88
Manufacturers' Trust (New York, New York), 7
Marco Polo, 1
marketing. *See also* branding
    branding function, 17
    future prospects, 191–93
    site planning, 39
mechanical room, HVAC systems, 101–2. *See also* electrical systems; HVAC systems; plumbing
medieval Europe, 1
Medley, Bill, 193
Merchants Bank of Winona (Minnesota), 4
Microsoft, branding, 24

INDEX

modernization. *See* remodeling; retrofitting
monetary note, 1
motion sensors, lighting, 107
Mountain State Bank (Cumming, Georgia) case study, 167–68
multi-floor design, 84–86
Myfeski Cook Architects, 59

National Bank Act of 1863, 3, 12
National Credit Union Administration (NCAU), 6–7
National Credit Union Association (NCUA), 15
National Credit Union Share Insurance Fund (NCUSIF), 7, 15
National Farmers Bank (Owatonna, Minnesota), 4
nationally-chartered banks, functions of, 13
National Monetary Commission, 3
NCR Company, 125
NewGround, 20–23, 61, 161–63, 168–69, 186–87
night depositories
  service, 125
  specialized equipment, 134–35
Norlarco Credit Union (Fort Collins, Colorado) case study, 61, 152–53
North Fork Bank, Long Beach Branch (Long Beach, New York) case study, 180–82
North Fork Bank (New York, New York) case study, 23–24
North Shore Community Bank & Trust (Chicago, Illinois), 59
North Shore Credit Union (Vancouver, British Columbia) case study, 18–20, 69

Office of the Comptroller of the Currency (OCC)
  commercial banks, 13
  creation of, 3
  functions of, 9–10
  listings for, 198
Office of Thrift Supervision (OTS)
  functions of, 10
  savings and loan associations (S&Ls), 14
offices
  acoustics, HVAC systems, 103
  building design, operational space, 88
  floor plan considerations, 62
  HVAC systems
    acoustics, 103
    conditioning zones, 98
    lobbies, 102
    radiant effect, 102–3
  programming, 29, 88
Old National Bancorp Headquarters (Evansville, Indiana) case study, 163–65
online banking. *See also* automated teller machine (ATM); electronic banking
  building design, 82–83
  floor plan, 62
openings, energy efficiency, HVAC systems, 100. *See also* entrances
open-space offices, building design, operational space, 88
operational space. *See* building design, operational space
overhead pneumatic tubes, drive-up banks, 35, 37, 59, 126. *See also* pneumatic tubes

Panic of 1893, 3
Panic of 1907, 3
paper money, 1
parking
  access, building codes, 92
  drive-up banks, 35
  site planning, 39
permits
  drive-up banks, site planning, 45–46
  signage, site planning, 59–60
personal digital assistant (PDA), 193
personal teller machines, 127–30
personnel. *See also* business hours; productivity
  future prospects, 191
  remote teller system, 70
  staff training, teller pod stations, 67
  teller pod stations, 67
Philadelphia Savings Fund Society (Pennsylvania), 6
Philp, Bruce, 23, 79
Pilot Bank (Tampa, Florida) case study, 61, 161–63
plantings, site planning, 39. *See also* landscaping; site planning
plumbing
  floor plan considerations, 62
  requirements, 103–4
PNC Bank (Pittsburgh, Pennsylvania), 95–96
pneumatic tubes. *See also* culverts; overhead pneumatic tubes; trench installations
  drive-up banks, 33, 35, 37, 44, 48, 50, 51, 59
  floor plan, 62, 66–67, 69, 72
  LEED ratings, 72
  remodeling, 72, 78
  specifications, 127–28

INDEX

Post, Karen, 17
power supply, electrical systems, 107. *See also* electrical systems
Prairie Style, 4
predesign. *See* programming
prefabrication
    safe deposit vaults, 135–40
    trailer units, temporary facilities, 42
premanufactured freestanding drive-up ATM enclosures and canopies, 148
preservation. *See* remodeling; retrofitting
Price, Sanders, Cooper and Rhees (The Architects Office), 188–90
The Private Bank, 83–84
private banking, building design, 83–84
private offices, building design, 88
productivity. *See also* business hours; personnel
    cash dispensing and cash recycling, 64
    remote teller system, 70, 72
programming, 27–32
    application and implementation, 30, 32
    checklist for, 27–30, 40
    components of, 27
    floor plan, 61
    lobby and waiting areas, 87
    offices, 29, 88
    site planning checklist, 40
project process. *See* construction process
property lines, site planning, 40–41
Prosper.com, 192
prototypical design, architectural styles, 80
Purcell, William G., 4

Queen Anne style (English), 3

radiant effect, HVAC systems, 102–3
ramps, building codes, 92
Reconstruction Finance Corporation (RFC), 194
recycling. *See* cash dispensing and cash recycling
regulatory agencies, 9–12
    Bank Protection Act of 1968, 11–12
    deregulated services, building design, 84
    dual banking system, 12
    Federal Deposit Insurance Corporation (FDIC), 12
    Federal Reserve System, 10–11
    listing of, 195–98
    Office of the Comptroller of the Currency (OCC), 9–10
    Office of Thrift Supervision (OTS), 10
    state authorities, 12
remodeling, 72–78. *See also* retrofitting
remote cash dispensing and cash recycling, 65–66
remote deposit capture, 8, 193
remote teller room
    equipment checklist, 29
    floor plan, 69–72
    remodeling, 77–78
Renaissance, 1
Resolution Trust Corporation, 194
rest rooms. *See* toilets
retrofitting, Ascend Credit Union (Murfreesboro, Tennessee) case study, 21–23. *See also* remodeling
Revolutionary War (U.S.), 1, 2
Richardson, Henry H., 3
River Bank (Osceola, Wisconsin) case study, 61, 165–67

Rock Springs National Bank (Rock Springs, Wyoming) case study, 168–69
Romanesque style, 3
Roosevelt, Franklin D., 6–7
RSMeans Co., 94–95

safe deposit vaults, 135–45. *See also* vault(s)
    boxes and lockers, 142
    building design, 90
    composite safes and lockers, 144–45
    prefabricated, 135–40
    safes and security chests, 143–44
    security lockers, 143
    teller lockers, 143
    vault doors, 140–42
St. Cloud Federal Credit Union (Sartell, Minnesota) case study, 178–80
savings and loan association (S&L), 14, 194
savings bank, function of, 14
seasonal changes, temperature levels, 97–98
Second Bank of the United States, 2, 12
Second Empire style (French), 3
Second Life virtual currency, branding, 24–25
security
    alarm and building security systems, 148–50
    cash dispensing and cash recycling, 64–65
    drive-up banks, 37
    floor plan, 62
    lighting, 104–5
    site planning, 39
    teller pod stations, 67
security chests, safe deposit vaults, 143–44

INDEX

security equipment, electrical systems, 109
security lockers, vaults, 143
Seibert, Paul, 18
service representatives. *See* customer service representatives
sewage, building design, 94
sight lines, drive-up banks, floor plan, 66–67. *See also* glare; lighting
signage
    site planning, 59–60
    specialized equipment, 150
Signature Branch, Madison National Bank (Merrick, New York) case study, 160–61
single-floor design, 84–86
site planning, 39–60
    automated teller machine (ATM), 53–55
    canopy design, 55–59
    checklist for, 41–42
    drive-up banks
        commercial lanes, 52–53
        conventional, 44–47
        direct-bury and trench installations, 51–52
        face-up lanes, 47–50
        tandem island customer units, 50
    floor number considerations, 84–86
    information sources, 41
    location recommendations, 41
    overview, 39–40
    signage, 59–60
    temporary facilities, 42–44
    utilities, 94
    zoning, 40–41
site soils. *See* soils
Skidmore, Owings & Merrill, 7
SmallBiz magazine, 24
social networks, electronic banking, 82–83

soils
    pneumatic tubes, drive-up banks, 35
    site planning, 41
solar orientation
    canopy design, 55
    HVAC systems, 102–3
    signage, 60
    site planning, 39
space, programming, 28, 32
Spanish Mission style, 80
specialized equipment, 125–50. *See also* equipment
    alarm and building security systems, 148–50
    automated teller machine (ATM), 145–48
    building design, 108–9
    drive-up banks
        conventional, 125–26
        remote, 126
    floor plan considerations, 62
    forms dispenser, 150
    lighting, 150
    manufacturers of, listed, 201–7
    night depositories, 134–35
    overview, 125
    personal teller machines, 127–30
    programming checklist, 30
    safe deposit vaults, 135–45
    signage, 150
    window and drawer units, 131–33
sprinkler systems, fire and lawns systems, 103–4
staff. *See* personnel
staff offices. *See* offices
staff training, teller pod stations, 67
state authorities
    banking regulatory agencies, 12
    listing of, 199–200
state-chartered banks, functions of, 12–13

storage vaults. *See* vault(s)
stormwater, building design, 94
Strickland, William, 2
styles. *See* architectural styles
Sullivan, Louis, 4
supermarket locations, building design, 81
surveyors, site planning, 41
sustainability, building design, 95–96

Tab Products Co. LLC, 122
tandem island customer units, drive-up banks, site planning, 50
task lighting, 104
technology, branding, 24–25
technology rooms, HVAC systems, 103
telephone systems, building design, 109
teller
    access to, building codes, 92
    drive-up teller
        floor plan, 66–67
        placement of, 33
        programming checklist, 29
    equipment requirements, 122
    floor plans, 63–64
    remote teller room equipment, programming checklist, 29
    under-counter equipment, 111–15
teller lockers, safe deposit vaults, 143
teller pod stations
    floor plan, 67–68
    future prospects, 191–93
    remodeling, 77
teller room equipment, programming checklist, 28
temperature controls, 102
temperature levels, 97–98
temporary facilities, site planning, 42–44
thermostats, 102
through-wall drive-up ATM, 147